# THE DARK SIDE

## Also by Steve Paikin

*The Life: The Seductive Call of Politics*

# THE DARK SIDE

## THE PERSONAL PRICE
## OF A POLITICAL LIFE

# STEVE PAIKIN

VIKING
CANADA

VIKING CANADA

Penguin Group (Canada), a division of Pearson Penguin Canada Inc., 10 Alcorn Avenue, Toronto, Ontario M4V 3B2

Penguin Group (U.K.), 80 Strand, London WC2R 0RL, England
Penguin Group (U.S.), 375 Hudson Street, New York, New York 10014, U.S.A.
Penguin Group (Australia) Inc., 250 Camberwell Road, Camberwell, Victoria 3124, Australia
Penguin Group (Ireland), 25 St. Stephen's Green, Dublin 2, Ireland
Penguin Books India (P) Ltd, 11, Community Centre, Panchsheel Park,
New Delhi – 110 017, India
Penguin Group (New Zealand), cnr Rosedale and Airborne Roads, Albany, Auckland 1310,
New Zealand
Penguin Books (South Africa) (Pty) Ltd, 24 Sturdee Avenue, Rosebank 2196, South Africa

Penguin Group, Registered Offices: 80 Strand, London WC2R 0RL, England

First published 2003

1 2 3 4 5 6 7 8 9 10  (FR)

NATIONAL LIBRARY OF CANADA CATALOGUING IN PUBLICATION

Paikin, Steve, 1960–
The dark side : the personal price of a political life / Steve Paikin.

Includes index.

ISBN 0-670-04328-1

1. Politicians—Canada. 2. Prime ministers—Canada—Provinces.
3. Women politicians—Canada. 4. Canada—Politics and government—1935– I. Title.

FC26.P6P33 2003     324.2'2'0971     C2003-903774-6

Visit the Penguin Group (Canada) website at **www.penguin.ca**

*To My Parents*
*Marnie and Larry Paikin*

*This book may be about the dark side,*
*but life with you two has been oh-so-bright*

No memory of having starred
Atones for later disregard
Or keeps the end from being hard.
—*Robert Frost*


A good way to get in trouble is to get into politics.
It is like putting your head in a pail
and asking someone to hit it.
—*Billy Hepburn, father of former*
*Ontario premier Mitchell Hepburn*

# THE CONTENTS

# THE INTRODUCTION

I guess I just prefer to see the dark side of things.
The glass is always half-empty. And cracked.
And I just cut my lip on it. And chipped a tooth.
—*Actor and comedian Janeane Garofalo*

Two years ago, Penguin Canada published my first book, *The Life: The Seductive Call of Politics,* which told stories of the wonderful, even noble, reasons why public-spirited folks enter the political arena. To my delight, *The Life* received kudos for getting away from the typical approach to covering politics, which starts from the assumption that anyone who is interested in public life is an egomaniacal jerk, anxious to leech as much as he or she can out of the system.

Having done that, let's be candid. As Janeane Garofalo suggests in her witty quote above, there is plenty in life—and especially public life—that is not noble, altruistic, or public-spirited, and events do not unfold as people wish they would. Even the most successful politicians have to shake their heads at the horrendous pitfalls they encounter.

It never ceases to amaze me how steep the learning curve is for first-time politicos. I've seen it time and time again in more than twenty years of covering public life in Canada. Even candidates who have a reasonably solid sense of what's in store for them express shock when confronted with reality.

And the biggest shock comes when it's all over.

"The public don't understand just how vulnerable we are," says Frank McKenna, the former New Brunswick premier. "Most of my colleagues really landed on their rear end, not on their feet. When you're defeated, you're *persona non grata* for a period of time. So you end up with a lot of very sad cases."

Politicians often speak of their attraction to the political arena. This book tells you what it's like when a pride of lions is waiting for you in that arena, ready to rip you limb from limb. The vicious campaigns. The betrayals. The toll this life takes on families. The issues that zoom in from out of nowhere, to cut short promising careers. The first ministers who, upon defeat, experience a unique loneliness few of us can understand. And what's truly surprising is that even those who barely escape intact still won't close the door on giving it another go.

Go figure. It's the perplexing, sometimes inexplicable, sometimes dangerous, dark side of the life of politics.

*—Steve Paikin*
Toronto
September 2003

# THE BETRAYAL

I can see we've already cultivated a special understanding.
I scratch your back, and you stick a knife in mine.
—*Rimmer to Queeg on* Red Dwarf, *BBC-TV*

I've always said that in politics, your enemies can't hurt you,
but your friends will kill you.
—*former Texas governor Ann Richards*

For too many canadians, politics is a discredited, loathsome profession. The minute you enter it, your motives are suspect. The public finds it impossible to believe that anyone participates without a sinister, self-aggrandizing agenda. That's why it's astonishing that so many men and women are still attracted to placing their names on ballots and standing for office. After all, the majority of people who do that will lose. Of the winners, the overwhelming majority will not achieve either the personal or professional goals they established before entering politics. And, of course, a significant percentage of politicians will end up leaving the arena before they're ready to go, when for one reason or another the electorate does not invite them to continue in their jobs.

Politics can be a noble calling. But it can also break your heart in deeply profound ways—beyond losing an election. Over and over during interviews for this book, politicians have confirmed that their most deeply disturbing moments occur not when a critic skilfully slices and dices them in public. That they expect. But when a colleague does it unexpectedly or surreptitiously—at a closed-door meeting, perhaps—the wounds are deeper and often never heal.

Back in the late 1980s, I attended a Queen's Park press gallery dinner in Toronto. This is an annual event where journalists and the politicians they cover temporarily sheathe their knives and schmooze the night away. Comedy is an important feature of the evening. Every party leader goes up on stage and does a few minutes of stand-up. On the evening in question, the Liberals' David Peterson was unable to be there, so one of his caucus mates— David Ramsay—performed in his stead. It was an unusual choice because Ramsay had been a Liberal for only a short time. He first won election in his northern Ontario riding as a New Democrat. He then became one of the very few politicians in Canadian history to cross the floor to another party and win re-election anyway. Ramsay did his comedy bit, which wasn't bad. But that view was not universally held. I was sitting at a table with Bob Rae, the NDP leader, and he never once cracked a smile during Ramsay's routine. In fact, Rae didn't even look at his former caucus mate as Ramsay left the stage and returned to his seat. I asked Rae whether he was aware of his strained response. He certainly was.

"I'll never speak to him again," he said in a soft but clearly angry voice. "When somebody betrays you like that, you never forget it."

Betrayal. By colleagues. It is the seamy underbelly of politics that the public hears little about. Our newspapers are filled with stories of strategic battles between parties. But the wars among colleagues are often far more vicious, and much less publicized.

Michael Bryant is an intelligent, gifted speaker from midtown Toronto. He's had more formal education than probably 99 percent of people in politics (bachelor and master's degrees from the University of British Columbia, law degree from Osgoode Hall, and another master's degree from Harvard; to boot, he was a former clerk at the Supreme Court of Canada for the current chief justice).

Almost five years ago, I met him at a political function. He was bright-eyed and bushy-tailed and couldn't have been more than thirty-five years old. He stuck out his hand like a pro and said, "Hi Steve, nice to meet you, I'm Michael Bryant. I'm going to win the Liberal nomination in St. Paul's, then beat the Tories for the seat during the [Ontario] election." These were the first words out of his mouth. I smiled my "I-know-what-you're-in-for-and-you-don't-and-besides-I've-heard-that-speech-before" smile, but his enthusiasm and ambition were infectious. By the end of the conversation, I suspected that wasn't the last I'd see of Michael Bryant.

Sure enough, on Ontario election night 1999, there was Bryant's name at the top of the lists in St. Paul's riding. Despite a renewed majority for Mike Harris's Conservative government, Bryant went against the province-wide trend and won big.

Several months later, I ran into him again and asked him how it was going. He was candid.

"Steve, I never would have believed it. The feuding. The internecine warfare. The back-stabbing. And you know what?"

"What?" I asked.

"I love it!"

I love Bryant's story too, but most people, when confronted with the dark side of politics, don't have quite as much fun. In fact, to the contrary. They become depressed at how tough it is to survive, let alone thrive, in such a rough business.

David Goyette, for example, used to be a political consultant in Toronto before he got sick of the game and dropped virtually all of his political contracts. He was a senior adviser to then Toronto mayor Art Eggleton in the early 1980s, and thereafter worked for several Liberal cabinet ministers in the Peterson government. He remembers well the advice he gave one junior minister, who reported to a senior minister and was a rookie to politics.

"I told her that her greatest threat on the job was going to be from the inside," Goyette says.

The junior minister disagreed, insisting the opposition parties were her real problem. She was convinced that, if she knew her stuff and dealt with her opponents effectively, she would be okay. And so she approached cabinet, satisfied in the knowledge that her colleagues would assist her in securing a certain amount of money for an important project under her jurisdiction.

Everything was proceeding along smoothly until the final cabinet meeting on the issue. The senior minister then proceeded, without any warning or advance word to her "colleague," to cut the junior minister's legs out from under her. She declared at that meeting that the money for the project would be significantly less than the amount agreed upon earlier. The junior minister's wonderful plans, dependent on the kindness of her senior minister, were dashed.

"This junior minister had no knowledge that this was coming," Goyette recalls. "She was heartbroken, fell into tears, fell into depression for a couple of days and thought, 'Oh my God, I've been Brutusized!' To me, that's been the one thing that most new members are constantly surprised about. It's my friends that are going to get me, it's not my enemies."

Michael Marzolini, chair and chief executive officer of Pollara, the Liberal Party of Canada's polling company for more than a decade, says his concern about politics is that the relationships are ever-changing. "Somebody who purports to be your best friend today may try to stick a knife in you tomorrow. And vice versa. It's the nature of the game and it's a shame." Marzolini thinks business is more "cards-on-the-table." He's seen too many cabinet ministers try to make one another look bad, in hopes of getting some future promotional advantage.

One incident that left a nasty taste in Marzolini's mouth took place at the 1984 federal Liberal leadership convention to replace Pierre Trudeau. Laurence Decore, mayor of Edmonton at the time, controlled a bloc of delegates who voted for cabinet minister Mark McGuigan on the first ballot. But before the first-ballot results were even announced, Decore bolted from the McGuigan section of the hall and made a beeline for John Turner's box.

"It was so opportunistic," Marzolini recalls. "There was no loyalty."

Likewise, Sharon Carstairs remembers the day the man she thought would succeed her as Manitoba Liberal leader pulled a fast one on her. Jim Carr had been privately planning to leave Manitoba politics to take a job at the *Winnipeg Free Press*. He didn't breathe a word of it to his closest caucus colleague, Carstairs, until literally minutes before he called a news conference. "It was the biggest disappointment for me," says Carstairs, who by the time of our interview was leader of the government in the Senate. "I was absolutely astounded. This was a man with whom I'd chaired everything for six years. And I'd always seen him as the natural successor."

ONE OF THE MOST EXTRAORDINARY TALES of betrayal in Canadian politics took place just a few years ago. It happened to a politician who had made history by becoming the first woman ever to lead a major political party in her province. She took her party from no seats to official opposition status in a relatively short space of time, only to be knifed—not in the back, but in the front—by her colleagues.

What's most unusual about the betrayal of Lynda Haverstock is that her brother Dennis Ham, seven years her senior, had watched virtually the same thing happen to his leader during his time in public life.

Ham was there at the rebirth of the Conservative party in Saskatchewan in the 1970s. The Conservatives hadn't been in power since 1934, and had won just one seat over the next forty years. But in 1975, Dennis Ham was one of seven Conservative MLAs who laid the foundations for a Tory revival. What he saw during his short time in the legislature disgusted him. He watched a plot unfold to oust Dick Collver as Tory leader, and the backroom machinations were so unpleasant that Ham not only quit politics but left Saskatchewan altogether. He hadn't been a Collver fan to begin with, but was convinced that the style of politics being practised in Saskatchewan amounted to borderline treason.

Twenty years later, Ham's sister described him in an interview as "still very distressed by the really appalling behaviour that he saw lodged against Dick Collver, by this group that wanted the power"—the very group that Ham suspected would ruin Saskatchewan financially, and eventually did.

(Collver's name may ring some bells. After he was turfed by the Tories, he sat as an independent member of the legislature and started his own quasi-western-separatist movement, the Unionist Party. He was also an acquaintance of fellow MLA Colin Thatcher, who often spoke to Collver of his hatred for his ex-wife, JoAnn Wilson. Collver tried to get Thatcher to reach a fair settlement with Wilson. But Thatcher would have none of it and subsequently was found guilty of killing his ex-wife. He is serving a life sentence.)

Dennis Ham's cautionary tale should have been all the warning Lynda Haverstock needed to avoid public life. She certainly thought it was.

"Public life seemed devoid of anything of real principle," Haverstock recalls thinking at the time. "And so I made the proclamation that never, ever, ever would I ever enter public life."

Haverstock had another, more private reason for concluding that politics wasn't for her. Her own "sordid past," as she jokingly describes it, also made her an unlikely candidate to make history in a province that is used to creating its own political heroes and then exporting them all over the country.

Lynda Haverstock grew up in Swift Current, Saskatchewan, got married at age fifteen, dropped out of school and had a baby at age sixteen, then found herself left to her own devices in the raising of her daughter when her husband literally disappeared. She hasn't seen him since.

"Thirty-six years ago nobody ever had a baby and kept it," she says. "Thirty-six years ago, I felt I was the only person who did what I did. And that was a very isolating thing."

In fact, ten other girls also got pregnant at Haverstock's high school. But she says they all "disappeared. And when they came home they didn't have a baby. I chose something different."

Apart from all that, Haverstock had to contend with painful form of rheumatoid arthritis for a decade. She got around in a wheelchair for a year, then graduated to arm canes and eventually crutches.

Instead of folding her tent and giving up on life, Haverstock went back to school and earned her master's degree in education, and a doctorate in clinical psychology. She began to develop an expertise and a reputation for helping farm families cope with Saskatchewan's ever-present agricultural crisis.

"What frightened me so much in the 1980s was watching my culture die," Haverstock says. There was no shortage of people fighting the good fight for the "agri" part of agriculture. But not enough people understood the "culture" part of the equation.

Haverstock was both moved and outraged at the farm crisis. Suicide rates were up. Families were falling apart and going under financially. "My 1980s experience with the people of my province was more than I could bear," she says. "I could work eighteen-hour days, seven days a week, three hundred and sixty-five days a year with farm families in crisis. And I would put a dent in nothing."

And so, despite her brother's experience and her "sordid past," Lynda Haverstock reached out to politics. At the time she was a therapist at a mental health clinic, a university professor, and a researcher working at the University of Saskatchewan's Centre for Agricultural Medicine, trying to put on paper some ideas for long-term solutions to the farm crisis. She had tried on several occasions to get a meeting with Grant Devine, whose Tories had captured the highest number of seats in Saskatchewan history in the 1982 election. Devine was both premier and agriculture minister—definitely the man Haverstock needed to see. But she was having no success. So, to the chagrin of many of Devine's staffers, she buttonholed Devine at a conference in Saskatoon, and gave him her business card and her paper in hopes of getting him to read about solutions to Saskatchewan's dilemma, both "agri" and "cultural," that she regarded as more profound than anything the government had considered to date. The encounter did not go well.

"I was really appalled and found him a little prick who really wasn't all that interested," says Haverstock, who is speaking from her office and knows my tape recorder is rolling at the other end of the phone line but evidently doesn't care how she describes the former premier. She felt Devine had no comprehension of the depth of the problem, other than to go to Ottawa and beg for a billion-dollar bailout—admittedly an expensive band-aid, but a band-aid nonetheless. A subsequent meeting with Devine provided her with further proof that he had little commitment to what she viewed as longer-term solutions.

Earlier, in her university student days of the 1970s, Haverstock had flirted with and rejected the New Democratic Party. Now she'd been rebuffed by Premier Devine a decade later. So in 1987, she decided to see what Saskatchewan's Liberal Party was all about. She discovered that the party, which had governed her province for thirty-four of its first thirty-nine years of existence, was now, itself, virtually non-existent. The Liberals were registering 4-percent support in public opinion polls.

Nevertheless, Haverstock accepted an invitation to speak at a Liberal policy convention and evidently turned heads because some party officials asked her to get more deeply involved. Why not, she figured, and they promised to be in touch. But, consistent with the party's utter disorganization at the time, it was rare for anyone to follow up on such a promise.

Haverstock made the follow-up move herself.

In 1988, the Liberals were in the midst of a leadership race. Ralph Goodale had resigned as party leader to enter federal politics. Haverstock attended an all-candidates' debate that was held at the University of Saskatchewan as part of the run-up to the leadership convention.

"I went and left there completely demoralized," she recalls. "I was so devastated. And all I thought about was, there is no hope. I don't want to be cruel, but I just felt that there was no one articulating anything in terms of a vision."

And then something unusual happened: one high-ranking party member started pressuring Haverstock to run for the leadership herself, even though the race was well under way. It seemed a ludicrous idea. Leadership contests are usually won by the candidate with the biggest Rolodex and the best organization. He (it always had been "he" in Saskatchewan) who knows and impresses the most party members, and who can put together a finely tuned campaign machine, is almost always victorious.

Which meant Haverstock had two problems. She had no apparent base of support in the party, having never campaigned for other candidates, gone to fundraisers, or hit the rubber-chicken circuit extolling the party's virtues. Worse, never mind that she had no organization to speak of, she had no organization at all.

Besides, her plate was already plenty full. She was teaching university, supervising graduate students in clinical work, doing other work through the Saskatoon Mental Health Clinic, and leading farm stress workshops at night.

The pressure continued to mount. Remembering her brother's experience, she called Dennis, who was now living in Calgary, for advice. Naturally, he tried to dissuade her from entering the fray. Not because he doubted she could do the job—he was, in fact, supremely confident of his sister's abilities to bring the Liberals back to political respectability. But he was terrified that what had happened to his leader would happen to his sister—that she would rebuild the party, only to be chucked overboard for another leader (undoubtedly a man) when the party was within striking distance of power. Dennis assured her he'd be there for her if she did take the plunge. But his advice was clear: If you go, watch your back. Watch your front. Watch everything.

There was someone else whose blessing Haverstock needed to obtain before she would consider entering public life. She had been both mother and father to her then 24-year-old daughter Dani almost from the beginning. Haverstock needed Dani to know that if she entered politics, she couldn't always be there for her—the time pressures and travel commitments of the job would be enormous. So she struck a pact with Dani, which included five personal commandments that to this day, she has kept private between them. She promised her daughter that if she even *thought* about breaking one of those commandments, she'd quit. Dani signed on the metaphorical dotted line and gave her blessing too.

So Lynda Haverstock did something extraordinary, maybe unprecedented, in Canadian political history. She threw her hat into the ring knowing that she had signed up none of the delegates attending the leadership convention. Her strategy was simple: campaign like hell in the time remaining, give the mother of all speeches at the convention, and hope to carry the day through dedication and inspiration.

And that's just what she did. On the April Fool's Day weekend of 1989, in the Regency Ballroom of the Hotel Saskatchewan in Regina, Lynda Maureen Haverstock became the first woman to lead a political party in Saskatchewan history. She captured 89 percent of the votes in a smashing first-ballot victory.

In most political parties, that kind of victory would constitute a significant mandate to lead. Come to think of it, you'd think Haverstock had earned carte blanche to do whatever she wanted to whip the party back into fighting shape. But she was about to learn some quick lessons about politics in the Saskatchewan Liberal Party.

First, the schisms were unbelievable. Regina Liberals hated Saskatoon Liberals. Where federal allegiances were concerned, John Turner supporters hated Jean Chrétien supporters. (Turner was still the national Liberal leader at this point, but on his way out, having lost two consecutive elections to Brian Mulroney.) Even the cleavages from the previous provincial leadership run between Ralph Goodale and Tony Merchant hadn't yet healed. The internecine entanglements were constant.

That was the pack of wolves Lynda Haverstock had signed on to lead. And she didn't have to wait long before the party would test her mettle.

During the course of Haverstock's first year as leader, the federal Liberals held a convention to replace Turner. While Saskatchewan Liberals divided primarily into the Jean Chrétien and Paul Martin camps, Haverstock stayed on the sidelines and played neutral. It's the kind of approach that both William Davis and Peter Lougheed took in the 1983 federal Progressive Conservative contest. The thinking was that the provincial leader was going to have to be on very good terms and work closely with whichever candidate won the federal contest, so why risk alienating anyone? While Ontario's Davis and Alberta's Lougheed were praised for their practical approach to leadership politics, Haverstock was vilified. Each camp thought she was secretly supporting the other. It was the first of many run-ins with the party brass.

Nevertheless, Liberals approached the next provincial election, in 1991, with considerably more optimism. Haverstock had helped transform a party that was $300,000 in the red, with two lawsuits pending, into a party that was $155,000 in the black (which is, coincidentally, exactly what the Liberals spent on that '91 campaign). The Tories under Grant Devine were imploding, thanks to policies that had ratcheted up the debt to unprecedented levels. The PCs were also dealing with a nightmare of political corruption. Several key advisers and cabinet ministers would be the subject of criminal prosecutions, including Eric Berntson, the deputy premier, who was eventually convicted of fraud in February 1999. Some Tories even went to prison.

On election night—October 21, 1991—the Liberals found themselves with almost 24 percent of the total votes cast, a huge improvement from where the party started before Haverstock's leadership. The other good news was that, unlike the other two parties, Liberal voters weren't overwhelmingly in urban Saskatchewan, the NDP's stronghold, or the rural parts of the province, which had been Tory territory the previous decade. The votes were split evenly between the two. This suggested that the Liberals were perhaps poised to put together a broad-based urban-rural coalition, which could take the party over the top on some future election date.

But there was bad news too. Because of the way the votes split, Haverstock's Liberals won just one seat—her own, in Saskatoon Greystone, the largest urban constituency in the province. The NDP, under Roy Romanow, returned to power after a hiatus of nearly a decade, matching Devine's record-busting fifty-five seats. The Tories were fortunate to maintain ten seats.

"The fact that, in an NDP landslide, these people chose to go against the trend and vote for me was just a tremendous, tremendous honour," says Haverstock, who despite running a province-wide campaign recalls still managing to knock on every door in her constituency.

"The very, very difficult part of that day was realizing I was going to the legislature alone," she adds. "So what was actually a victory was not."

Still, Haverstock quickly set her priorities. She wanted to continue to rebuild the party, which meant lots of travelling around Saskatchewan. At the same time, she wanted the Liberal voice to be heard in the legislature. Given that the Conservatives were an utterly discredited bunch, she hoped—if it didn't sound too presumptuous—to be the constructive conscience of the House. She'd attack the NDP where warranted, but not just for the sake of attack.

This strategy would come back to haunt her because many of her fellow Liberals wanted a more predictable, oppose-everything style of opposition. But Haverstock was determined to practise politics differently, and thought she had the mandate from her leadership-convention win and her election-night vote count to do so. When the new NDP government introduced its Speech from the Throne, Haverstock did something highly unusual. She listened to it. She reflected on it. And she actually voted in favour of it. She felt the government needed a break, to start repairing the damage the Tories had left behind. She was sure the general public, which had just handed the New Democrats a massive majority, would see it the same way.

The public may have been tuned in to Haverstock's self-styled "new politics," but the old politicos definitely weren't.

"I believed that the new government needed to be given support," she says, "that what the people needed was to see that we were coming together to work on their behalf."

Years later, Haverstock admits it was awfully naive of her to think she could have convinced the political establishment to practise politics differently. "Neither the NDP nor many Liberals ever let me forget that vote," she says. "They acted like I was just a fool. But I still believe I was right."

Former Saskatchewan premier Allan Blakeney understands the quandary in which Haverstock found herself. "She wasn't able to turn her back on the old politics without making it sound like she was turning her back on the old politicians," he says.

Haverstock continued to do politics her way. Against the wishes of many in her party and again forgoing a tactical opportunity to make life miserable for the NDP, she supported the government's gay rights legislation. And paid a price.

"How absolutely unconscionable that there are people to this very day that see this as some kind of game," she says. "Like, it's some bloody performance. I don't think so."

If there is one absolute truth of Saskatchewan politics, it's that virtually all governments get a second chance. Roy Romanow won three elections. Grant Devine got two terms. Allan Blakeney was there for eleven years. Ross Thatcher won two elections. Tommy Douglas was premier for almost seventeen years. You can go all the way back to Saskatchewan's origins in 1905, and only once has a party failed to win consecutive elections (the exception was a minority Conservative government during the Depression).

So to think that Lynda Haverstock was going to break a nearly century-old trend and defeat the incumbent New Democrats was unrealistic. And sure enough, she didn't. But on June 21, 1995, Haverstock's second election as Liberal leader, the party's fortunes again improved significantly. Haverstock took the Liberals' total vote to 36 percent, once again evenly split between rural and urban ridings. And ten new Liberal MLAs would be joining her at the legislature, forming Her Majesty's Official Opposition to a reduced

NDP majority. In most provinces, in most parties, that would constitute steady, successful growth. For many Saskatchewan Liberals, who already objected to Haverstock's new style of politics and freelancing on issues, it constituted failure. While observers from across Canada saw a rebirth in Liberal fortunes, others in Saskatchewan were ready to move in for the kill.

Some people suggested in media interviews at the time that the Liberals should have taken twice as many seats. Others privately groused about the strict new personal code of ethics Haverstock imposed on her caucus or the new fundraising guidelines. On occasion she would veto fundraising efforts by backroom officials because, in her view, "they absolutely weren't kosher."

Before Haverstock could even gather her new caucus together for its first meeting, a coup was afoot. A significant part of the new caucus met privately to plot its next move. When the whole caucus eventually did meet some days later, Haverstock faced her enemies head-on.

"I told them the truth," she says. "I said, 'I know that there are people here who want my job. But it's important to learn your own first. Our job now is to earn what the people have given us, and that is the privilege of being able to represent them.' And this just went right over their heads, because [their plan] was already in motion."

A few months later the Liberals held their leadership review. It was on November 11—certainly a day to remember for Haverstock and her supporters. Saskatchewan's Julius Caesar was walking into the proverbial senate house. That same group of enemy MLAs approached Haverstock behind closed doors and gave her an ultimatum. They didn't like her new rules, her new style, or her new politics. Now that the Liberals were on the verge of power, Haverstock was being forced out. It was just as her brother had prophesied seven years earlier.

"There were people in that room who were scuzz-buckets. I mean, you know, they just were," she says, still with evident disgust.

Ironically, Haverstock expected to be done in by some ambitious colleagues. In fact, she predicted it during an interview with a business magazine, shortly after winning the leadership. "I understood that for many people to have a woman as leader would be difficult," she was quoted as saying. "And that in all likelihood, once the party had been built, I would be seen as expendable and a man would be brought in as leader." (This brings to mind an article that then senator John F. Kennedy wrote for *Everywoman's Magazine* in 1956. In it, he mused about the qualities a woman president needed to have: "The wisdom of Eleanor Roosevelt, the leadership of Joan of Arc, the compassion of Queen Victoria, the cleverness of Clare Booth Luce, the determination of polio nurse Sister Kenny, and the courage of Helen Keller." Apparently, the same might be said for female party leaders at this time in Canada.)

What must have been particularly galling was seeing not only the leaders of the coup but the silent colleagues who were watching the drama unfold more as spectators than participants. Haverstock thought she had developed friendships with some of those who now stood idly by, watching their leader suffer the equivalent of a political lynching. "You know what?" she says. "There are people who simply don't have courage. There are people who are just afraid. There are people who are followers, not leaders."

Now the ball was in Haverstock's court. She could confront her adversaries and fight another Liberal civil war. She could stay on as a kind of lame-duck leader and give in to their demands. Or she could pick up the ball and go home.

"I could have chosen to play politics their way, taken them on, and won," she insists. "But if I had done that I would have become exactly like the kind of people in politics I was trying to not be like."

Fighting meant violating some of the five commandments Haverstock swore to her daughter she'd never violate. So she left that unfriendly gathering, went up to her hotel room, and talked to her husband Harley Olsen, her daughter, and her closest political adviser, Elaine Hughston. She told all of them she was finished leading the Liberal Party of Saskatchewan.

Haverstock returned to the convention floor and announced her resignation. Her leadership of the party would end where it began—in the Regency Ballroom of the Hotel Saskatchewan. She said the news would no doubt come as a surprise to many and a relief to some. The most dramatic speech of her political life was delivered with no speaking notes: she ad-libbed it. Some delegates began to scream at her to reconsider. Others simply cried. And then came the media onslaught.

"This must be the worst day of your life," suggested one reporter, perhaps not completely aware that the woman in the middle of the scrum had been a single mother in high school.

"It doesn't even come close," Haverstock shot back.

For most politicians, the story might end there. But, as you've no doubt gathered, Haverstock doesn't give up easily. Rather than quit altogether, she continued to sit in the legislature as an independent Liberal. Not only that, she occupied a chair literally a few feet away from her former caucus mates, who had not only done her in but had the temerity to rescind her Liberal party membership. The Speaker of the legislature told her privately he could never, ever, ever, ever have sat in such proximity to that gang.

With Haverstock gone as leader, the Saskatchewan Liberal Party began what looked like a return to irrelevance. One of the few Liberal MLAs who had stayed loyal to Haverstock—and the party's only Aboriginal member—eventually resigned his seat, ostensibly because relations with his fellow Liberals were so bad that his colleagues weren't even telling him when caucus meetings were being held. So he sought and won an NDP nomination, and was victorious in the ensuing by-election. Buckley Belanger would go on to become an NDP cabinet minister in Saskatchewan, responsible for the environment and northern affairs. (Belanger later sent a picture to Haverstock that he'd inscribed: "What could have been and should have been.")

Still others left to create the new Saskatchewan Party, a coalition of rural Conservatives, Reformers, and disaffected Liberals, all championing tax cuts and smaller government.

Haverstock finished her term, but did not exactly go gentle into the night. She became a talk-show host on Saskatoon radio station CJWW, from where she could continue to press her issues and stay in touch with people.

On September 16, 1999, without Haverstock at the helm, the Liberals' support in the ensuing election plummeted to just 20 percent—good for three seats—a thrashing by any definition. But as luck would have it, they were three crucially important seats. The bottom fell out of the Romanow government's support, which was reduced to twenty-nine seats and minority status. The upstart Saskatchewan Party came out of nowhere to shock the province's political establishment. In a rare error, the CBC-TV election-night broadcast had to eat some serious humble pie. Early in the evening, the station's "Decision Desk" had declared that the NDP would renew its majority status. But the longer the night went on, the more it became apparent that something extraordinary was happening. In its first election run, the Saskatchewan Party captured twenty-six seats. Less than two weeks after the election, Premier Romanow and the new Liberal leader, Jim Melenchuk, formed a coalition government of what they called "equal partners." Two of the Liberal MLAs got cabinet posts (Melenchuk took the education portfolio), while the third was appointed Speaker of the legislature. Haverstock called the scenario "the unholy alliance."

The end of the Haverstock story? Not by a long shot. Haverstock took her daughter Dani, who has multiple sclerosis, down to Florida to consult medical specialists. While in the Sunshine State, she got a message to call an Ottawa phone number that she didn't recognize. With an active itinerary in Florida, she figured she'd wait until she got back to Canada before returning the call.

But the caller was persistent. The next message said the call was from the prime minister's appointments office. Haverstock assumed she was being approached for advice on some Saskatchewan citizen who might be considered for an appointment, so again she didn't rush to return the call.

But eventually she rang the number. And she got the shock of a lifetime. Prime Minister Chrétien wanted to know whether Lynda Haverstock, one-time high school dropout and single teenaged mother, would consider accepting an appointment as the next lieutenant-governor of Saskatchewan.

*Well, I am stunned,* Haverstock remembers thinking. "I was stunned because, trust me on this one, this was not in the mix of my life, you know? I just never believed that I would ever, ever get some consideration like that."

Once again, Haverstock consulted with her daughter and husband. She enjoyed her radio gig. She had a packed schedule of farm crisis workshops on the go. And one of the things she liked about not being in public life was the time she now had to spend with Dani and her two grandchildren, her three stepchildren, and her step-grandchild. Harley Olsen, her husband, had also just finished convincing his employer to move his job from Regina to Saskatoon. Now he would have to sell them on moving the job back to Regina, without sounding as if he'd just flown in from Mars.

After a good discussion, they all came to the same conclusion: Lynda Haverstock belonged back in public life.

"I think that this is the perfect fit for you," Dani told her mother.

"I think this is the job you were made for in your life," said her husband.

"I was very moved," Haverstock says. "I felt very supported."

She called the Prime Minister's Office and said yes, she'd be honoured to be considered. The next evening, Jean Chrétien called and offered her the job. Even though they had both been Liberal leaders at the same time, Haverstock and Chrétien had never been terribly close. When he had come through Saskatchewan, they had met to discuss party business and provincial issues. But she had made it a point never to call Ottawa just to schmooze. She respected Chrétien too much to waste his time. Haverstock points out, in very un-vice-regal terms, "As you have probably been able to figure out, I learned very early on that life is too short for bullshit."

But not too short to meet the Queen, which Haverstock did with Olsen after taking the job. A private audience on the Queen's home turf, no less. Their limousine pulled up at Buckingham Palace just in time for the ever-popular Changing of the Guard, which meant that hundreds of people were at hand when they arrived.

"I felt so sorry for them because they thought someone important was going through the gates to meet the Queen," Haverstock jokes.

I suggest to Her Honour that some part of her being must have lapped up the delicious irony of her appointment. After all, her enemies in the Liberal party who were so pleased to see her gone from Saskatchewan politics now had to face a different reality. Most of them had lost their seats. Conversely, she had staged a triumphant return and would be a fixture on the provincial scene for at least five years.

Haverstock insists she experienced no feelings of vindication. From virtually any other politician, the claim would not be credible. From her, it is, and the following personal history lesson will explain why.

For more than thirty years, Lynda Haverstock's daughter has received virtually nothing from her biological father. Not a Christmas card. Not a birthday card. Three separate payments of fifty dollars constitute his total contribution to Haverstock's child care expenses.

At first, Haverstock was furious and bitter. "I thought, someday that guy is going to know what he did," she says. "And he will live with regret."

Then, when her daughter was eight years old, Haverstock got a phone call from Dani's father, totally out of the blue—the only contact she's had with him since his disappearance. He was incoherent and sobbing uncontrollably. She discovered her feelings of anger and betrayal had disappeared.

"I don't need to get even," she says. "I don't. It comes at too much of a cost."

And now Lynda Haverstock seems to have the job that she was, in fact, meant to have all along. "I get to be around people everywhere, from every walk of life," she says. If she serves out her entire five-year term, she'll be Saskatchewan's lieutenant-governor on January 1, 2005, when the province celebrates its centennial in Canada. It's a celebration she yearns to be a part of.

"I get to say exactly what I care about, what I believe, what I feel deeply committed to," she says. "But nobody's suspicious as to why I am giving them that message, because I am not in public life any more as a politician."

In some respects, that's a sad commentary on the state of political discourse in Canada. We have so trivialized our politicians, and many of them have themselves so discredited the profession, that only when they leave do we give credence to what they say.

Haverstock finishes our conversation by wishing me well and then says, "Adios amigo." Not at all your typical vice-regal send-off. But perhaps appropriate from one of the inspiring survivors of political betrayal.

IMAGINE BEING A MEMBER of Prime Minister Pierre Trudeau's cabinet. You've had a front-row seat for some of the most important national debates in Canadian history. Then imagine that you've also been a politician since you were in high school, and end up walking away from the only job you've really ever loved when you realize that your enemies have taken over your party. But your story is not over. Years later, to add insult to injury, you're hounded by law enforcement officials, who accuse you of having misused funds in your department while you were a minister. You know the charges are bogus, but the allegation costs you almost a decade of your life—you lose your reputation, your family, and virtually every dime you've got to fight back. Eventually, you're exonerated from all the charges, but the victory has almost killed you. Yet, through it all, you find you've still got the itch to run for office again. And you try to mount a comeback. But your former friends, who have taken back control of the party, have rigged the game to prevent you from making that comeback. When you call on your former cabinet colleague, who's since become prime minister, to ask for help to pay your astronomical legal bills—help you're entitled to receive—he makes you wait another six years, endure more trauma, and hit rock bottom before finally coming through. Talk about feeling betrayed.

And despite all that, you still want to run for office *again?*

Some would say that you need to have your head examined. Others prefer a different interpretation. Welcome to the life and times of John Carr Munro.

If you lived in Hamilton, Ontario, in the 1960s and '70s, it was impossible not to know John Munro. He was as ubiquitous a presence in the Steel City then as Sheila Copps is today—probably more so. He was the political gatekeeper of the city. He knew everyone and had his fingers in everything. His influence around town was legendary.

Munro's political memories actually go back to the days of William Lyon Mackenzie King, who was prime minister when Munro started at Westdale High School. The young Munro liked King and the way he handled the conscription debate, but Munro didn't have a lot of company in his affections for the prime minister. He thinks thirty-nine of the forty people in his class hated King. And Munro's maternal grandfather, Leeming Carr, was a big-C Conservative, having served in the cabinet of Ontario premier G. Howard Ferguson.

Mackenzie King may deserve the credit for John Munro's political awakening. But it was a tough-as-nails militaristic school principal, known to his students as "Baldy" McQueen, who planted the seeds of Munro's commitment. Colonel McQueen ran a tight ship. He had students marching down the halls to class with army-like precision. Munro wasn't much of a fan of the colonel's management style, and he let the principal know how he felt. He may have had wider political views that didn't mesh with those of his fellow students, but Munro's classmates appreciated his taking the lead when it came to the in-house matter of the bald colonel. Munro successfully ran for president of the student council, only to have McQueen threaten to void the election—so concerned was he about the young whipper-snapper he'd have to deal with. Eventually the principal thought better of it, although he would suspend Munro from the school for a few days over a future disagreement.

"We were storming into the administration offices and demanding the colonel withdraw some of his recent edicts," Munro recalls. "Even making excuses for the excesses of youth, I think he was a little too militaristic."

Osgoode Hall Law School in Toronto was Munro's next stop. During his first year there, he had to deal with a family tragedy. His father died, and rather than leave his mother alone in Hamilton, Munro decided to commute to school every day. One of the other

Osgoode law students in his car pool was Lincoln Alexander, who would go on to become a Conservative MP from Hamilton and lieutenant-governor of Ontario.

Munro's political ambition was clear to everyone who watched him take on "Baldy" McQueen. So no one could have been terribly surprised when, at the tender age of twenty-three, he successfully ran for Hamilton City Council.

But he overreached in his next effort to move up the political ladder. He challenged Ellen Fairclough in the 1957 general election. Munro lost badly. Fairclough became Canada's first female cabinet minister, in John Diefenbaker's government.

Undeterred, Munro tried again in 1962, this time opposing Quinto Martini, who was one of Dief's parliamentary secretaries and Canada's first MP of Italian descent. This time, Munro won election as an Opposition backbencher. He was thirty-one years old. Nine months and another election later, he was an MP in Lester Pearson's Liberal government.

Munro bided his time on the backbenches, normally not a fun place for ambitious, impatient young MPs. But, even with the benefit of forty years' hindsight, Munro remembers that as one of the most satisfying times of his life. Pearson appointed him parliamentary secretary to the minister of health, Judy LaMarsh, who put Munro on the committees that would push medicare and the Canada Pension Plan through the House of Commons. Munro worked closely with the legendary New Democrat parliamentarian Stanley Knowles—a key alliance given the Liberals' minority government status. Munro also chaired a committee of the Liberal caucus whose chief task was to resist buckling under the pressure of the insurance industry, which deeply distrusted the new CPP and medicare legislation. After Pierre Trudeau became prime minister in April 1968, Munro performed the same function for the new health minister, Allan MacEachen, regarding the passage of medicare.

But bigger things were in store for John Munro. Trudeau appointed the Hamilton MP to his first cabinet in 1968. He would only be a minister without portfolio, but then again, only for two months. When Trudeau won a smashing majority victory later that year, he appointed Munro the minister of national health and welfare. Obviously, Munro knew the portfolio and the issues inside-out.

As politicians, Pierre Elliott Trudeau and John Carr Munro couldn't have been more different. Trudeau was the wealthy, elegant philosopher king from Mount Royal. Munro was a middle-class, look-out-for-the-little-guy street fighter from blue-collar Steel City. But the prime minister liked something he saw in Munro. The Hamilton MP had reliable antennae. He knew what the average Canadian thought about any and every Trudeau government move.

When it came to running a department, Munro knew something too: that it was bloody difficult to get anything through. Today, the conventional wisdom on the Trudeau government is that it was too left-wing, with too much spending and too little concern for budget deficits. And yet even a self-proclaimed left-winger such as Munro, who wanted more program spending to help lower-income people, found himself stymied by what he perceived as conservative elements in the government, and particularly the bureaucracy.

"We were mortified that at times they orchestrated endless meetings to really disable the elected people," Munro says of the mandarins of the time. "It was an exhaustive round of meetings and so on. We were just generally neutralized, and Canada became a place where there was really bureaucratic control.

"You could form alliances, which I was bound and determined to do, or else you'd be totally disarmed," he says. So, "The Big Spenders," as they were called in cabinet, stuck up for one another. *You need something in Prince Edward Island? No problem. I'll back you at Treasury Board if you back this project I need in*

*Hamilton.* Ron Basford, a one-time minister of justice from Vancouver, used to joke that he liked being sent to Hamilton to give speeches because he wanted to see where all the government's money was going.

Deal by deal, Munro brought millions to the southwest tip of Lake Ontario. If you thought that added to his local lustre—and it did—think about what having an exclusive meeting with one of the Beatles might do for his reputation.

It's doubtful that John Munro got into politics so he could rub shoulders with rock 'n' roll legends. But two days before Christmas 1969, that's just what the minister for health and welfare did. A good percentage of Canadians remember John Lennon and Yoko Ono visiting the Parliament buildings for an hour-long meeting with Prime Minister Trudeau. Many fewer people remember that the next meeting on the ex-Beatle's itinerary was with Canada's chain-smoking health minister.

"They were sitting in my office discussing the decriminalization of marijuana," Munro recalls. "It was a fun meeting. They were different."

Meeting rock legends may have been one of the stranger perks of the job, but Munro knew that was not why he was in politics. His working-class constituents on Barton Street and Kenilworth Avenue in Hamilton's east end sent him to Ottawa eight times to fight for them. Ironically, one of his greatest achievements in that regard would also break his heart.

More than anything else, Munro wanted Canadians to have a guaranteed annual income. He thought it was a progressive way for the government to hand out social benefits. He also saw the policy as a means of bypassing the bureaucrats. "There was a nauseating stigma to them delving into people's lives, making them answer all sorts of questions," Munro says. "It was just a licence for abuse of power over individuals."

Munro liked the idea of a guaranteed annual income for a variety
of reasons. After months of "horrifying study," as he puts it, he
believed this approach would rationalize all the different plans the
provinces had in place, make the system more efficient, eliminate
duplication, not to mention remind Canadians that the Liberal
government was playing a meaningful role in their daily lives.

The problem with it was that it required a massive investment
upfront, and it would be some time before the savings would be
realized.

"In politics, that's tough," Munro says. "And when it's big,
upfront money, almost all your colleagues leave you. Many of the
other ministers that were really your friends, on the progressive
side of cabinet, started saying, 'If Munro gets all this, there won't
be anything left for our portfolios.'"

Munro came to despise a system of government that pitted not
friend against foe, but friend against friend.

The cabinet office organized spending in so-called envelopes
rather than by department. There would be only so many dollars in
the social policy envelope. Munro knew the thinking behind it all:
"We'll put all the progressive ministers in the one envelope. And the
others had their money all locked up in their envelopes, and then,
we'll get all those guys killing each other," Munro says. "They
wanted a fractured cabinet, and disabled a lot of the progressive
element in the cabinet."

Munro was running out of time, and allies. Then he met with
Prime Minister Trudeau.

"Well, I'm going to do something for you, John," the prime
minister said. "I'm not gonna shoot this whole thing down. We'll
give you a guaranteed annual income, but we won't do it for all the
people. We'll do it for the senior citizens."

It was a bitter pill to swallow, but it was something. Seniors
already automatically got old age security. But Munro's plan

would become an added benefit for low-income seniors. "You file your own income statement. And you'd get a cheque based on that income statement," he says. "We inaugurated that right through Canada, and hundreds of thousands of people got it. Even more so today," he says with a pride that's kept in check by the fact that the program was only a fraction of what he wanted. In one of the oddities of public life, Munro had to traverse the country singing the praises of the new policy, when in reality he was deeply disappointed.

"But if you resigned over it, then you're totally disabled," he says. "You get nothing."

Thirty years later, Munro can afford to be a little prouder of what he accomplished.

"It wasn't one of those colourless, emotionless transfer payments that people never see—a bookkeeping entry between two levels of government," he says. "It *really* went to them. And I think it was a significant force for national unity."

Munro would spend four years in the health portfolio, then another six stormy years as labour minister, where he had to deal with organized labour's disgust with the government's wage and price control program. But he remained a favourite of Trudeau's, and spent his final four years in government as minister of Indian affairs and northern development. It would prove to be a job of historic import for Munro's political career, but not for the reasons he'd hoped.

John Munro thought he was going to make history as a forward-thinking minister of Indian affairs and northern development.

"The whole Department of Indian Affairs is considered a swamp," he says. "They had to put up with paternalism run rampant." Having two portfolios was also a huge challenge. "You're always on the road," he says. "And I had northern affairs too so you're always near a state of exhaustion."

Munro did put a year of blood, sweat, toil, and tears into getting an Indian anti-discrimination bill through Parliament, only to see his efforts fail by one vote in the Senate. He found the heartbreak on this one even worse than losing the guaranteed annual income debate, particularly because he felt a Liberal senator betrayed him on the vote (Munro won't discuss the senator's identity).

There were better days. It was Munro who got to announce that, at long last, the federal government would support the creation of Nunavut, a third northern territory.

But four years into his tenure in Indian affairs, Munro's champion in cabinet went for a walk in the snow. Pierre Trudeau was quitting. The leadership race was on, and Munro wanted a piece of it. Everyone knew this was a two-horse race—John Turner versus Jean Chrétien. However, the man from Hamilton East wanted to use his candidacy to improve his clout at the cabinet table. Munro thought Native Canadians always had a tough job getting their fair share of the pie in Ottawa. He found his colleagues treated him a whole lot better when they knew he might control a sizable bloc of delegates at the convention.

"You could just sense it," he recalls of those cabinet meetings. "You didn't need to sit in a backroom and sign a piece of paper. They knew the realities. They were hoping to please me, marginally. My clients, the Indians, were fighting desperately for money. And I guess I wouldn't think too kindly of a guy who's giving me a bad time for money for my own people."

The convention itself was anticlimactic for Munro. The day before the all-important speeches, he came down with a debilitating case of laryngitis. You could feel the sympathy in the hall for someone who desperately wanted to articulate his vision of the country but could barely get his vocal cords to cooperate.

That wasn't Munro's only problem that weekend. As he got to the podium to speak, he noticed an almost complete absence of supporters nearby. This was certainly puzzling, since the party had allocated a certain number of so-called floor spaces to each candidate. Munro was supposed to have 150. The party had even sent him a bill for several thousand dollars to cover the cost of those spaces. Munro's campaign team investigated the matter further and discovered that Team Turner had somehow outmanoeuvred the Munro convention forces and taken all of Munro's floor spaces. "So I raised a bit of a stink on this and said, 'Look, John Turner's paying this bill. I want no part of it,'" Munro recalls. Turner paid the bill, he adds.

Floor spaces or not, Munro hung in for one ballot, then moved to Jean Chrétien for the second ballot. Everyone knew Turner would take it on that next ballot (and he did), but Munro just couldn't go to Turner. "We differed on almost everything," he says of the man who would win and then fritter away the prime ministership in embarrassing fashion.

Nevertheless, with Turner in the driver's seat, Munro did the unthinkable. After twenty-two years in federal politics, he walked away. His re-election in Hamilton East was as guaranteed as anything in politics can possibly be. But he concluded that not having the job he loved was better than serving under John Turner.

"After all those years in cabinet," Munro says, "to go back to the backbench with John Turner, who didn't want any part of me . . . I would have been totally isolated."

"Were you depressed at the thought of leaving politics?" I ask.

"Oh, very. Yeah, I was very unhappy."

"Did it take a long time to get that out of your system?"

"I don't think you ever get it out of your system," he says. "Politics is your life. It *was* my life, and it was a great challenge despite all its ups and downs, and despite its vices. I miss it. Yeah, I miss it. I'd like to be back there, in cabinet."

Munro spent the next four years on the sidelines of politics, but still found a way to help the powerless, whose causes he'd championed throughout his time in cabinet. He put his legal skills to work helping immigrants come to Canada, which provided some measure of satisfaction. But nothing could replace the buzz of winning an election and getting back into the game. Midway through Brian Mulroney's first mandate, Munro resolved to make a comeback. Initially, he looked at the Broadview–Greenwood riding in Toronto, since his immigration practice was there and he was spending enormous amounts of time in the constituency. However, those plans went off the rails when Munro's second marriage began to disintegrate (Munro was married to Lily Oddie Munro, who was a provincial cabinet minister in David Peterson's government). He decided to move back to Hamilton primarily, he says, to protect his custodial rights to his son.

He also decided to run for a seat near his old stomping grounds. This time he chose Lincoln, just east of his old riding (where he was unable to run because Hamilton East was now the prime real estate of Sheila Copps). He signed up members like crazy and won the Liberal nomination.

The Tories were evidently concerned enough about a potential Munro comeback that the prime minister put Lincoln's MP, Shirley Martin, into his cabinet as minister of state for transport just a couple of months before the 1988 election.

"Norman Atkins targeted me personally," Munro alleges, referring to the senator who was the Progressive Conservatives' national campaign manager for Mulroney's two successful majority government runs. (For his part, Atkins denies there's any bad blood between Munro and him. "I think he's smoking something," Atkins says. "We would have done everything we could to help Shirley Martin but there was nothing we did to damage John personally. He did that himself.")

Martin's promotion to cabinet hurt, but not nearly as much as an article published by the *Ottawa Citizen* that would send Munro spiralling into a special kind of hell for the next decade of his life. The newspaper reported that the Liberal candidate in Lincoln was the subject of a criminal investigation by the Royal Canadian Mounted Police. Munro never did find out the source of the Mounties' leak to the newspaper, but the timing couldn't have been worse for his candidacy. It was enough to return the seat to the PC fold. Shirley Martin won by four hundred and thirty-eight votes, out of more than fifty thousand cast; Munro had lost by less than one percentage point. As bitter as the taste of that election defeat would be, it paled in comparison to the hurricane of events over which he was about to have no control. He would call it his "nightmare decade."

For four years, the Mounties had been investigating his stewardship of the Indian Affairs Department. And then, in late 1989, they nailed him. The central allegation focused on a $1.5-million government grant to the National Indian Brotherhood (now known as the Assembly of First Nations). The Mounties alleged Munro and several Indian leaders had conspired to funnel the money back into the minister's leadership campaign. They laid thirty-seven charges.

It was a devastating development. It suggested that Munro's life-long efforts to make things better for the worst off in society were just a facade for his corrupt personal ambitions. The truly difficult part of it for Munro was that the charges carried an aura of believability. Munro did represent a very tough part of Hamilton, where organized crime had fairly deep roots. While no definite links between Munro and the less savoury figures on the Hamilton social scene were ever proved, it was presumed that on occasion Munro ran with a rough crowd.

It emerged that Munro had shown up for work one day with a black eye, claiming he'd slipped in the shower. The explanation may have been true, but it seemed few of his constituents were buying it. Munro's hometown newspaper, *The Hamilton Spectator*, ran a cartoon that reflected the mood of the community. The sketch showed a prisoner on a bunk bed asking his cellmate what he was in for. The cellmate, a shower stall, explained he was doing time for striking a cabinet minister.

In other words, as much as John Munro had a reputation for garnering millions in federal money for his city, he also had a knack for getting into some awkward public relations jams. And that was hurting his efforts to plead his innocence.

Nevertheless, Munro spent everything he had doing just that. He was convinced he was the subject of a witch-hunt, and he was going to prove it, if it was the last thing he did.

It almost was. Munro became a pariah in a hometown that he loved and that had previously loved him. He was *persona non grata*. The opinion leaders, with whom he'd always worked to accomplish things for Hamilton, crossed the street rather than face him in an awkward encounter. The stress took its toll.

"You become so overcome with total despair that you look for help, and I looked to God and a commitment to Jesus Christ as my personal saviour," Munro says, immediately going on the defensive with the comment: "I know what you think on that, but that's exactly what happened."

Munro went to trial in Ottawa, and for nine months, when he wasn't in a courtroom he was scouting out churches. It didn't matter what denomination those churches represented. He just needed to be there to pray that he'd get through another day.

"So, imposing the personal discipline to live a day at a time, and a commitment to religious belief, I believe, was the key," Munro says. "And I got through it. Without that, I don't think I could have done it, because it was too awful, just horrifying."

After nearly a year of hearings, Munro was finally delivered from the valley of the shadow of death. In 1991, Ontario Court Judge Jack Nadelle threw out most of the charges, calling the evidence circumstantial and troubling. The Crown withdrew the remaining charges. The entire exercise had cost taxpayers almost $4 million.

"It was better than an acquittal," Munro says, referring to the fact that the judge threw out the case before the accused even had to call a single witness. "It was a complete exoneration."

The story wasn't over. Munro had lost a chunk of his life, and now he wanted some of it back. So he sued the federal government for malicious prosecution. And on the bright side, at least people were now stopping him on the streets again.

"It was, 'Gee, Munro, are you still alive? I thought you were dead.' That sort of thing," he quips.

Munro's fight for compensation was truly bizarre. The tradition in Canada has been for the public to pay the legal fees of cabinet ministers and civil servants who are charged in the course of their duties. Munro seemed a potential beneficiary of this tradition after the charges were laid, and even more so after he beat the rap. He also *thought* he had friends in high places. Some of his former cabinet colleagues, including Prime Minister Chrétien, were still in government. Yet few in the Liberal government appear to have lifted a finger to address his case in a timely fashion. Munro felt betrayed.

"In actual fact, I felt badly for John's legal situation," says David Smith, a former cabinet colleague whom Chrétien appointed to the Senate in 2002. "I urged the government very strongly to make the settlement with him that they finally made." Smith says both he and Hamilton cabinet minister Sheila Copps met with then justice minister Allan Rock to try to secure a settlement for Munro. "I was very supportive of his situation, as was Sheila," Smith says.

Munro seems ready to spit nails when he hears what Smith's side of the story is. "David is a complete and absolute liar," he says. "I never heard of David Smith ever once calling me or friends or talking to any other members of the Liberal Party about urging a settlement." (Smith emphatically denies Munro's charge.) Munro says that, as far as he knows, only Senators Allan MacEachen and Jerry Grafstein went to bat for him.

When I inform Smith of Munro's comments, the congenial senator sends a miffed reply.

> Notwithstanding his insult I thought the government should cover his (Munro's) expenses. Sheila Copps and I took Allan Rock, then minister of Justice, into the kitchen during a national caucus dinner at the Loew's Concord Hotel in Quebec City in January of 1997 to press the issue on what we both thought was a question of principle. I am not a liar. John owes me two apologies, but I don't expect to receive any, and perhaps that's why I haven't spoken with him since 1996. I regard these incidents as rather sad.

In fact, in a story that has never been published before, it was Doug Fisher, the dean of the Ottawa press gallery, who may have put the wheels in motion for a settlement for Munro. Fisher came to public attention in stunning fashion, having upset the legendary wartime cabinet minister C.D. Howe in the 1957 election. He was elected on the Co-operative Commonwealth Federation banner in the riding of Port Arthur (now Thunder Bay), Ontario, and won four successive election victories. Fisher was instrumental in helping Munro implement many policies, both as an MP and a journalist with the *Toronto Telegram*. The two became friends.

Fast-forward to the end of the 1990s. Fisher was celebrating the forty years he'd spent in a variety of guises on Parliament Hill. He was the guest of honour at a cocktail party at which Prime Minister Chrétien was in attendance. (In fact, the mischievous Fisher invited three people who had become complete pariahs in political circles by running afoul of the law: Alan Eagleson, the former head of the

National Hockey League Players' Association; former Mulroney crony Pat MacAdam; and Munro.)

Just minutes after delivering his thank-you speech, Fisher tore a strip off Chrétien during a private conversation with the prime minister. He told him he was shocked and disappointed at the way Munro was being treated and found the whole thing inexplicable.

"There was foot-dragging all over the place," the octogenarian Fisher says today from his Ottawa home. "I was disturbed at what had happened to Munro. I thought he got a bad deal. It was a particularly sad case."

The dressing-down must have made an impression on the prime minister because within a matter of days, then deputy prime minister Herb Gray was on the file, having been directed to bring the matter to a conclusion.

"Many months followed before a final settlement was reached," Munro says, "but without Doug Fisher's intervention, there's no doubt that the situation would have remained unattended to."

Fisher says he had to meet with Prime Minister Chrétien as many as four times before the compensation package for Munro was finally a done deal. One of the PM's staffers told him that a couple of cabinet ministers and senior bureaucrats were "being sticky about it," but no names were mentioned.

"There was a feeling in the upper apparatus that Munro had gone too far in criticizing the party," Fisher says. "They weren't looking to do him any favours."

When the compensation package finally came though, Munro was "so bloody relieved," Fisher says. "He needed and deserved a break. He was one of the good ministers."

In the midst of Munro's legal travails, another prime minister came and went. Brian Mulroney was gone. Kim Campbell had taken over the reins of the PC party, the 1993 election was approaching, and once again, Munro badly wanted back into public life. However, once again, a series of events conspired to prevent his much-desired return to Parliament.

Munro's old friends in the party may not have helped him with his compensation claim against the government, but they were downright adversarial as it related to his comeback. Munro was not going to be handed the nomination in Lincoln on a silver platter. This time, he was going to have to fight hard for it. And Munro alleges that one of his former colleagues did everything possible to sabotage his nomination fight.

Party nominations are worse than elections. You're not challenging your enemies in another party: you're challenging your own friends in the same party. As a candidate, you spend months signing up party members in the hope that they will come to a nomination meeting and choose you to carry the party's colours into the next election. But there are a myriad of rules surrounding nomination fights, and Munro feels the party went out of its way to change the rules to hurt him.

Campaign teams don't just sign up new members. They also have to register those memberships with the party before a certain cut-off date. The party isn't supposed to say when that is, but if head office favours one candidate over another, they might let slip to one campaign team that a certain deadline could be approaching and it might be a good idea to get those memberships registered as soon as possible. If the memberships aren't registered before the deadline, they're invalid. And that's what happened to Munro.

"They'd make rules retroactively to give an advantage to the people they liked," says Barbara Jackman, the highly regarded immigration lawyer who helped Munro mount a challenge to what they considered an arbitrary abuse of power. Jackman, on Munro's behalf, filed a suit in Ontario court against what she called the party's "dirty tricks," after a face-to-face chat with one of the party's ultimate insiders proved fruitless.

"John complained directly to David Smith, but it was a complete waste of time," Jackman says. "We shouldn't have even bothered opening our mouths."

Munro telephoned Smith to confront him directly. As far as Smith was concerned, it was simply a coincidence that Munro's opponent had submitted a huge batch of party memberships just before the cut-off date.

For his part, Smith denies that interpretation of events. "I never really figured out why John was so mad at me," he says. "I have no ill will towards the guy whatever. Any thought that the rules were prejudiced against him deliberately is just totally erroneous."

David Smith and John Munro were both Liberals and both in Pierre Trudeau's cabinet from 1983 to 1984, but that's about all they had in common. Munro was on the left of the party, Smith on the right. Munro represented First Nations communities, and Smith was minister for small business. By 1993, Munro was desperately trying to get back into politics, while Smith, even though no longer an elected politician, had never left. When he was defeated in the Mulroney landslide of 1984, Smith slipped into the role of party apparatchik very naturally. By the time Jean Chrétien took over the party, Smith had become the Liberals' national campaign chair from his perch as chairman of a blue-chip national law firm.

When Munro and I talk about Smith, it's the one time during our three-hour interview when I get the sense that steam might come out of Munro's ears at any moment. (Our interview is in the basement of his home, and at this point Munro starts shifting his position a lot on the couch. He's been sitting rather comfortably up till now.)

"If I hadn't been such an integral part of the party for so long," he says, "I might not have been able to identify the abuses of David . . . whatever his name is . . ."

"Smith," I offer helpfully.

"Smith," Munro spits out. "At some point, the party will have to correct the abuses of the Dave Smiths of the Liberal Party."

But it wasn't just Smith. Munro admits his old friend Jean Chrétien was opposed to his coming back into politics. "They all wanted new faces," he says.

For much of the 1990s, John Munro had made it his quest to improve the state of democracy in the Liberal Party. He felt victimized by the way the party played him in the Lincoln nomination. He also despised the fact that the prime minister appointed a handful of high-profile candidates in that 1993 campaign, with no regard to the wishes of the local riding association. He made that part of his lawsuit as well, saying the move effectively violated candidates' rights, under the Charter of Rights and Freedoms, to seek office.

In fact, Munro was so disturbed at the prime minister's right to appoint candidates that he went to Ottawa and had a private meeting with Chrétien to discuss the matter.

"It's an odious practice, Jean, and fundamentally undemocratic," Munro recalls telling his old friend of more than a decade. "I dare you to appoint somebody in Lincoln to oppose me."

The conversation was getting loud and heated. Chrétien tried lowering the temperature by laughing and saying, "I would never do that to an old friend," Munro recalls. Then as Munro was leaving, Chrétien put his arm around him and said, "Don't worry John. I'm only going to appoint two or three more at most." In fact, Chrétien did *not* appoint a candidate to oppose Munro. But Munro is convinced the prime minister did the next worst thing. He nailed him with a retroactive membership cut-off, effectively killing Munro's chances of winning the nomination.

Munro tells another story about a Liberal gathering he attended. About fifty former cabinet ministers were celebrating the retirement of Allan MacEachen from the Senate. Both Munro and David Smith were at the event, both having served with MacEachen in one of Pierre

Trudeau's cabinets. Smith spotted Munro and went over to shake hands. Munro declined. "David, there are a lot of Liberals in this room, and you're the only one I won't shake hands with," he told him. They haven't spoken since.

By suing his own party, John Munro realized he was running the risk of looking like a cranky old man. But it's almost as though he can't help himself.

"I'm not gonna surrender," he told me. "Giving up is surrender, or pretty close to it."

"I like John," former Liberal foreign affairs minister Lloyd Axworthy told me a week after my interview with Munro. "He did some great things at Indian affairs. But some guys just don't know when to let go."

From the day the charges against him disintegrated, Munro spent eight years fighting the federal government for compensation. And finally, his efforts paid off. In the spring of 1999, the feds gave him $1.4 million, almost all of which went to his lawyers and creditors. At the news conference announcing the agreement, Munro was asked, now that his troubles were behind him, whether he had an "itch" to get back into politics. Munro suggested that at sixty-eight years of age, if he got an itch, he sought medical treatment. It was a cute throwaway line by a man who had every right to be twisted and bitter about his ordeal, but didn't seem to be—and still doesn't.

"Do you allow it to so colour you and embitter you that you become just sort of a walking pillar of hate and animosity?" he asks rhetorically. Apparently not.

That's the thing about John Munro. He can't let go. He may be seventy-two years old now, but he still believes he has one more successful campaign in him, one more term of service to perform. And that's why, on June 28, 2000, he announced that he would run for mayor of the newly amalgamated City of Hamilton. Hamiltonians weren't as interested in his coming back to public life as he was.

Running on the slogan "Return to Greatness," Munro came fourth in the mayor's race, capturing less than 10 percent of the votes.

"I desperately wanted to win," Munro says, with a sadness and passion in his voice. "But I didn't want there to come a moment in my life where I'd be ashamed of myself for having an opportunity and I didn't take it.

"Yeah, I miss it," he says. "I'd like to be back there. Politics, you know, it was my life. And it was a great challenge despite all its ups and downs, and despite its vices. I don't think you ever get it out of your system."

Just when you think that the only luck this man experiences is bad luck, something unusual happened to Munro. Something good.

If you drive to 9300 Airport Road in Mount Hope, just outside Hamilton, you will see a sign for the Hamilton International John C. Munro Airport. After enduring one of the most turbulent careers in and out of politics that any Canadian has, John Munro was delightfully surprised that several colleagues lobbied privately to have the airport named after him.

"Oh, Steve," he says of the official naming ceremony, "It was incredible."

Is John Munro finally done with politics? Does this sound like a man who's finished with politics?

"I suppose I'm down on myself now that the trial's settled and everything, that I haven't found a way to make a contribution again," he says. "I know I want to. I know I will, if I get a chance. It's just that I haven't been able to assess where that chance lies or even indeed if there is one.

"But I'll certainly look until I die, I guess."

*(Sadly, for John Munro there will be no more opportunities to return to the life he loved so much. He suffered a fatal heart attack at his home in Hamilton in August 2003, just before this book went to press. He was seventy-two years old.)*

# THE COLLATERAL
# DAMAGE

The highest reward for a man's toil is not what he gets for it,
but what he becomes by it.
—*attributed to John Ruskin, artist, scientist, poet,
environmentalist, philosopher, and art critic*

IT'S NOT HARD to understand why successful politicians love
public life. They get the opportunity to influence the nation's
agenda, the potential to leave a positive mark on history, and the
chance to make a difference in the lives of constituents—not to
mention the ego boost of being close to the action.

What's harder to understand is where the attraction lies for
politicians who are at the opposite end of the spectrum of success.
Particularly compelling are the stories of well-intentioned
Canadians who seek the life for the all the right reasons, but then
get caught up in a maelstrom of events not necessarily of their own
making. Some are professionally destroyed by the experience; some
are personally ruined. Others are both. Some of these politicians
even continue to seek jobs in public life, despite experiencing
emotionally gut-wrenching political falls from grace.

My favourite U.S. president would never be found among the
likes of George Washington, Thomas Jefferson, or Abraham

Lincoln. As a watcher of current events, I'm much more drawn to leaders such as Richard Nixon or Bill Clinton—brilliant men who, through some fatal flaw, will be remembered by history for all the wrong reasons.

In Canada, we haven't seen anything quite as dramatic as the resignation or impeachment of the leader of the free world. But this country has had its share of tragic figures. Through the years, many Canadian politicians have experienced the sensation of being in the eye of the hurricane. Their enemies have them trapped. They wake up every day dealing with the knowledge that everyone they know is following their descent into political hell—some with concern and trepidation, others with delight. Very often these men and women get themselves into their own mess, but sometimes they're just in the wrong place at the wrong time and they're powerless to change the outcome. For members of the media who like a good story above all else, it's like watching a train about to derail. You know there are going to be casualties, but you can't take your eyes off the impending disaster. And, of course, you can't wait to report on it.

Perhaps 'twas ever thus, but it seems that over the past twenty years in Canadian politics, the electorate has been particularly unforgiving. Today's heroes are tomorrow's ghosts. In British Columbia, Social Credit is dead. In Ontario, dozens of Tories, then Liberals, then New Democrats lost their jobs in successive elections in the mid-1980s and 1990s. In New Brunswick, the Progressive Conservative Party disappeared for a decade. Nationally, more than 100 Liberal MPs lost their jobs in the Mulroney landslide of 1984. And then the wheel turned, and more than 150 Tory MPs (and their staff) all hit the job market at the same time in 1993. For most Canadians, a new election just means a new cast of characters to complain about. The former politicians are out of sight, and definitely out of mind. But, for those politicians, a trip to the political graveyard can be emotionally painful and financially disastrous.

Perhaps the toughest transition from politics back to what is sardonically termed "real life" happened to the MPs who made up Brian Mulroney's second Conservative mandate. Rarely has a government in Canadian history been so reviled. Rarely has the sentence been as harsh—from 169 seats in 1988 to just 2 in 1993. In their efforts to punish Mulroney, Canadians lashed out at his caucus, whose members became collateral damage. They may have been merely low-ranking officers and not generals, but their defeat was absolute. They lost their government, their seats, almost their whole party. Try getting a job when the people in your constituency have spoken loudly about how much they hate you, and the new government has been waiting for nine years to put its own people into patronage positions.

"They don't understand just how vulnerable we are," says Frank McKenna, the former New Brunswick premier. "Most of my colleagues really landed on their rear end, not on their feet. When you're defeated, you're *persona non grata* for a period of time. So you end up with a lot of very sad cases."

That view is echoed by David Goyette, a one-time consultant to more than a hundred politicians at all levels of government, including Jean Chrétien, John Turner, Bob Rae, and Art Eggleton. Goyette quit dispensing advice after tiring of the stink of the game.

"I've seen very nice people who come from smaller, rural communities and have risen to positions of authority," Goyette says. "They become quite egomaniacal about themselves, knowing their deputy minister will say, 'Yes sir, no sir, three bags full.' And the day it ends, all that goes away. And it's a crushing blow. It's like falling off the psychological edge of a cliff, and finding yourself at the bottom, looking up and saying, 'Where are all these people now that I need them?'"

Major-General (retired) Lewis Mackenzie, a PC candidate in the 1997 federal election, is right to point out that politics isn't actual war, contrary to what one of his campaign advisers once foolishly suggested. But some parallels exist. In the pursuit of power, politicians, like soldiers, are drafted or volunteer. Their enemies won't necessarily decimate their bodies, but they can kill their spirit, their soul, or their self-image. And participants in this ruthless struggle have responded in many different ways. Some are temporarily wounded, requiring months or years to get back on their feet. Others believe they still have a contribution to make. They are determined that their last battle not be their last battle. And then we remember that there are some for whom "politics" means a body-contact sport, and others who see it as a euphemism for collateral damage assessment after a war.

PAUL DICK REMEMBERS the exact moment when lightning struck. He was a seventeen-year-old kid living in Arnprior, near Ottawa, when he heard that a popular politician would be coming to town. So he cut class for the afternoon and drove with his mother to hear John George Diefenbaker speak. It was 1957.

"A seed was planted, yeah," says Dick. "Ever since then, I've always said I'm going to be a politician." Eventually, Dick and Dief would become caucus mates for seven years—and develop a love-hate relationship.

"I loved him for rebuilding the Conservative party in this century," Dick says. "And hated him for staying too long and helping to drive it back down again."

Even though he'd waited fifteen years to run for office, Paul Dick was, in a sense, an accidental candidate. It was a bit of a fluke that he was on the ballot at all for his first campaign. By 1972, the bloom had come off Pierre Trudeau's rose. So Dick sought the Progressive Conservative nomination in Lanark–Renfrew–Carleton, an Ontario riding just outside Ottawa, but lost to a high-school principal.

Then Trudeau did Paul Dick a big favour. He called the election on September 1, 1972. Election day would be October 30. The principal feared that if he failed to win the riding for the Tories, he'd be out of a job for the entire academic year. So he gave up the nomination, forcing the riding association into the unenviable position of having to hold another nominating meeting after the election had already been called. The second time around, Paul Dick would not be denied.

He may have been the official Tory candidate at a time when Tory fortunes were rising. But it was still going to be an uphill climb to wrest the riding away from the Liberals. Nonetheless, Dick had a good feeling about what he was hearing at the doorstep. He even suggested to his wife that he thought he might take the riding by a slim 2,500-vote margin. And what did she think of his prognostication? "She later told me she just about puked," Dick laughs. "She said, 'This poor, misbegotten kid thinks he's going to win this election, and he's not going to win it.'"

But he did. By four thousand votes. For Paul Dick, the dream was now taking shape. For his wife, the excitement was a little less palpable. After all, she had given birth to twins on August 1, just six weeks before the second nomination meeting.

"She must have hated your guts then," I suggest to him.

"Well," Dick says with just a tad of understatement, "it was a point of discussion."

Still, nothing could take away from the joy he felt when he took the oath of office as the new MP for Lanark–Renfrew–Carleton.

*Well, Jesus, here I am,* Dick recalls thinking. *I made it. Since age seventeen, I wanted to be a member of Parliament, and now I'm thirty-two and I got sworn in today. Holy shit! Now, where do I find my office?*

It didn't take Paul Dick long to discover that one of the most enjoyable aspects of being an MP involves the activity that the public is perhaps most skeptical about—doing little things for constituents.

There was an elderly woman in Renfrew who was living on a miserly sum. Hers was a classic tale of woe, inasmuch as she didn't quite fit into any neat bureaucratic category that would allow her to improve her lot. But Dick went to bat for her, and with a little massaging of the system here and there, managed to get this woman a small, extra monthly pension. One day he walked into his office and found a five-pound box of Laura Secord chocolates from the woman—her way of saying thank you.

"And my first feeling was, we can't take this," Dick recalls. "We have to send it back. And then I realized you'd just destroy the lady if you did that."

Pierre Trudeau's infamous observation of MPs as nobodies once they're one hundred yards away from Parliament Hill has endured. But the truth is slightly different: part of the lure of public life is that an MP can be a somebody in his or her own constituency, particularly in rural Canada. Politicians love being deal makers. They are horse traders. Some of that is to fulfill the ego and show off whatever modest influence they have. But the public also has to acknowledge that, oftentimes, some good can come of it.

For Paul Dick, a problem at the Union Carbide plant in Arnprior offered him the opportunity to strut his stuff and play let's-make-a-deal. The plant was on the verge of closing because it couldn't get any caprolactam.

"Well, what the fuck is caprolactam?" Dick asks in relating the story. "I had never heard of it before."

"I've never heard of it either," I tell him. "How do you spell that?"

"I have no idea," he says. "I barely learned to pronounce it."

(In fact, caprolactam is a toxic, leaf-like solid used in the manufacture of synthetic fibres.)

"We're in 1974, and we're into the oil crisis," Dick says. "And they're going to close a plant down with three hundred and sixty employees in a town of five thousand." Economically, socially, psychologically, politically—any way you wanted to look at it—the loss of the plant would have been a disaster. So Dick met with the Liberal energy minister, Alistair Gillespie, to find a solution.

"We ended up getting caprolactam from Russia," he says. "And they took it to New Jersey and had to upgrade it, and brought it back up and shipped it into Arnprior. And the plant's still open."

And dollars to doughnuts, it's a good bet that virtually no one in the community knows how it all happened. "That's what your job is," Dick says. "You're an expediter. You're trying to make things happen."

Dick won re-election in 1974, but had a difficult decision to make midway through that second term. Robert Stanfield had resigned as Conservative leader, and the party was in the throes of a divisive leadership convention. Dick thought the party needed to do much better in Quebec, so he supported Claude Wagner.

"He was a francophone. He's from Quebec," Dick says, explaining his choice. "I thought he was an extremely good leader of men. He was charismatic." Dick wasn't at all sold on Brian Mulroney. In fact, as he puts it, "I did what some people would call some 'dirty tricks' that helped jeopardize [Mulroney] in '76."

What Dick did was initiate something that became a real thorn in Mulroney's side. Just one week before the leadership convention, Dick secretly started a petition of Conservative MPs who said they would refuse to sit in Parliament if Mulroney became leader. Forty members signed the petition—almost half the entire PC caucus. "It was good enough for a headline," Dick says. Actually, it was much more. It was a devastating blow to Mulroney's leadership aspirations and, of course, the future prime minister would not make it to the last ballot at that '76 convention. Ironically, despite Dick's mischief, Wagner didn't win either. Joe Clark did.

For the next eight years, Dick continued to be good to his constituents and they continued to be good to him. He won re-election in 1979 and 1980, then changed his mind about Mulroney and supported him for leader at the 1983 convention. When Mulroney won his landslide in 1984, he called Dick to talk about a cabinet job. But the news wasn't exactly what Dick was hoping for.

"He had to put another woman in," Dick remembers the prime minister saying. "Okay. I understood those things." However, Mulroney added that Dick would get another phone call in twenty-four months inviting him to join the cabinet at that time. Mulroney said it was a promise.

Twenty-one months later, on June 30, 1986, the Prime Minister's Office called. Paul Dick became associate minister of national defence. For fourteen years, he'd been a backbencher, attending to the daily concerns of eastern Ontario. Within a year of Dick's new appointment, the prime minister would send him to Israel to meet with then defence minister Yitzhak Rabin to express the Canadian government's displeasure at Israel's handling of the *intifada*.

"And I think he thought, 'Oh, you poor little boy, you don't really know what you're talking about,'" Dick recalls of the meeting. "But he was very nice. We got along fine. It was very pleasant. It was probably one of the really interesting things in my career."

Another time, Dick was the prime minister's emissary at high-level talks with the Malaysian government. His job was to convince the Malaysians to give Bristol Aerospace in Winnipeg the maintenance contract for Malaysia's fleet of supersonic F-5A Freedom Fighter attack airplanes. "Those were the things that I guess make politics a bit of a thrill now and then," he says.

After Mulroney's Conservatives won a second term in 1988, Dick got himself a promotion. He asked for, and received, the portfolio for the Department of Supply and Services, which with a $6.5-billion budget was the largest purchasing agent in the country. And he discovered something quite extraordinary: the legendary C.D. Howe had held this very job during the Second World War. Once the Gulf War started in 1991, the government dusted off an old statute and Dick learned he actually had vast powers to regulate the economy.

"Oh, Christ, I could buy and sell companies at a whim," he laughs. "They had powers! That wasn't a democracy in those days. That was close to dictatorship, I tell you. If you blinked the wrong way, they'd say, 'Sorry, we just took over your factory.'"

They may have re-examined the act to see what Dick potentially could do in the event the Gulf War became more protracted. But Dick's real interest in that portfolio stemmed from his inability, while in Opposition, to get any government contracts for businesses in his constituency. To get contracts, you had to be on a list. As far as Dick was concerned, only friends of the civil service got on that list. After all, it was the bureaucrats who vetted all applications for government procurement contracts.

"There were so many ways in which an applicant could either be accepted or rejected," Dick says. "They had to qualify the right way, wink, wink, nod, nod. And all I found was that I had Liberals on the list and I couldn't get any Tories in the door."

So what did he tell his department officials to do?

"I said, 'Fuck, throw the whole list out,'" he recalls. "'We're going to get rid of them all and open it up to everybody.'" His proposal sailed through cabinet in a matter of minutes. Of course, the senior bureaucrats told him it could never be done. So Dick went over the heads (or in this case, under) and collaborated with secondary-level public servants who shared his belief in changing the system.

"I can tell you there's a hell of a lot more public service patronage than there ever was political patronage, from what I could see," Dick insists.

In any event, Dick wanted and eventually got a computerized, open-bidding system, where anyone could make a pitch for government business. Dick is no longer the minister, but the system he put in place endures.

Later in his term, he would merge Supply and Services with another department, Public Works—trimming seven thousand civil servants in the process—into a new Department of Public Works and Government Services. Even the Liberals who succeeded Dick said in their 2000–01 annual estimates report that the "efficiency and effectiveness of government operations cannot be overstated."

Dick was never one of the big stars of Mulroney's cabinet. But he knew his role and performed it well.

"I think he respected me," Dick says of his prime minister. "I didn't cause him any trouble, and I think I was one of those solid ministers who they knew they could give something and it would be done and done well."

Unfortunately for Paul Dick, this was as good as it was going to get in politics. He was about to encounter the other side of public life. And it was going to be very, very messy.

Paul Dick's political career was chugging along nicely, but his private life was another story. He was going through a very messy and very public divorce. Some days, when he arrived on Parliament Hill, the national press corps would be lying in wait to scrum him about the latest developments in his marital breakup.

It was the other side of public life. Because he was a minister of the Crown, the media decided his private life was news. And if he weren't in public life?

"Who would ever give a shit?" he asks.

*Frank* magazine, Canada's self-proclaimed satirical press, was having a field day with Paul Dick. The magazine covered the divorce in seven issues, even putting him on the cover once. The state of the Dicks' marriage was apparently of such national import that the Department of External Affairs shipped copies of newspaper articles about it to every embassy abroad.

Dick's twin sons were now in their late teens and getting a front-row view of how tough politics could be. Their father, some days, felt like going into hiding.

Does Dick blame politics for the breakup of his marriage? Not exactly. "If there's a weakness, politics is like a chisel you put on it. If you hit it with a hammer right on that weakness, it'll crack it right open," he says.

Politics was getting to be a very rough sport for Dick. But it was still a sport he loved to play. Trouble was, his days looked numbered. The Tories were stuck in a bad rut of unpopularity and seemingly could find no way out. On October 25, 1993, the public rendered its verdict on nine years of Conservative rule. Two MPs survived the bloodbath, and Paul Dick wasn't one of them. For the first time in twenty-one years, he was out of work. Dick, like most Tories, got stomped at the polls, losing his renamed Lanark–Carleton riding by eighteen thousand votes. Even if you combined the Tory and Reform votes (which you can't, but anyway . . .), you still wouldn't have had enough to overtake the Liberal victor, Ian Murray.

"I had originally gone into politics believing this would be my career for life, that I was going to be a professional politician," Dick says. "I wasn't ready to go out when I got tossed out."

Nor would he be ready for the rude reception he'd face trying to get a new job.

In some ways, the terrible public opinion polls that Paul Dick read three weeks before Election day in 1993 helped ease his transition to the ranks of the unemployed. Dick had already won six elections and knew there was no way he could win a seventh. So he started to think about something he hoped he would never have to face—life *after* politics. Election day was in October, so he figured he'd give himself a few months to chill out before embarking on his next career. The one thing he did need to do was buy a new car.

No matter how prepared a politician is to lose, there is always a period of mourning after defeat. Dick was no exception. He wanted to blame someone for the Tories' implosion but never thought Kim Campbell should bear the brunt of the responsibility. Instead, it was Brian Mulroney he was upset at.

"I went through a period where I was pretty pissed off at him," Dick says candidly. "I thought he abandoned the ship. He left us in the lurch." Dick wanted Mulroney to lead the party into the 1993 election, and is convinced the Tories would have won more than just two seats.

In any event, Dick didn't spend much time wondering about what might have been. He had to get a job. Before politics, he'd been a Crown attorney. But that was twenty-one years ago and he was just too far removed from the law to go back. Come to think of it, he'd been fired from his last Crown attorney's job, because he sought (and initially lost) the PC nomination for the 1972 election. He was told that he was obviously too partisan and wasn't wanted back. Ideally, he wanted to put some of the skills he'd learned around the cabinet table to work in the private sector. He'd become a bit of an expert on procurement contracts, and merging departments, and thought a career in administration or strategic planning would be interesting.

"I thought I had a lot of pretty good experience," Dick says. "But I found out that no one wanted Tories."

One management consulting company talked to him, then inexplicably stopped returning his calls. "All of a sudden, it died, fast, as if I'd just been pushed off a cliff," Dick recalls. He later found out a high-ranking civil servant advised the company not to hire him, because the Liberals were now in power. What good could a former Tory do?

Throughout his time as a minister, Dick had been approached by supporters who assured him that, as soon as his political career was over, a seat on their board of directors had his name on it. Now he tried to follow up on those offers, but they all disappeared. Apparently the offers were contingent on the Tories remaining in power, or at least not losing power as one of the most hated governments in Canadian history.

He had job interviews with law firms. He had job interviews with businesses. He had job interviews with former high-school friends. In total, Dick attended 144 job interviews, only to be told his experience managing a $6.5-billion department was irrelevant. *Thanks for coming out, but we don't want you.*

None of this surprises Tom Long, campaign co-chair for Mike Harris's two successful majority government runs in Ontario. Long, now a partner at the Toronto office of Egon Zehnder International, an executive placement firm, says he frequently pitches people with political experience for jobs. But his private sector clients are leery.

"There's just a natural bias against it," he says. "There's not an appreciation of the kind of intrinsic value of the experience these people have. People tend to pigeonhole us. I find Canadian decision makers are very conservative in their decision making. I don't say that entirely positively."

With his prospects looking desperate, Paul Dick remembered something his ex-wife had once told him—that if he ever got out of politics, he might make a good stockbroker. So he approached a friend at a brokerage house in Ottawa, who gave him an entry-level position. There he was, fifty-four years old, working alongside twenty-two-year-olds just out of university. He put in seventy-hour weeks developing a new client list. In his first year, 1995, he made $36,000, compared with his cabinet minister's salary of $114,120 (not to mention a car and a driver). All he could think was, *thank goodness for my MP's pension,* which meant the hit on his lifestyle wasn't as dramatic as it might have been. The hit on his pride, however, was deep.

"You can sit here and cry about it, but that's not advancing you," Dick says. "If you dream about the past you're wasting time."

Paul Dick has now been selling stocks for eight years. Those lonely days of phone calls not being returned seem far in the past. In 2002, he earned double what he used to make as a cabinet minister.

"So it turned around. I'm not starving at all," he says. "I paid off all the bills and just came back from two weeks in Europe. It was the first time I was able to afford to travel like that."

Considering the bumpy ride he's had over the past decade, life has been pretty good for Paul Dick in recent times. One of his sons, Wyatt, started working with him at CIBC Wood Gundy in Ottawa. The other, Andrew, has been working with a hedge fund in London. Even his personal life improved. By mid-2003, he had been in a relationship for eleven years. And he was on speaking terms with his first wife, for the first time in a decade.

Does Paul Dick miss politics? Of course he does. But you won't catch him getting too nostalgic.

"Some guys have the wherewithal to say, 'hey, move on,'" he says. "And other people are going to sit there and look out the window and dream about the past. And I'm sorry. If you dream about the past, you're wasting time."

LIKE PAUL DICK, Brian O'Kurley's first political memories are of John Diefenbaker. O'Kurley's father was a travelling salesman, selling farm machinery in small, rural communities in northern Alberta. When his father wasn't doing that, he was working on Diefenbaker's electoral fortunes. Dief was all for farmers and talked a lot about getting a better price for wheat. That was music to the O'Kurley family's ears.

Brian O'Kurley's first encounter with politics happened in Lamont, Alberta, about fifty kilometres northeast of Edmonton. He was in Grade 2. Valentine's Day was coming and all the children in the class had to make little cards, each bearing one student's name, and put those cards in a box. The victors would be crowned the King and Queen of Hearts. Even at the age of seven, little Brian was a competitive sort: he wanted to win this, his first, election.

"I remember working that classroom and saying, 'I'm giving you one. Will you give me one?'" he says.

O'Kurley did win his first election and did become the King of Hearts. A young girl named Bernadette Eleniak was crowned Queen of Hearts. In a twist of fate worthy of a Hollywood motion picture, Brian and Bernadette, the king and queen, would become husband and wife nineteen years later.

Whether it's the thrill of competition or the high of seeing others offer their support, O'Kurley's not sure. But he continued to contest elections through his formative years. He logged his first upset victory, capturing the presidency of his junior-high school union. Even though he was a tender thirteen years old, he intuitively understood political strategy. The junior-high president may have represented Grades 7, 8, and 9, but it was always a Grade 9 kid who won—until Brian O'Kurley came along and won as a Grade 8 student.

"I just did the basic math," he says. "You realize that if you could get the seventh graders and the eighth graders, that's more numbers than ninth graders." He pulled the same trick in senior high. He won that presidency, despite being in Grade 11. (Bernadette won the election the following year, in Grade 12.)

In 1979, O'Kurley decided to become a teacher; the best position he could find for a first job was teaching prisoners at Fort Saskatchewan Correctional Institute northeast of Edmonton. Once that contract expired, he married his Queen of Hearts, Bernadette, and started looking for another job. He discovered, through a friend, an opening in the foothills of the Rocky Mountains. The town was called Edson, located in the federal riding of Yellowhead, which happened to be represented by a guy named Joe Clark.

Clark may have been a laughingstock in much of the country for blowing the Tories' first shot at power since Diefenbaker's government. But that hardly mattered to O'Kurley. He liked what he saw, dove in, and soon became Clark's membership chair, then first vice-president on the riding executive.

And he wasn't done. O'Kurley had been bitten badly by the political bug. He got involved in Alberta politics, too. He served on the provincial executive with Premier Peter Lougheed, and on five other provincial constituencies; and he acted as campaign manager for several municipal politicians.

"So I sort of had my hand in it," O'Kurley says modestly. In the 1980s he would also manage to go back to university, to get a graduate degree in educational administration, and welcome the arrival of four children.

Things were, you might say, busy—and about to get a lot worse.

Just as he'd done to become the King of Hearts in Grade 2, Brian O'Kurley continued to work the rooms of Alberta politics. But his efforts met a roadblock in 1983, when his friend and MP, Joe Clark, lost the Conservative leadership to Brian Mulroney. O'Kurley feared what that might mean for his future in politics. But when he met Mulroney in Calgary, he was pleasantly surprised. The new Tory leader was friendly, and seemed to have time for political chit-chat and picture taking, which O'Kurley appreciated.

The Tories, under Mulroney, crushed the Liberals in the ensuing election. But O'Kurley was still not a candidate. He continued to enjoy working at all three levels of government and was cautious about not wanting to step on others' toes. But when five new ridings appeared in Alberta in time for the 1988 election, O'Kurley figured this was his moment. He talked to Clark, Alberta cabinet ministers, and members of the provincial executive, and got the green light to contest Elk Island, one of the new ridings.

"I didn't want to just blast in," he says.

Even though he'd spent the past eight years in Yellowhead, O'Kurley had deep roots in Elk Island. It encompassed the area northeast of Edmonton where he and his wife had been born and raised. He still had loads of friends in the riding.

Of course, O'Kurley wasn't the only Albertan who thought he had his name on Elk Island. Two other candidates vied for the PC nomination, which in those days was as good as a win on election day. O'Kurley's campaign loaded up bus after bus with family friends and business acquaintances who were also turned on by the thought of participating in a political drama.

O'Kurley took the nomination on the second ballot. "That was a really, really exciting thrill," he recalls. "I'm thirty-five years old, it's my first kick at politics, and there I am."

Six months later, O'Kurley would win his first election with more than 48 percent of the vote—more than double the percentage for the second-place NDP. Reform, showing early signs of becoming the dominant western party, came third with 20 percent, while the Liberals didn't get their deposit back. Even with a reduced majority government, the Tories took twenty-five out of twenty-six Alberta seats (the New Democrats' Ross Harvey prevented a province-wide PC sweep).

The O'Kurley family was about to find out how exciting political life would be for Brian, and how drop-dead exhausting it would be for his wife.

At work, Brian O'Kurley was like the proverbial kid in the candy store. He was a teacher in his mid-thirties from small-town Alberta, suddenly thrust into some of the most brutal national politics of the century. Free trade, the goods and services tax, the increasing effects of globalization on the country, and the eventual rise of the Reform party were issues visiting his doorstep on a daily basis.

Meanwhile, his home life was in a state of near-crisis. He had three young children and another on the way when he became an

MP. During the nomination fight, the family had some sense of how tough politics was going to be on their lives. While O'Kurley and his wife got up at six in the morning every day to sign up new members, his parents looked after the couple's two boys, and her parents watched over their daughter.

"Once we had made the decision [to run], we just sort of absorbed all the punishment that came with it," O'Kurley recalls.

But being an MP was a different story. During the week, O'Kurley lived in Ottawa, leaving his pregnant wife and three kids to fend for themselves back in northern Alberta.

"Then I'd come home on a Friday night with a bagful of laundry and say 'How's everybody?'" O'Kurley says. Saturday morning and afternoon meant meetings with constituents and other local events. On Saturday night, it was the rubber-chicken dinner circuit: making a speech at another event. Sunday morning was for church. The family might have lunch together, and then it was off to the airport and a flight back to Ottawa.

"I was virtually absent from home and it wasn't much of a life," O'Kurley admits. So he moved the entire family to Ottawa, figuring they'd at least all sleep in the same house four or five nights a week.

That was the positive side of the equation. The negative side was that Bernadette didn't know a soul in Ottawa. In Alberta she at least had her family and friends to draw on for support.

O'Kurley soon discovered what every MP whose riding is more than a couple of hours outside of Ottawa learns. His only daughter was having a third birthday party and he was more than two thousand kilometres away in a village in Elk Island. He approached a small engine-repair shop, begged to use the phone, and sang "Happy Birthday" to his daughter. He could understand missing that important family function to save a life or deliver a baby.

"But there were times when I'd be invited to functions and you felt like it didn't matter if you were there or not," says O'Kurley, who was trapped in the classic politician's dilemma—the pressure to be visible in the riding versus the needs of your own family. He wanted to be at his daughter's third birthday party. But he also knew there were provincial and municipal politicians living in northern Alberta twelve months a year, some of whom might love to make either O'Kurley's new Ottawa address or his lack of attendance in the riding an issue in the next campaign.

It's an aspect of public life most voters never think of, let alone have sympathy for. "No doubt, you are insulated from certain realities. But you get pounded in other ways," O'Kurley says. "I found myself sitting in Pearson airport at one o'clock on a Saturday morning and saying, 'What am I doing here? I haven't seen my family for two weeks.'"

Yes, O'Kurley has heard all the arguments about truck drivers and construction workers who spend lots of time away from home.

"That sort of shuts you up a little bit," he admits. "But then, nobody's criticizing the truck driver. There isn't somebody in the newspaper that's saying, 'By golly, Bill the trucker ran the red light or cut me off.' He doesn't have the same pressure to be accountable to such a diverse group of interests."

Four fascinating but tumultuous years later, O'Kurley was running for re-election. The Tory numbers in Elk Island were down about 14 percent from the 1988 campaign, but O'Kurley was still in first place, hanging on to a one- or two-point lead over the Liberals, whose support had tripled with Jean Chrétien as leader. Reform's vote was actually down a few points from the 1988 election results.

Then Kim Campbell called the election. And the rest was history. The Tory vote collapsed; the Liberals actually maintained their support (good for second place); but the Reform vote skyrocketed, with the party taking twenty-two of Alberta's twenty-six seats (the Liberals snagged four Edmonton area seats). And Brian O'Kurley's political career was over after just one term.

"You could just feel everything crumbling under you," O'Kurley remembers of election night. "And it's so sad."

In a riding of 90,000 people, only 5,714 went to the polls on October 25, 1993 to vote for Brian O'Kurley. He was constantly disillusioned by friends who told him that they just couldn't support him this time 'round. Conversely, he was astounded at the guts shown by a smaller number of others who, despite the tide away from the Tories, still volunteered to help O'Kurley's re-election hopes.

"They'd walk into the coffee shops in the small towns and they'd just get kicked," he recalls. "That was one of the hardest things for me to see—some of my supporters being abused when it wasn't their fault. They just wanted to say, 'We think O'Kurley's a good guy.' When things are going well, that's easy to do. That's pretty tough to do when things are going against you."

Things would continue to go against O'Kurley for some time yet. He was learning first-hand what unemployment was all about. The vast majority of his colleagues at least had a pension waiting for them when they were defeated, because they'd had two terms in Parliament. O'Kurley only had one term—not enough to qualify. Moreover, he'd been out of teaching for four years and discovered none of his Alberta experience counted for much in Ontario—not his seniority, not his pension contributions, not much of anything. And since the election had been held in October, after the school year had already started, all of that year's full-time teachers had already been hired.

Even though the O'Kurley children had all grown up in Ottawa, the family wanted to move back to Alberta, where their roots were deep and they would be living close to good friends and family.

But this was a time when the provincial government under Ralph Klein was implementing major changes in education. School boards were amalgamated. Money was tight. Teachers were being laid off, not hired. Some former associates wanted to help O'Kurley out, but how would it look, laying off a couple of dozen teachers, then hiring a former Tory backbencher.

O'Kurley tried everything. He touched base with his provincial government connections. The education sector. The broader public sector. The private sector. He couldn't find anything.

"People who would call me because they wanted some help from government when you were an MP, you'd call them and they'd say, 'Well, he's in a meeting now,'" O'Kurley recalls. "You wouldn't get the call back. And it was tough."

O'Kurley learned another unpleasant truism of politics. When things are going well, everyone's in it together. His caucus stuck together. In the beginning, his supporters hung together. And then came the 1993 election.

"All of the sudden you feel like your ship's been blown out of the water," he says. "It's almost like that *Titanic* movie. You're hanging on to a piece of rubble, or something floating in the sea, and you're just sort of hanging on. You're waiting for the ship to come and it ain't coming. There's nobody. The phone isn't ringing.

"Initially you're sort of looking around and you're saying, 'Where's the medic?' You're out on the battlefield and you're saying, 'Medic, medic.'"

So the debate as to whether to return to Alberta really wasn't a debate after all. The O'Kurleys would stay in Ottawa and try to make the best of it. The former MP started all over again. He dusted off his resumé, began making phone calls at 6:30 every morning, and hoped for the best. He got his first job as a substitute teacher in some of the most challenging classrooms in the Ottawa area. "The jobs that nobody else wants," is how O'Kurley puts it. "They'd be giving me jobs that my qualifications might not necessarily match but my enthusiasm certainly did. And if they said, 'Go teach kindergarten,' I taught kindergarten."

It was quite a difference from the previous year, when O'Kurley was one of the Canadian delegation's representatives to the Earth Summit in Rio de Janeiro. There he was rubbing shoulders with the elder George Bush, and with Mikhail Gorbachev, Helmut Kohl, and Fidel Castro. Now, as the old vaudeville expression goes, no one wanted to know from him.

In the three years after the 1993 election, O'Kurley heard from precisely three friends from his days in Alberta politics. In our conversation, he's very careful not to whine about his predicament. He understands that people have to get on with their lives. But the dearth of people reaching out to him clearly still hurts him. He mentions no fewer than eight times the fact that his phone went silent after his election loss.

"You're looking for some little bit of a boost, morale or otherwise," he says. "But you're on your own."

In some ways, politicians can't win. O'Kurley's been out of the game now for twice as long as he was in it. But when he's back in Alberta, say, at a reunion or a wedding, he's still seen as "that former politician."

He's finally settled his campaign debt from his nomination meeting. O'Kurley paid for the privilege of seeking the Tory nomination in Elk Island by taking out a personal line of credit and incurring nearly $30,000 in debt. He's paid it off, bit by bit, by not taking vacations with his wife, not buying her new clothes, not eating out at restaurants, and driving his 1985 Chevy Impala into the ground.

"That's my car," he says almost proudly. "That's what I drive to work. Every year I think, 'Well, maybe one more year.' And the boys and I do a lot of the mechanical work ourselves and save a few bucks there."

Believe it or not, the O'Kurley kids tease their father, asking him when he's going to make the big comeback. Despite the bumps and bruises he's sustained in public life, O'Kurley says under the right circumstances, he would think about getting back in.

"There's a certain honour in saying, 'Look, I can take a punch,'" he says. "I'm not going to complain about it. I'm going to keep on going."

FOR ALL OF HIS PERSONALITY FLAWS—and he had many—Canada's eighteenth prime minister seemed to have one aspect of his job in remarkably fine perspective. You might think Brian Mulroney would have had the most excruciatingly difficult emotional transition to life after politics. After all, was there ever a politician, who loved the trappings of office, the international stage, the ego boost of feeding off of his caucus's loyalty, not to mention the accomplishment of back-to-back majority governments, as much as Mulroney? If there was, it escapes me.

And yet Mulroney spared himself much of the typical post-political-life depression by understanding, much better than most, how ephemeral the job was in the first place.

"I used to tell the kids at Harrington Lake, 'Look, none of this belongs to us,'" Mulroney recalls. "'When Daddy's finished with this, we're going back to Montreal and start all over again.' They had a very clear understanding of that from the beginning." Apparently, so did the prime minister.

I've met hundreds of politicians over the years, and I'm constantly surprised at how ill-prepared many of them are for life after politics, particularly if they're starting that life after an election loss. There's a sense of disbelief that it's all come to an end. One moment, you're the toast of the town, your picture's in the newspapers, microphones are thrust in your face as journalists breathlessly await your sage words on some major initiative of the day. You're invited to an endless list of community events; assistants and various hangers-on follow all your orders. The next moment, it's all gone.

Former political consultant David Goyette has shared many of those painful moments with politicians for whom the ride has come to an end. He tells me the story of one cabinet minister whose party was unceremoniously tossed out by the electorate. As the soon-to-be-unemployed former politician was cleaning out his office, his wife came to visit. She had been most unhappy with their lives during his time in power. Their family lived a long way from the provincial capital, and the couple had grown apart. Packing up all those years of memorabilia brought a flood of emotions to the surface.

"They just broke down and the two of them hugged each other and cried," says Goyette, who himself becomes emotional remembering the scene. "We talked about the return to private life and how this had to be spun as a good, positive thing and you will recover and you will do well. But he didn't get over the hump." The last Goyette heard, this one-time executive and minister of the Crown had a low-level job at a provincial agency that was paying him a fraction of the salary he had once earned.

More collateral damage in a war that is politics.

# THE THIRD LAW

For every action, there is an equal and opposite reaction.
—*Sir Isaac Newton's third law of motion*

FOR MUCH OF THE TWENTIETH CENTURY, the province of Ontario had a reputation for foisting some of the least interesting politicians in the country on its citizens. Former premier William Davis used to joke that his job was to run the government, not entertain reporters. He seemed to be following a tradition and a style by which virtually every premier of Ontario lived. Perhaps Davis's most famous answer to any reporter's question about why he was so bland was, "Bland works." And indeed it did for the forty-two consecutive years that the Tories governed Ontario, from 1943 to 1985.

But in the early 1980s, two men—who were from the same generation and assumed the leadership of their parties around the same time—changed the course of Ontario history. There was absolutely nothing bland about them. They were fierce political adversaries. But they did come together, as their supporters might say, for one brief shining moment in 1985, and utterly transformed Ontario politics, both for better and for worse. Their reward for doing so was to be subjected to some of the worst humiliation and opprobrium public life has to offer. They will probably not like my saying so, but they are the best example I can conjure up of Newton's third law of motion (quoted above) coming to life in politics. Even though the two men represented different parties, neither could have become premier without the other. One helped bring down a dynasty to make the other premier of Ontario. Then that premier made one fatal miscalculation, which ironically gave the job to the other guy.

David Robert Peterson could not have become premier without Robert Keith Rae. And the converse is true, too.

David Peterson was the product of a partnership between two people whom he describes as having genuine intellectual curiosity and a passion for social justice. His father was originally from Saskatchewan and always active in politics. Clarence Peterson was, for example, a signatory of the Regina Manifesto, which set out the goals and principles of the fledgling Co-operative Commonwealth Federation in 1933. After moving to Ontario, he served on London City Council and twice ran unsuccessfully for provincial parliament, at a time when Liberals couldn't buy a seat at Queen's Park. Still, Clarence always reached high, as evidenced by his running as a Liberal against future Ontario premier John Robarts in 1955. He lost, but almost every non-Tory lost in that election. Premier Leslie Frost's Conservatives won eighty-four of ninety-eight seats. To seek public office when you know you're going to be clobbered reflects an impressive commitment to public life, and Clarence Peterson had that.

BOB RAE'S FAMILY was also immersed in politics, but in a different way. Rae's father, Saul, was part of the federal civil service. High-ranking cabinet members dropped by the Rae household on a regular basis. Saul Rae worked directly for Lester Pearson when the future prime minister was external affairs minister. When Pearson assumed the presidency of the United Nations General Assembly, little Bobby Rae, age five, would go to New York and watch the sessions.

The first election Rae remembers was in 1956, when his father was Canada's ambassador to the United States and the family was living in Washington. (Rae was actually Richard Nixon's paper boy at the time.) He may have been only eight years old, but Rae was spellbound listening to radio coverage of the Democratic Party's convention floor fight over who would join Adlai Stevenson on the presidential ticket—John F. Kennedy or Estes Kefauver.

In 1957, Rae was still too young to be invited to the embassy party where diplomats and journalists gathered to listen to the radio hookup of the Canadian election returns. But he does remember his father coming home after the event and telling his son how surprised he was to hear that the Liberals had lost and John Diefenbaker was about to become the prime minister.

Rae's first direct contact with politics was actually as a backroom boy, running Chuckie Rendelman for student body president of Horace Mann Public School in Washington. But he would not have to wait long to discover his true métier was as a candidate. He first ran for student council in Grade 8, even then fascinated by the "great human contest."

"I enjoyed the theatre of it, I enjoyed the public-speaking part of it, I enjoyed meeting people, I enjoyed the salesmanship of it," Rae says. "I enjoyed convincing people of the merits of my point of view versus someone else's point of view. And I think just a sense of service, too."

WATCHING HIS FATHER campaign and listening to his mother remind him that he had to "give something back" to his community made David Peterson think about what kind of contribution he wanted to make to society.

"To this day, it was the most formative influence in my life," he says of his parents' example. "If you have something, you owe it back. You have no right to just sit there and assume you've got a divine right to whatever gifts that you have acquired either by luck or by chance or perhaps by talent. If you've got the talent, you're lucky you were born with it."

Given his father's history, politics was an obvious channel for Peterson's efforts. But strangely enough, he never even thought of running until he was already in his thirties. While exercising at the YMCA in London, Ontario, he bumped into an old friend named Ted McGrath (pronounced *McGraw*). The two got talking about provincial politics and Peterson realized he wasn't at all pleased with the way things were being run. The Davis government tried to portray itself as an impressive team of fiscal managers, yet never presented a balanced budget. Furthermore, the Tories had been in power for thirty straight years.

"I thought they were just a bunch of cigar-smoking men in the backroom running the place," Peterson says of the Tories. "It was a very limited space and I thought the whole place should be opened up."

Peterson had also been very involved in national issues while at law school at the University of Toronto. He chaired a group that made a submission to the Royal Commission on Bilingualism and Biculturalism around 1970. But he had never really given any serious thought to standing for office himself, until Ted *told* him he should. So he thought about it, and decided to go for it.

Peterson and McGrath next figured they should drive to Toronto to meet Robert Nixon, then leader of the Ontario Liberals. For two men who would go on to become fast friends and work closely together at the highest levels of government, Peterson and Nixon didn't get on all that well at the outset. The party leader seemed more interested in talking to McGrath than Peterson.

"He didn't much care about me," Peterson remembers with a laugh. "He wasn't particularly enamoured with me." If Peterson was hoping Nixon might court him a bit, he left disappointed. But, in the end, it didn't matter. He had already made up his mind to run.

If some people were surprised that David Peterson intended to run for the Liberals in London, they could hardly be blamed. London was solid Tory territory, and the home base of former Ontario premier John Robarts, one of Peterson's political heroes. On top of that, Peterson had just attended, in the spring of 1974, a national Progressive Conservative convention at which his father-in-law, Don Matthews, sought re-election as party president. So when David Peterson announced he'd seek the Liberal nomination in London Centre, "I think everybody thought I was nuts," he says.

Peterson won his nomination, then hit the hustings with his wife, Shelley, whom he'd met in October 1973, then married exactly two and a half months later. Having had little first-hand contact with political campaigns, Peterson found himself blown away by volunteers who would knock signs into front lawns for hours at a time, for thirty straight days. "And it's just because they believe in you, they trust you, they're having fun, and in some way you're connected with them in making the world a better place."

When Bob Rae returned to Canada in 1974 after completing a Rhodes Scholarship, he too began to explore whether politics might be the best outlet for his passionate interest in social and economic justice. But Rae wasn't sure what party he ought to be in. After all, he came out of a family that, politically, was scrupulously neutral, although small-l liberal. However, he did know what he wasn't.

"I always had a sense of the Conservative party as being the party that defends privilege," Rae says. "It was a sense that I had from an early age, and certainly a sense that I developed very strongly in England. And I was never keen about that aspect of the Tory party."

Once back in Ontario, Rae discovered the New Democrats espoused the kind of politics he was interested in. The Lewis family was out on the front line: the fiery and brilliant orator Stephen Lewis was leading the provincial party, while his father, David, represented the conscience of the nation in Parliament as federal

NDP leader. The Liberals under Robert Nixon actually seemed a more rural, conservative group. The NDP was clearly left wing and more responsive to emerging urban issues.

But in politics timing is everything. By the time Rae graduated from law school and decided he wanted into the arena, Ontario voters had just gone to the polls. It was too late for him to get in that door. However, there was a federal by-election in Toronto's Broadview–Greenwood riding in October 1978. So Rae made his entry into national politics then and there.

Rae's parents had figured this day would come eventually, but they were surprised that their son was heading into politics so quickly after graduating. Rae hadn't even been called to the bar yet, and would now have to postpone writing his bar admission exams to run for Parliament.

Rae wasted little time making an impression in Ottawa. His keen mind and brilliant speaking style rocketed him to prominence, even though he was only thirty years old.

His most significant day in Parliament came toward the end of 1979, when he moved the motion of non-confidence to pull the plug on Joe Clark's nascent government. The very next morning, Rae found himself writing his bar admission exams. Sitting three seats in front of him was Maureen McTeer, Clark's wife.

"She was staring daggers at me," Rae laughs. "She wouldn't talk to me."

No kidding. In the ensuing election in 1980, Clark's Tories lost thirty-three seats and the right to govern. They were The Blue Blip. The New Democrats picked up six seats and sealed Rae's name in Canadian history books forever.

MEANWHILE, DAVID PETERSON'S STAR was also on the rise. Peterson and two other Liberals shocked the Ontario status quo by winning all three seats in very Tory London in the 1975 provincial election, and cutting Bill Davis's government down to minority status. Davis took only 36 percent of the total vote. Journalist Charlotte Montgomery wrote a much-discussed article, telling her readers to "watch Peterson." But the Grits as a party came third, behind Stephen Lewis's NDP, which vaulted into the official Opposition role by edging out the Liberals thirty-eight to thirty-six in the seat count.

Peterson's first caucus meeting was also a shocker. After Nixon welcomed his new group of MPPs to Queen's Park, he announced he'd be resigning as leader. When the meeting broke up and the members emerged, reporters thrust their cameras and microphones into Peterson's face.

"Are you going to run for leader?" they asked.

"Look, I haven't even found the washroom, how can I run for leader?" Peterson responded. In fact, Peterson had only ever been to the legislature twice—once to meet Nixon before running, then again to hear his leader quit. He was thirty-two years old, wet behind the ears, but getting lots of pressure to reach for the brass ring. So he did. He didn't know many Liberals. He didn't know the province. He didn't have a firm grasp of many issues.

"And I damn near won," he says. Peterson lost by just forty-five votes to Stuart Smith, a psychiatrist from Montreal who had moved to Hamilton. Ultimately, Peterson was seen as perhaps a little too young and a little too conservative. Smith started the process of transforming the Liberals from a rural rump into a more sophisticated urban force, which ironically would never pay dividends for him, but would for the man he defeated.

"It was very premature in a lot of ways 'cause there was so much I didn't know," Peterson admits. "But I'll tell you, [in running for leader] you learn a hell of a lot in a hell of a hurry."

One thing he learned was the power he possessed to make little changes in people's lives, which made a world of difference. Sure,

Peterson figures he inadvertently helped a few "scam artists" cheat the system along the way. But, overwhelmingly, there were people who captured his heart, such as a woman named Cathy. A single mother of three children, Cathy came to Peterson for help. He responded by getting her better housing and a healthier family benefits cheque, and he encouraged her to upgrade her skills.

"And she went on and got into school, got a better job, met a nice guy, married, he was nice to her children," Peterson recalls. "You follow their lives along and they invite you to their wedding and they send you pictures of their kids. That is very real." Twenty-five years later, this hard-nosed veteran of many nasty political wars still gets misty-eyed recounting the story.

Stuart Smith continued the Liberals' efforts to end the Tory dynasty. He moved the party back into official Opposition status after the 1977 election, this time edging the New Democrats by one seat. And he continued to hold Davis to a minority government. But Ontarians grew to admire and trust Davis more over the next four years. When the premier went back to the polls in 1981, the public rewarded him with his biggest victory yet—44.5 percent of the votes and a solid majority. Stuart Smith was finished. So was the new NDP leader Michael Cassidy, who had replaced Lewis after the '77 campaign. But David Peterson was just getting started. And so was Bob Rae. In 1982, both Peterson and Rae would win their party's leadership, Rae having decided to parlay his stardom in Ottawa into bringing the provincial wing of the party to a prominence it had never enjoyed before.

Initially, Peterson must have thought he'd won a booby prize. He'd watch his party suffer some terribly demoralizing moments. Sheila Copps, whom he defeated for the party crown, quit to move to the federal arena. So did MPPs Don Boudrias, Albert Roy, and Eric Cunningham. Ian Scott, the extraordinarily gifted Toronto lawyer and star candidate who had run unsuccessfully for the party in 1981, started to drive out to Peterson's cottage one day to announce that he wouldn't be running again either. But halfway there, he turned his car around. He knew his departure would be too crushing for Peterson to bear, and just couldn't inflict that on him. Scott would offer his name up for election next time out, and never regret doing so.

Ironically, it was Peterson's chief political opponent who gave him some of the best unsolicited advice during his time in public life. "God bless Bill Davis," Peterson says admiringly. When he offered his advice, Davis was no doubt thinking of another party leader from London—his own predecessor, John Robarts—who was admired politically but whose personal life was a mess. Davis urged Peterson to move his entire family to Toronto, which he did.

"Robarts was my hero as a premier, but he was also the antithesis of where I want to be in my personal life," Peterson says bluntly of his fellow Londoner, whose marriage, and life, both ended prematurely after his political career was over.

Rae, too, had a rough start. He didn't have a seat in the legislature, and Premier Davis was in no hurry to accommodate the NDP leader's need to get in there and raise a fuss. For some reason, Rae also seemed much less comfortable in the leader's role than he did in Ottawa as the much-praised finance critic. Journalists started writing stories about whether they had misjudged the social democratic wunderkind.

Meanwhile, Peterson needed a miracle to remain relevant on the Ontario political scene. He got two of them. A financial scandal broke among three of the province's more venerable trust companies. Davis was on vacation in Florida, while Peterson soaked up valuable ice time in question period, demonstrating an impressive grasp of complicated financial issues.

Rae, too, began to make his presence felt. Former NDP leader and long-time party stalwart Donald C. MacDonald resigned his

York South seat in working-class west end Toronto, forcing Premier Davis to call a by-election. Rae found himself fighting his fourth election in five years, but at last he had a seat in the legislature, defeating future MP John Nunziata.

Then, both leaders caught one of those breaks you only dream about in politics. Instead of exploiting his unprecedented popularity and calling an election he certainly would have won, Bill Davis announced on Thanksgiving weekend in 1984 that, after twenty-five years, he was retiring from politics. It meant the next election would be contested by first-time leaders for all three major parties.

The Ontario of the mid-1980s was going through significant demographic changes. It was no longer the dull, WASP-ish place of yesteryear. Southern Ontario was ready to bust out economically after a miserable recession in the early 1980s. Emerging issues included ethnic diversity, a new female business class, and the rising power of urban voters, all of which the tired Tories were ill-equipped to understand. Peterson looked good, had a gorgeous wife and three kids, jogged a lot, and seemed to be the incarnation of a thoroughly modern Ontario family man. New PC leader Frank Miller, thoroughly decent but older than Davis, didn't.

On May 2, 1985, David Peterson had a very good feeling. Liberals hadn't been in power at Queen's Park in forty-two years—coincidentally, Peterson's entire life. But after visiting the polls in his riding on election day, the Liberal leader, totally at peace, talked to his wife, Shelley.

"We're going to win this son of a gun," he told her.

A quarter-century later, Peterson remembers the incredible sensation he experienced on election night, even though his party actually came second in the seat count.

"There is something I think that good politicians—and I don't pretend I am one—can almost pick up by osmosis. Good politicians can read a lot from a crowd or from people. You just sort of soak it up in your pores. I could just sense that we were identifying with the people. We had so much momentum."

Had the election taken place a few days later, Peterson would probably have won a majority government—that's how badly the Tory vote was sinking. As it was, he had to content himself with the fact that his Liberals actually won more votes than the Tories but came up four seats short because of the vote splits—forty-eight seats to fifty-two. Still, Miller's lead was tenuous and his minority government would be short-lived. Bob Rae's NDP held the balance of power with its own solid showing of twenty-five seats.

"I knew I was going to be the premier after the election in '85," Peterson says. "I knew that the NDP couldn't support the Tories. They just couldn't because there was no intellectual justification for doing it."

Maybe Peterson knew it, but the rest of Ontario didn't. The NDP resolved to hold negotiations with representatives of both parties. Whoever would best accommodate Bob Rae's agenda would get his party's support. Peterson was convinced it would be him.

"They didn't want an election," Peterson says of the NDP. "And I said, 'Let's call another election. I'm happy. Let's ask the people.'

"'Cause I figured we could go back and win it. So I was the only guy who was prepared to go to the people again. And that gives you a lot of strength. If you're not afraid to go to the people, it gives you a bit of a moral advantage."

In fact, the Peterson–Rae collaboration simply made too much sense. Because the two parties were in concert on so many issues, they agreed to sign a formal accord outlining which measures would be acted on and when. One of the most important elements in the agreement was implementing full public funding for the province's Catholic school system. William Davis had announced his intention to introduce full funding for the separate system, but retired before the bill was actually passed. It was left to the Liberals, with backing from the NDP, to draw up and pass the bill.

The Peterson–Rae accord turned out to be one of the most credible documents in the history of any government in Canada. Traditionally, governments outline their agendas in a Speech from the Throne, which is read and then, more often than not, forgotten a day later. After Peterson and Rae signed the accord, they adhered to its tenets quite faithfully. As an aside, there was some discussion about having the two leaders photographed together at the time of signing. Peterson absolutely refused. "This was not a coalition government and I didn't want to give the impression that it was," he says. "*We* were running the joint, not them." Rae concurs with Peterson's recollection of events. "Nothing would have given me more pleasure than to have had a photo op on that occasion," he says.

Another significant proviso of the accord was stability in the Ontario Legislature. Peterson had to promise not to call an election for two years.

At the time, some Ontarians thought the closeness of the 1985 election would result in some kind of constitutional crisis. What if, upon losing the confidence of the House, Frank Miller had asked the lieutenant-governor to dissolve the legislature and send the people back to the polls? Could the lieutenant-governor ignore the wishes of an elected official? Could he refuse a first minister's request and offer Peterson a chance to govern?

In the end, the questions were moot. Miller admitted his government couldn't survive and less than two months after election day, Lieutenant-Governor John Black Aird asked Peterson to form a government, which he did with the NDP's backing. Once Peterson became premier, he appointed former leader Robert Nixon as his treasurer. And in a truly ironic bit of political trivia, David Peterson became the first Liberal premier of Ontario since Nixon's father, Harry, had left the job in 1943.

Day One of the new Liberal government was unlike anything anyone had ever seen before. Instead of swearing in his new cabinet in a small private ceremony, as had been the custom, Peterson took advantage of a beautiful June day to stage the event on the front lawn of the legislature. Thousands of citizens attended and accepted the invitation of their new premier to tour Queen's Park. This was a well-intentioned but almost disastrous gesture by Peterson. With thousands of people wandering the halls of the legislature, it later emerged that the second floor almost caved in due to the unprecedented traffic. Luckily, nothing happened and shortly thereafter, the building underwent a serious renovation to make it sturdier.

Whether you agreed or disagreed with the agenda set out in the accord, there was one indisputable fact. The next two years featured some of the most activist, ambitious, and far-reaching governing in Ontario history, particularly when compared with the steady-as-she-goes approach of the Tories during the dying months of their dynasty.

Were Ontarians nervous about the first non-Conservative government in four decades? Apparently not. Peterson's poll numbers shot up as he began to fulfill the pledges made in his agreement with Rae. His government banned doctors from charging their patients extra for medically insured services, a practice known as extra-billing. There was a nasty doctors' strike over it, but the government wiped the floor with the docs in the battle for public opinion. Peterson wanted a much more transparent government, so he passed the most ambitious freedom of information law in the country. As the economy improved and significant revenues started flowing into provincial coffers, the government reached further. It eliminated income taxes for its poorest citizens. It abolished the regressive health insurance premiums people had to pay to gain access to the health care system. It passed the strictest environmental protection legislation in Ontario history. It extended

French-language services to the province's half-million franco-
phones, and passed a new law prohibiting discrimination against
gays and lesbians in the areas of employment and housing.

There were simple gestures, too. During their years as opposition
MPPs, Peterson and Nixon had seen far too many poor families
suffer through miserable winters, unable to afford adequate winter
clothing for their children. The premier remembered "Cathy" and
what he'd been able to do for her.

"When you proceed up the ladder into cabinet and you get to be
first minister, you say, well if I could do that for Cathy, why can't I
do that for two hundred thousand people?" Peterson says.

So he did. Poor families received a bonus cheque so they could
buy winter coats for their kids.

"Some people would say, 'I'm not going to give it to them, they'll
drink it up in beer,'" Peterson acknowledges. "I'm not saying some
people didn't go out and buy beer. Maybe they did. But I think
probably a bunch of kids got coats they wouldn't have got."

It was classic, activist, unabashedly liberal governing.
Expenditures and taxes went up significantly, but the economy was
so supercharged that widespread tax revolts never materialized. As
Ian Scott, who became attorney general, told his cabinet colleagues
during one meeting, "The people elected us to spend." Given that
the Liberals and NDP combined for 63 percent of the votes cast in
that 1985 election, the claim wasn't without some merit. Members
of Peterson's cabinet were motivated by the notion that the province
was falling behind in too many areas because the Tories had stub-
bornly refused to make much-needed investments. They were
determined to make up for what, in their view, were years of
neglect. And they did so with a vengeance.

David Peterson might never have been premier without Bob Rae's
assistance. But it was becoming increasingly clear that the public
was rewarding the Liberals, and not the NDP, for the achievements

of the government. When the two-year accord period expired, Peterson called an election and marched to one of the easiest majority governments in provincial history. The polls barely moved from start to finish. It was a summertime campaign and, again, Peterson took advantage by attending a ton of community barbecues and projecting an image of youthful success. The generational change was complete. Ontario was no longer being governed by conservative men in their mid- to late-fifties. It was now the domain of forty-something, young, urban professionals. The Liberals took an astonishing 95 out of 130 seats, almost all at the expense of the Conservatives. They captured more than 47 percent of the votes. It was the highest percentage of the total vote count since Peterson's hero John Robarts had tracked almost 49 percent nearly twenty-five years earlier.

For Bob Rae, the election appeared to have mixed blessings. The complete collapse of the Tories meant Rae moved up to Opposition leader. And his party actually attracted a greater percentage of the vote on September 10, 1987 than it had in 1985. But the NDP also lost six seats from the prior campaign and no longer held the balance of power.

David Peterson no longer needed Bob Rae to be premier of Ontario.

For Peterson, it was a spectacular victory. He was the most popular politician in the country, with limitless potential. It seemed he could be premier of Ontario for as long as he wanted. What he didn't know was that he was on the verge of one of the worst humiliations in Canadian political history.

Considering that Peterson had won the first Liberal majority government in Ontario in fifty years, his first speech to his new, ninety-five-member caucus, in hindsight, seems extraordinarily prescient. Almost half the MPPs in the room were rookies, elected solely on Peterson's coattails. They knew it and so did he.

"I got you elected this time," the premier told his caucus. "But next time, you'll have to get me elected." It was as if Peterson instinctively knew his second term was going to be much more challenging than his rookie session. And it was.

"I never get carried away about success or failure," Peterson says of his unusual caucus address. "They are very fickle mistresses. You can't sustain that kind of popularity forever. You pick up barnacles and baggage as you go forward."

The media, seeing two tiny opposition parties in the House, got much tougher in its coverage of the governing Liberals. The opposition politicians, Bob Rae in particular, went for the political jugular as never before. And there was less willingness to forgive rookie mistakes. Peterson set unusually high standards of conduct that his ministers had to live up to. Many couldn't and didn't and were replaced.

But upon his return, other issues continued to take some of the shine off Peterson's government. Promises of lower auto insurance premiums that couldn't be kept; interminable disputes with municipalities over changes to Sunday shopping laws; and a fundraising scandal that prompted Peterson to call a public inquiry and eventually resulted in a jail term for Patricia Starr—a friend of several Liberal cabinet ministers.

But the second term also featured major achievements. On the social policy front, Peterson's government held extensive hearings into improving the lives of welfare recipients, and then implemented an extensive set of reforms costing billions. The program, called "Transitions," may in fact have been too successful. The government received little credit for trying to make the lives of Ontario's worst-off citizens better. And the province faced the bewildering spectre of seeing its economic performance constantly improve, but its welfare rolls continue to swell. (In 1995, one of the first orders of business for the new Mike Harris government would be a 22-percent cut to the generous welfare benefits introduced by the Peterson government.)

And then there was Meech Lake. From as far back as he could remember, national affairs had captivated David Peterson. He desperately wanted to secure Quebec's signature on a constitutional agreement, for both patriotic and personal reasons. Peterson knew Ontario premiers were expected to play a major role in nation-building. Against all odds, John Robarts convened the Confederation of Tomorrow conference in 1967. William Davis was instrumental in the repatriation of the Canadian Constitution in the early 1980s. Now, David Peterson could join that pantheon by assuring Quebec's future in the Canadian constitutional family with the ratification of the Meech Lake Accord.

The Meech negotiations featured some of the most intense moments Peterson would experience in politics. At one point, when things weren't going well, Peterson and Robert Bourassa had a private conversation. The Quebec premier tried to tell his Ontario counterpart the precariousness of his position. Bourassa couldn't appear to be too bullish on Meech, lest the sovereignist movement cut him to shreds. But he couldn't be too tough on the federalists, or the other premiers would throw their hands up in anger and kill the negotiations.

"I'm walking a tightrope all the time, David," Bourassa said. "If I take one step the wrong way, I could get killed. And you know what?"

"What?" Peterson asked.

"I love it!" Bourassa told him.

The failure of the Meech Lake Accord in June 1990 was David Peterson's saddest moment in politics. It was the file he cared about the most. For a while, it looked as though he had played the role of hero among the first ministers, volunteering to give up six Ontario seats in the Senate, so Quebec could maintain its historic 25-

percent chunk of representation in the chamber of sober second thought. Ontario was playing its traditional role of great compromiser to assure national unity, a triumph that would make all the other crises over auto insurance, fundraising, and ministerial scandals go away. But it failed.

"Lots of people argue, and they might be right, that I had lost perspective on that one," Peterson admits. "I spent so much time and attention on it. We were so damn close."

According to former New Brunswick premier Frank McKenna, Peterson had a premonition that his attention to the constitutional file might come back to haunt him.

"I saw David Peterson put his political life on the line for national unity, even though he knew it would hurt him politically," he says.

Dalton Camp, the late *Toronto Star* columnist and former PC party president, predicted in the summer of 1990 that the first premier who "picked his head up" after the Meech Lake negotiations would be severely punished by the voters.

David Peterson was that premier. Less than two months after the eleven first ministers left Ottawa with an apparent agreement, Peterson called an election for September 6, 1990. If he was hoping for a repeat of the breezy, successful summer campaign of three years earlier, he would be sadly mistaken.

His campaign kickoff was hijacked by a demonstrator, who excoriated Peterson's environmental record—an odd topic to choose, since it's widely acknowledged that environmental protection received higher priority under Peterson's government than it has under any other Ontario government before or since.

Peterson also had no answer to the basic question: Why are you calling this election less than three years into a five-year term?

The Liberals' polling numbers were still far and away superior to their opponents', which was a significant part of the reason why

Peterson went to the electorate early. The Tories still seemed out of the game and, in Mike Harris, had a new leader that few people knew. The New Democrats, of course, couldn't win. They never had. That had been the simplest truism in Ontario politics from time immemorial.

But there was something strange in the air in Ontario in the summer of 1990. The aftermath of Meech, the early election call, an economy starting to cool off, and an ill-advised mid-campaign promise of a sales tax cut (it looked like a desperate bribe to stay in office) all proved a toxic mix to the Liberal campaign. Candidates told the leader's office to keep Peterson out of their ridings. Eventually, some MPPs stopped canvassing altogether. Their mere presence at front doors was losing them votes. Treasurer Robert Nixon, an icon in the party and in his riding, found himself on the receiving end of vicious tongue-lashings from constituents. Nixon's handlers had to drag him out of supermarkets, where he was campaigning, because he was losing his temper and telling voters to go procreate copiously—except in somewhat more colloquial terms.

And then Ontarians did something they had never done before. In their efforts to send David Peterson a message, they unexpectedly threw him overboard. Receiving less than 38 percent of the votes cast, Bob Rae's New Democratic Party won a *majority* government. Only three years earlier, David Peterson had been the most popular politician in the country. But on election night 1990, he conceded defeat and resigned on the spot as party leader. "That was my way of taking full responsibility for the losses," he says. The wounds were deep and in plain sight. Peterson was heartbroken, and the harsh second-guessing that was about to begin wasn't going to make him feel any better.

"One thing I learned while I was on the boxing team at the University of Toronto is that when they've hit you, don't let them know they've hit you," Peterson says of that night. "You can't sit there and whine and weep. You have to carry on. You force yourself to do that. People in public life by and large accept criticisms that very few others can take."

David Goyette, who worked for many of Peterson's cabinet ministers, says politicians may be great performers while in office. But that pales in comparison to how they perform once they're dumped and have to make a concession speech for all their friends and enemies to see.

"Although all politicians will tell you they prepare for that, I'll tell you the truth," Goyette says. "Most politicians don't really prepare too seriously for a loss. That's the greatest acting job of all. Because it's the first time you are once again yourself, alone, and you know that in two minutes, when you finish your speech, you are going to be desperately alone."

With the advantage of hindsight, we can now add that almost *every* signatory to the Meech Lake Accord faced the wrath of the electorate soon after the agreement failed. William Vander Zalm was hounded from office in British Columbia. Alberta's Don Getty left politics an unhappy man. In Saskatchewan, Grant Devine was crushed in his re-election bid. Quebec's Robert Bourassa, and Joe Ghiz of Prince Edward Island both declined to seek re-election. Nova Scotia's John Buchanan took a Senate appointment and ran, before he could be tossed out on his ear. Only Frank McKenna broke the mould as the one Meech Lake signatory who would go on to enjoy future electoral success. It may well be because he arrived in Ottawa in June 1990 as a constructive critic of the accord, having campaigned against it and won every seat in his province. (Eventually, he came around and endorsed a compromise proposal.) The two consistent opponents of Meech—Gary Filmon of Manitoba and Clyde Wells of Newfoundland—both handily won re-election.

Meanwhile, David Peterson wouldn't have to wait long for the post-election insults to begin. At the Liberals' first caucus meeting, the MPPs who had survived the debacle actually debated whether to allow Peterson to attend. The Liberals' defeat was so complete that the premier lost his own seat—just the third time in the province's history that a sitting premier suffered such an indignity. Some MPPs figured that no seat meant no right to attend caucus. Many party members couldn't wait to distance themselves from their fallen leader. If that hurt, Peterson wasn't about to let on to his former colleagues.

Conversely, New Democrats could not get over their good fortune. Stephen Lewis, the former party leader, told CBC-TV's Kelly Crowe at an election-night party, "This exceeds my wildest fantasies."

Regardless of your politics, it was hard not to feel a little goodwill toward Bob Rae that night. (Well, maybe very partisan Liberals didn't feel much goodwill.) The Rae family had recently endured two unbearable tragedies: the death of Bob's brother David from leukemia, despite Bob's donating his own bone marrow, an extremely painful procedure in its own right; and the death of Rae's in-laws in an automobile accident caused by a drunk driver.

I was hosting the CBC-TV election broadcast that night. When I mentioned those tragedies during a one-on-one interview with Rae, and asked whether he considered his electoral triumph some form of "payback," he allowed that he had talked to his mother earlier in the evening, and she had voiced the thought that it was "about time that the Rae family had a party."

Even some NDP opponents got into the spirit of Rae's victory. A group of long-time PC party loyalists, including former leader Larry Grossman, gathered in a hotel room at the Sutton Place Hotel in Toronto to watch the returns. When it was announced that the NDP had won, the group spontaneously rose in a standing ovation (no doubt mostly inspired by the group's delight at Peterson's downfall).

A day after the election, I telephoned veteran Liberal Robert Nixon to get his views on the election debacle. Nixon had spent a quarter of a century on the opposition benches, waiting for a chance to move to the other side of the House. Having finally succeeded, he was now about to lose his job as treasurer after just five years.

"Do you think Ontarians are freaking out at what they've done?" I asked him.

"No," he said, "I think they think this is pretty neat."

Certainly, the first swearing-in of an NDP government in Ontario was a pretty neat event. It took place at Convocation Hall at the University of Toronto on a beautiful October day. The hall was packed, and an overflow crowd gathered outside to watch the festivities on television. A sense of humour showed when the faithful took their seats to the background strains of "Side by Side" (which begins: "Oh we ain't got a barrel of money . . ." and wouldn't that prove to be prophetic). The lieutenant-governor, Lincoln Alexander, added to the upbeat tone of the day just before he administered the oath of office to Ontario's twenty-first premier. He jokingly asked the audience, "Do I know Bob Rae?" then proceeded to remind everyone that it was Rae's non-confidence motion that ended Alexander's career as the minister of labour in Joe Clark's government back in 1979.

Ask Bob Rae ten years later what his best day in public life was, and astonishingly, neither election night nor inauguration day make the list.

"Those were fun but you always know that sort of triumph is very short-lived," Rae says. "Election night is a great high. It's a day of great excitement. And the inauguration day is a day of great excitement. But you know that's fleeting. It's here today, gone tomorrow. But the sort of satisfaction you get out of a day when you've really accomplished something from a personal standpoint, those are great days."

Still, inauguration day *was* a great day. The lieutenant-governor administered the oath of office to a record number of women cabinet ministers. The eleven women included Zanana Akande, the first black woman ever to sit in cabinet; Marion Boyd, the woman who defeated David Peterson in his own riding; and Frances Lankin, a former jail guard.

Spicing up the cabinet mix was Peter Kormos, a wacky maverick who drove a Corvette, wore cowboy boots, and had a rap sheet for civil disobedience.

The dean of the cabinet would be a short, unassuming former community college teacher from Walden, near Sudbury, named Floyd Laughren, who had been an MPP for almost twenty years. Laughren's father was an illiterate farm worker from Shawville, Quebec. And here was young Floyd: deputy premier, treasurer, and minister of economics in the country's biggest province.

One MPP, Peter North, was thrilled to be in cabinet and one day said so to Laughren during a flight to Thunder Bay.

"Don't get too excited about it," Laughren told him. "It's just Thunder Bay."

"No, it's not that," North replied. "It's my first trip on a plane."

The first couple of months for Bob Rae's new government must have seemed like a magical mystery tour. Most Ontarians quickly came to agree with Bob Nixon's post-election observation, because after just two months in power, the NDP had skyrocketed to 60-percent popularity in public opinion surveys. When Laughren mentioned the poll result in the legislature one day, Rae quickly responded, "Don't inhale!"

Despite the euphoria of the first few months, Rae's first year as premier wasn't much fun at all. He wasn't sleeping well. Then he contracted pneumonia in the middle of the summer. It was all related to the stress of doing a job he frankly never expected to get. Ironically, as Ontario's fiscal news got worse, Rae's health improved. He had a heart-to-heart talk with his wife, Arlene Perly, his closest friend and adviser, who somehow convinced him to start enjoying the job more and fretting less about what he couldn't control. The reality was, during his entire political life to that point, Bob Rae had never been the decision maker. He had only ever been the decision critic. It may well be that the adjustment was harder on him than he'd anticipated.

As Ontario went into the recession everyone had anticipated, the numbers started to get downright scary. Tax revenues plummeted, but the NDP was determined to cushion the blow as much as possible. Ontarians were accustomed to seeing annual deficits of $2 billion, even $3 billion, on budget day. But when Laughren announced the deficit would hit *$10 billion,* the public's love affair with the NDP began to disintegrate.

Somehow, both Rae and Laughren were able to portray a reasonably calm front, despite the constant onslaught of bad news. Rae found some simple yet tried, tested, and true methods of dealing with it all. He'd shut the door and read a great book. Or he'd listen to music. Any kind of music.

"I still do that," he says. "I still find it has a huge affect, a huge impact. And watching a funny movie or a funny video. *Fawlty Towers.* Just laugh and get it out of your system. That's one of the ways I get re-tanked and recouped and able to come back."

In fact, Rae, who was often described as one of the most notoriously aloof politicians around, attributes that reputation to the times he is with people but simply zoned out. "It's just a coping mechanism, just a way of saying, I can perform 90 percent of the time, but not all the time. I need some other space. I've always been that way."

Behind the scenes, the premier and his treasurer even managed to laugh a little. One day, an assistant told Laughren that Rae was on the phone for him. The treasurer went to his office to take the call in private.

"Hi Floyd, it's Bob. I've got some good news," Rae said.

Laughren hung up on him. The phone rang again.

"Floyd, it's Bob. I guess we got cut off," Rae said.

"No Bob," Laughren said. "I hung up because I know that anybody that phones me with good news is bullshitting me and I haven't got time for it."

Meanwhile, for the first time in his life, David Peterson was out of a job. His rise and fall in politics had been so fast that he had given almost no thought to what he might do after his career was over. Today, Peterson says even if he had won that 1990 election, it would have been his last one.

"I didn't have any desire to set any records," he says. "I would have gone three to four years in order to give the party time to transition." Peterson actually had his eye on a potential successor—the University of Toronto's president at the time, Rob Prichard (who was to become president and chief executive officer of Torstar Corporation), whom he unsuccessfully courted to run for the party.

Peterson's immediate task was figuring out what to do next. For fifteen years, provincial politics had been his entire professional orientation. Now, in a business where "What have you done for me lately?" is so often the key, Peterson was forced to turn his back on the life that had just rejected him.

"I had to go on and put all my energies into building a new life," Peterson says. One of the first things he discovered about life after politics is that no one does you any favours.

Peterson took a few weeks to lick his wounds before re-emerging. He needed the time to figure out his next move, after suffering one of the worst body blows a Canadian politician has ever taken. And then he began the rebuilding process. He got himself ensconced as a senior partner and chairman in the blue-chip Toronto law firm Cassels, Brock & Blackwell. And then the directorships started coming in: chairman of the board of Chapters; founding chairman of the Toronto Raptors basketball team; director of Rogers Communications Inc. The timing of his arrival into the private sector wasn't what he had wanted. But Peterson was building up the new life that had been thrust upon him.

"Nobody owes me anything. I can't expect anything," Peterson says from his law office on the twenty-first floor of Toronto's Scotia Plaza skyscraper. "I don't just sit in this office and expect things to happen. I have to make things happen. I have to get the clients in, put the deals together. And the minute I lose my capacity to chair a board or to chair the law firm or to add some value, I'm out on my butt. Nobody's going to carry me."

However, Peterson has also come to appreciate a freedom from the kind of scrutiny politicians at his level endure. One day, he was walking in downtown Toronto when someone approached him.

"David Peterson," the man said, "I'm so glad you're not the premier any more. You were a terrible premier. And we're lucky to be rid of you."

Peterson listened, then responded: "Sir, one of the great things about not being in public life any more is that I don't have to listen to senile old assholes like you any more." And with that, Peterson walked away.

"I felt that it was one of the most liberating things that I've ever done in my entire life," Peterson sheepishly admits. "I shouldn't have been proud of myself, but I was. I felt good, I did."

Even though Ontario's financial picture continued to deteriorate, and with it his poll numbers, Bob Rae was determined to leave a positive and distinctive mark on his province. He had tried to spend his way out of the recession, but that only sent Ontario's deficit skyrocketing and left Wall Street bond rating agencies freaking. Raising tax rates actually brought in less revenue. He discovered he could direct his minister of finance to spend $1 billion on direct job creation, and the unemployment rate would decline by just one percentage point. Every option seemed quite hopeless.

But in the midst of all of this were some triumphs, which Rae is proud of to this day. It was the NDP that negotiated a unique partnership with the private sector to build Ontario's first privately financed superhighway—the 407 across the top of Toronto. Rae established a royal commission on education, whose recommendations for standardized testing, better report cards, a new curriculum, better teacher training, and greater parental input didn't sit on some dusty shelf. In fact, Mike Harris's Tories embraced the agenda, took credit for it, and implemented much of it.

In addition, there are thousands of people still manufacturing Dash 8 airplanes at de Havilland in Toronto, because Bob Rae interceded on their behalf and helped save the company from going under. The same could be said for Algoma Steel (where he put former premiers Bill Davis and Allan Blakeney on the board) and St. Mary's Paper in Sault Ste. Marie. Rae was perhaps uniquely positioned to negotiate terms that would keep those companies alive. He was a smart lawyer who understood the needs of business. He also represented a party that enjoyed a special relationship with labour and could maintain credibility with unionized workers. Laurent Beaudoin, chairman of Bombardier, called Rae the most intelligent politician he'd ever worked with.

"But would you vote for him?" I once asked Beaudoin at an event at de Havilland.

"No," he admitted, then, quickly recovering, added, "because I'm from Quebec."

It may have been a throwaway line, but it was indicative of the dilemma in which Rae found himself. Many business executives enjoyed their dealings with Rae—his intelligence, his integrity, his wit. But they couldn't or wouldn't publicly support him or raise money for his party. The chairs of Bay Street boards just didn't do that sort of thing for the NDP. What Bay Street big shots did in public was castigate the government for failing to lower the deficit, while at the same time lobbying Rae privately for more funds for a local hospital. Simultaneously, leaders within the private sector union movement, many of whom thought Rae was a little too centrist for their tastes anyway, wouldn't stick by him when their members started losing their jobs in droves.

Rae also made a decision that, to him, made perfect sense. But his political enemies were appalled. The premier appointed David Agnew, his chief of staff and former campaign manager, to become secretary of the cabinet—in effect, the province's top civil servant. For their first two years in office, New Democrats constantly grumbled that the Ontario public service was thwarting their efforts to implement their agenda. In opposition, David Peterson had complained that the civil service was stocked with too many Tories, and promised to clean house if he ever got in. When he did become premier, he completely changed his tune. He found the civil service to be far more professional and non-partisan than he had anticipated and the house cleaning never happened.

But such was not the case for the NDP.

"We had to appoint David," says Ruth Grier, the former NDP cabinet minister who, after leaving politics in 1995, became a weekly contributor to *Fourth Reading* on TVO. "We couldn't get anything through the civil service."

Maybe so. But the opposition had a field day with the appointment. It didn't take too much imagination for Rae's critics to accuse him of politicizing the impartial civil service, or even worse, giving one of the best-paying, most influential jobs in government to one of his best friends. It would be impossible for Bob Rae ever to accuse another politician of patronage.

Meanwhile, as the deficit headed for the stratosphere, Rae's government realized it had to make some extremely difficult decisions. What it came up with it likened to a three-legged stool to find $6 billion in savings. One leg of the stool would see the NDP raise taxes by $2 billion. The second leg would require cutting program spending by $2 billion. And the final leg—the final $2 billion—would be saved by unilaterally opening up collectively bargained contracts between the government and unionized employees in the broader public sector. Nearly one million people in Ontario were paid by the provincial government—doctors, hospital workers, teachers, caretakers, university professors, hydro workers. If they would accept a three-year wage freeze, plus take twelve unpaid days off per year, the government could realize its $2 billion in savings and everyone could keep their jobs. The alternative was firing tens of thousands of public sector employees in the middle of the worst recession since the Depression, and the New Democrats did not want to do that.

They called it the "Social Contract."

"That seemed to be tough, but at least it was a balanced approach," says Rae's finance minister, Floyd Laughren, of his three-legged stool. The idea seemed to be that everyone in Ontario would share the pain. No one group should feel picked on. But rather than see the initiative for what it was meant to accomplish, namely save public sector jobs, union leaders declared war on Rae and his government.

"I still think that from a social democratic view it was the right thing to do," says Laughren. "I'm not so sure that's true politically." Politically, the government alienated its one true base of support, a breach that, to this day, hasn't been repaired.

In 1993, the Social Contract negotiations with the public sector unions broke down and the government unilaterally imposed the $2 billion in savings. Rae's government still had almost two more years before it had to go back to the people. But the premier sensed that, politically speaking, from this moment on he was living on borrowed time.

"The Social Contract was a fiscal success," Rae says. "But in terms of the impact it had on our party—I came to realize that it was going to be very tough for us to come back."

Fighting the recession and the deficit became an all-consuming effort for Rae and his cabinet, so much so that the party turned its back on policies with which it was most clearly identified. The NDP came to office promising to create a public auto insurance scheme, similar to plans in British Columbia and Manitoba. But on the NDP's first anniversary in power, Rae cancelled those plans, citing exorbitant costs. In opposition, Rae excoriated the Peterson government for giving individual municipalities the local option of allowing stores to be open for business on Sunday. Once the NDP was in power, wide-open Sunday shopping became commonplace. And even though there was no official plank in the NDP platform against casino gambling, it was widely acknowledged that party members were deeply opposed to it. Yet it was the Rae government that opened Ontario's first permanent Las Vegas-style casino, in Windsor, to take advantage of that city's proximity to Detroit and oodles of American gamblers.

Saving money and raising revenue simply became more important than pursuing the NDP's traditional agenda, which had been laid waste by the recession anyway.

A year later, there actually was a glimmer of hope that the government's popularity might recover. The economy started to improve. But then federal finance minister Paul Martin downloaded another $2 billion in cuts onto Ontario. Rae felt handcuffed: he was out of options.

"You can't jack the deficit back up," he remembers thinking at the time. "You can't raise taxes. You can't lower taxes in my view responsibly without having to cut expenditures more, which I didn't believe in. I thought, at that point, *It's called the end game, Bob.*"

David Peterson watched it all with mild bemusement. Maybe not so mild.

"I think what happened in the NDP is that they totally lost their soul in power," he says. "Everything they stood for in the face of principle they jettisoned. At least they used to represent a conscience, even if they were wrong or crazy. At least they had some principles. When they became pragmatic, they weren't very good at that either."

But for Bob Rae, none of that was the worst part of the job. He expected to have to make tough policy decisions. In January 1993, the premier's office decided to amalgamate some ministries and restructure the government. It meant firing a couple of cabinet colleagues and deputy ministers.

"I found that painful," Rae says. "I found that personally difficult. Telling people it was the end of the day, that it's time to go, is a hard thing to do."

In the spring of 1995, Bob Rae succumbed to the inevitable. He was in last place in the public opinion polls. He refused to let the legislature sit for a spring session or even bring in a budget, so convinced was he that both moves would simply give critics a chance to heap more scorn on his government. His critics accused him of ducking his responsibilities and cheapening democracy. Finally, he called an election for June 8 and hoped for the best, knowing he'd just set in motion a chain of events that would probably end his political career after seventeen years.

"What I always had—and I think it's what allows me to go on—was a sense of, are you doing the right thing? Are you a good person? Are you doing the best you can?" Rae asks rhetorically. "If you can answer those things in the affirmative, you carry on and learn to ignore the worst kind of news. Without sounding corny, when you've lost a loved one, you've been through some really difficult emotional times, you realize this is not life. It's not the end of the world."

The day Rae called the election was a strange one for his minister of finance, Floyd Laughren, and not just because he knew the end was near. Laughren had been diagnosed with prostate cancer that morning. After receiving the news, he walked to Rae's office and the two shared a moment of reflection.

"It's been a rush, eh?" Rae said to him.

"Bob, we're gonna make a very good second-term government. Better than our first term," Laughren smiled.

Of course, they wouldn't get the chance. Like his political adversary David Peterson before him, Bob Rae would be premier of Ontario for only five years. Like David Peterson before him, he'd see dozens of colleagues go down to defeat on election night. However, unlike David Peterson before him, Rae would keep his own seat. It merely delayed his departure from politics for a little longer.

MIKE HARRIS SUCCESSFULLY CONTESTED the 1995 election by convincing voters that the David Peterson–Bob Rae era represented "ten lost years" for the province of Ontario. In fact, for a large part of the electorate, some of the numbers were rather distressing. In those ten years, government spending had nearly doubled from $29 billion to $54 billion. From Confederation to the last Conservative budget in the 1985 fiscal year, successive Ontario governments had accumulated $33 billion in debt. By the time the Liberals were out of office, that figure had moved up to $40 billion. The Liberals held power during amazingly buoyant times, yet only balanced one budget, despite sky-high revenues due to dozens of tax increases and the booming economy. In fairness, they were also the first government in twenty years to balance a budget.

When the economy tanked while the NDP was in power, budget deficits routinely grew to more than $10 billion a year. The incoming Harris government said the deficit would have hit $18 billion had it not imposed some emergency cuts upon taking office. By the time the NDP left office in 1995, the debt had surpassed a breathtakingly high $100 billion.

David Peterson didn't get to choose the moment of his departure from politics. The voters chose that for him by making Marion Boyd the new member for London Centre. In some ways, it was a cleaner out.

But Bob Rae was in a tougher spot. True, his party had lost the election and suffered a significant repudiation. However, he could take some solace in the fact that the rejection was nothing like that sustained by Kim Campbell two years earlier, when her PCs were reduced to two seats. At least the NDP held on to seventeen ridings, including Rae's own. But clearly, going from premier to leader of the third-place party didn't hold that much interest for Rae. Not only that, he was starting to feel the pressure of not having made very much money during his seventeen years in public life. The first of his three daughters was approaching university age, and by losing the premier's job, he was about to lose tens of thousands of dollars in salary.

The problem was, nobody was seriously urging Rae to quit—in fact, quite the opposite. With the Harris Tories promising to slash every program in sight, New Democrats demanded Rae stay and fight to protect his legacy. Even his eldest daughter, Judith, adamantly wanted him to stick around.

"You won (your riding of) York South. People like you in York South and you should stay," she told him.

And for nine months, he did. "I think it's better to go when people want you to stay, rather than to stay when everyone wants you to go," Rae says. "Diefenbaker I'm not. I don't want to hang around when everyone says the bell has rung." And so, on February 7, 1996, exactly fourteen years to the day after he became NDP leader, Bob Rae announced his departure from politics. Shortly thereafter, he signed on with the Toronto office of the law firm Goodman, Phillips & Vineberg (now just called Goodmans), specializing in mediation, arbitration, international trade law, and public policy. He seems to have made the transition to private life quite seamlessly, no doubt aided by the fact that the timing of his departure from politics was more or less his own. But if you want to make Bob Rae wistful about politics, ask him what he would have done had he been fortunate enough to win a second term.

"That's been the hardest thing to cope with—what might have been," he says candidly.

Never mind that Mike Harris almost immediately upon taking office killed several of the NDP's proudest achievements (employment equity, anti-scab legislation, and maintaining generous welfare rates in the face of a miserable recession). Rae also mourns the fact that billions in infrastructure improvements, such as new subway lines for Toronto, may never see the light of day because of his government's defeat. Building social housing, which was expensive but did get people off the streets, was cancelled altogether. JobsOntario, which offered subsidies to business to create jobs (particularly for the hardest to employ), was also ditched.

"That's why I write books and do what I do," Rae says, referring to the fact that he hasn't exactly been a shrinking violet in retirement. "It's because I feel there's sort of a legacy. The press that our government got was terrible, and you don't always get the defence you want. So you sometimes have to provide your own."

Again, Rae's wife, Arlene Perly, offered perhaps the most singularly useful advice. She reminded her husband that even if he had won a second term, *not* being premier was going to occupy a greater portion of his future than being premier. Her advice: "Forget it. It's over. It's done now. Move on. You've got to do something else."

(Arlene Perly had another good line: What's the definition of a defeated politician? Somebody who gets into the back seat of a car and nothing happens.)

One of the other people most instrumental in helping Rae make the transition was the senior partner at his new law firm—long-time Tory backroom boy Eddie Goodman. A Second World War veteran, Goodman reminded Rae that when the war was over, the men who came home returned to a much different existence. They knew their lives would never be that intense again.

"Politics is like a substitute," Rae says. "In civilian life it's the only comparable experience you can have. It's the intensity of the battle. It's the friendships that you form."

Politics has changed a lot since David Peterson and Bob Rae began living that life back in the 1970s. For one thing, it's a lot meaner today.

"It's not politically correct to criticize anyone else today. But you can criticize politicians," Peterson says. "People blame politicians for virtually every evil."

Peterson remembers the days when legislatures were more respectful, more collegial. You'd bash each other's brains out during question period, then play cards and have a beer afterward. Back then the attacks were less personal. Today, if you don't call your opponent a liar, you're considered a softie. Sure the politicians themselves are partly to blame. But Peterson also sees a culture where people such as Jerry Springer and Howard Stern now dominate.

"People are more interested in crap than they are in the subjects," he says. "There's no shame anywhere. And most issues are terribly complicated in politics."

Peterson's hero in politics, John Robarts, used to say that by the time a major decision got to his desk, it was undoubtedly so contentious that it could be decided by a flip of the coin—so persuasive were the arguments on both sides. "If the issue was so easy to resolve," Robarts used to say, "it would have been, before it ever got to me."

Bob Rae agrees with Peterson's assessment, but with a caveat. "I can't complain about that 'cause I've dished out as much as I've taken." In fact, Rae was forced to apologize publicly to one of Peterson's MPPs, after falsely accusing the member of corruption. Rae was also the first Ontario party leader in memory to call the premier (in this case Peterson) a "liar" during an election campaign. However, Rae certainly received as many cheap shots during his five years as premier as he dished out as Opposition leader.

"It's a blood sport," he says. "It's a tough business in many respects. It's not particularly fair, but neither is life. And politics reflects that."

Despite the fact that both men were discarded by the electorate in rather harsh fashion, neither one regrets the time he spent in public life.

"From 1985 to 1995, I had a lot of impact on the public agenda in this province," Rae says. "And I'm very proud of that."

David Peterson thought some of his best moments came when he walked into the lions' den. As Opposition leader, he marched into Essex County in southwestern Ontario—a hotbed of anti-Catholic sentiment—and spoke about the need to extend full public funding to the Catholic school system. He was premier when a handful of idiots stepped on and burned the Quebec flag in Brockville; Peterson visited the eastern Ontario town and gave a speech entirely in French.

"I loved some of those big fights when I was so comfortable with my own view and I was prepared to fight about it," he says. "I guess what defines a politician are what issues you die for. What do you really care about? I don't care that much about car insurance. But there are things that I do care about. And on these issues, I'm going to hang it all out and if they don't like it, to hell with them. That was an important lesson for me."

Both Peterson and Rae have had their successes in their new lives. They have had their problems as well.

Peterson has not been totally welcomed back into the Liberal fold. During the 1999 Ontario election campaign, he hosted an event at his Rosedale home for his local Liberal candidate, George Smitherman, Ontario's first openly gay member of the legislature. It was a private gathering. Peterson spoke brilliantly and eloquently about how, in his view, Ontario had become a meaner, less civilized place thanks to four years of Harris-style rule. But the new leader's advisers would never let the public see that kind of performance, preferring to keep Peterson on the sidelines during the campaign.

When Mike Harris gave a luncheon address to a joint meeting of the Canadian and Empire Clubs during that 1999 campaign, it was former PC premier Bill Davis who introduced him. When Dalton McGuinty, the Liberal leader, did the same event a week later, David Peterson was at the head table, but not invited to introduce the leader. The snub was conspicuous, none of the explanations very credible, and although he never said a contrary word about it, Peterson was hurt.

In the business world, Peterson also ran into a rash of either bad judgment or bad luck with some of his directorships. When the Toronto Raptors were sold, the new owners dumped him from the board. A more infamous example related to a company called YBM Magnex, an industrial magnet manufacturer, which the Ontario Securities Commission accused of contravening securities laws. Proceedings were launched against the directors, including Peterson, who resigned from the board in August 1998. Authorities have alleged the company had ties to the Russian mob. No one said that Peterson was connected to those underworld figures. But the suggestion was, he may not have been as diligent as he should have been in making sure the company's activities were kosher.

In the spring of 2002, he was put into the uncomfortable position of having to testify at a public hearing of the OSC. The former premier maintains it was he who successfully convinced the company to bring in a special investigator to get to the bottom of the mess. But OSC prosecutors argued Peterson was so derelict in his duties that he should be prohibited from serving on corporate boards for up to ten years.

"We're all holding our breath for David," said Nancy Poole, a friend from Peterson's London days.

In July 2003, an OSC panel sanctioned five of the company's eight directors—but not Peterson, who was hit with no penalties at all. The panel expressed its disappointment that Peterson "did not offer more insight and leadership." It confirmed that he failed to adequately address obvious conflicts of interest on the board and did not do enough to probe YBM's alleged ties to organized crime.

But Peterson called the ruling "a complete and total exoneration." His explanation always focused on the fact that he is involved with some high-risk companies and these things happen. Bill Davis, for example, resigned from the board of Corel in the summer of 2000, once its financial troubles became particularly difficult. However, others have suggested that sitting on almost a dozen different boards has overextended Peterson, a claim he denies.

Bob Rae also finds himself in a bit of a strange, although different, situation. Even though he's a highly paid downtown Toronto lawyer, he is still not accepted as one of the gang by the Bay Street set. And Rae's efforts to get New Democrats and Liberals to consider some kind of new centre-left party—not to mention the still-powerful sense of alienation among organized labour leaders over the Social Contract—has made him a pariah among many of his former New Democratic colleagues. It was most awkward, at the leadership convention replacing Rae, to see the former premier sitting with a very few close friends, but approached by virtually no one the entire time. For a man who got into politics because he loved working with people, Bob Rae is strangely isolated at both ends of the political spectrum these days.

"I feel that and I don't mind," Rae says. "I accept it. That's the way things are at the moment. But I've got lots of friends and I see a lot of people and I'm relaxed about life and I enjoy it. I'm not comfortable with the reluctance of the NDP to keep moving forward. I'm really disappointed that the process has ground to a halt. There's not enough imagination."

With the huge ups and downs of Rae's political life, he has been quite clear in saying his departure from politics was a resignation, not a retirement.

"I do feel that something else is going to happen," Rae says. "I'm fifty-one years old. The movie isn't over yet."

In fact, unlike most other retired politicians, Rae still frequently finds himself in the spotlight. He has taken on several high-profile causes, such as saving the Toronto Symphony Orchestra from bankruptcy, or mediating a dispute between the federal government and the Assembly of First Nations over the lobster fishery in Burnt Church, New Brunswick. He's also chairman of the Ottawa-based Forum of Federations, a non-profit organization he helped establish after his political career ended. The forum aims to strengthen democratic institutions around the world, and has board members from Nigeria, India, Germany, and Brazil. In fact, in 2002 Rae travelled to Oslo and the wartorn island of Sri Lanka for the forum, contributing to the Sri Lankan peace negotiations. And in a rather bizarre twist of fate, Rae accepted an appointment to the board of Hydro One, Ontario's beleaguered energy transmission company, which had been at the centre of a brewing political controversy ever since former premier Mike Harris put it up for sale in 2001. In April 2002, a judge ruled the sale illegal, putting the company's status into limbo. To make matters worse, the utility's excessive spending habits on executive compensation resulted in Harris's successor, Ernie Eves, cleaning house. The board and some senior executives were turfed. Rae was appointed to the new board, bringing his expertise (not to mention political "cover" for the new Eves government) to the scene.

"I'm enjoying it and having a terrific time," Rae says of his new life. "It's a really interesting mix."

Peterson insists he'll never run for office again, but he too won't close the door on some form of public service in future, particularly if the issue concerned national unity or constitutional reform. Perhaps he's thinking again of his political hero, Robarts, who, in retirement, was tabbed by Pierre Trudeau to co-chair one of the most ambitious takings of the nation's temperature, the 1979 Pepin–Robarts Task Force on National Unity.

"The problem is that once you're a politician, you're always seen as a politician," he says. "There is such a strong identification in people's minds that people think you're always plotting the next comeback."

For the vast majority of politicians who lose their jobs on election day, the sting of defeat can almost always be explained away by pointing to someone else. Political experts have long shown that in most Canadian races, individual riding-by-riding campaigns influence only 5 percent of the votes cast. That's significant if you lose by 4 percent. However, most of the people who will win or lose on any given election day, nationally or provincially, will do so because their leader ran an effective, winning campaign, or an ineffectual, losing one. The reality of today's modern, leader-focused, television-driven campaigns is that success or failure nearly always hinges on the public's affection for and trust of one person—and if you're not the leader, that person isn't you.

That's why, when you're the premier, when you've experienced the exhilaration of winning power and vanquishing your opponent, losing all that is as brutal as anything you'll experience in your professional life. Because there's absolutely nothing professional about it. *It's all personal.* When you're the boss and you lose the right to govern, there's no one else to blame. You're in your own special little hell, and usually it's of your own making.

That's why these stories from the dark side of the lives of two of Canada's most prominent former premiers are so dramatic and instructive.

Peterson says of his former occupation, "It's arguably the most interesting job in the country. It's stimulating in all respects. You deal with twenty crises a day, plus you try to drive a long-term agenda. You're always on edge."

On that, these two rivals—who transformed Ontario politics for better and for worse—can agree.

# THE METEORS

Men of genius are meteors destined to
burn themselves out in lighting up their age.
—*Napoleon Bonaparte*

IT'S REMARKABLE TO SEE what happens when an ordinary
person experiences the big win in a political arena. On the one day,
you may be dealing with just another backbencher, or cabinet
minister, or municipal politician. The next day you have to say
"Premier."

The occasionally toxic combination of politics and the media
has a unique way of shining a light on potential talent, creating
rising stars, then destroying them with equal panache. If you look
in the night sky and see a falling star, what you're actually
witnessing is a meteor. A popular educational text describes the
event thus:

> The intense heat burns up the meteors, which leave a blazing
> trail of light as they fall. . . . Many meteors burn up completely
> before hitting the earth's surface.*

---

* *HomeworkSpot.com* of Evanston, Illinois. Accessed July 6, 2003.
<homeworkspot.com/know/fallingstars.htm>

It would be difficult to find a more perfect metaphor to describe what happens to many people who rise too quickly, then crash and burn.

IF THE MUNICIPAL COUNCIL IN SURREY, British Columbia hadn't wanted to turn a park into a gravel pit in 1963, Canadians might never have heard of William Vander Zalm.

Vander Zalm was part of a community group trying to save the park in question. He was already in the plant business, so he donated some of his wares and planted them in the park in hopes of convincing the councillors to change their minds. They didn't.

"We weren't being told so much that we were wrong, or that they were right," recalls Vander Zalm from his home in Ladner, B.C. "It was just a matter of, we were heard and they proceeded anyway. And I think that really got me."

And at that moment, a political career was born. Vander Zalm had no memories of political life in his native Holland, which he left after attending elementary school. As an adult he seemed quite content simply to flex his free enterprise muscles, which he did quite skilfully from the age of seventeen on. He took over his father's bulb-growing farm and then expanded his gardening empire thereafter.

But that debate over the park vs. the gravel pit really bothered him. So in 1965 Vander Zalm sought and won a seat as a Surrey district alderman. As luck would have it, he defeated one of the gravel pit's proponents, which seemed a nice bonus to winning. For a guy who hadn't thought much about politics, the experience apparently transformed Vander Zalm, because three years later he ran for Pierre Trudeau's Liberals.

"I know. It's crazy, but I did," Vander Zalm now says about his flirtation with Trudeaumania. "Politicians do crazy things."

He lost a close contest to the NDP's Barry Mather, the former Vancouver journalist who had the distinction of introducing the first-ever freedom of information bill in a Canadian legislature in April 1965.

"But in retrospect, looking back, it was probably the best thing that could have happened," Vander Zalm now says.

The following year he became the mayor of Surrey and gave British Columbians a hint of the political derring-do that would follow him for the rest of his life. Twenty-five years before Mike Harris would bring in Ontario's first work-for-welfare program, Vander Zalm was introducing a variation on it to Surrey.

"I wouldn't allow the Welfare Department to pay welfare to young 'employables' if there were strawberries or raspberries to be picked, or potatoes to be dug," he says. "And that became a controversy."

Once again, Vander Zalm tried to move up in the political world, running for the Liberals in the 1972 provincial election. And once again, the voters in Surrey preferred to keep him in municipal politics. He came a bad third, with only 17 percent of the votes.

For a man who would eventually take B.C. politics by storm, Bill Vander Zalm's political career seemed very much stuck in neutral. He was selling plenty of plants to British Columbians. But they weren't buying much else from him—until Social Credit and a premier not too affectionately known as "Mini-WAC" came along and breathed new life into Vander Zalm's flagging political career.

Twice Bill Vander Zalm had tried to move out of municipal politics, and twice the voters had denied him the chance. But 1975 would be different. The Social Credit party was making a comeback under William Bennett, son of the legendary B.C. premier W.A.C. Bennett. This time, Vander Zalm would run for the same seat he had run for previously (Surrey), against the same NDP opponent (Ernie Hall). But his days with the Liberals were over. He would run, and finally win, as a Socred.

After a sluggish start, Vander Zalm's career was about to take off. Premier Bennett appointed him minister of human resources, responsible for overseeing social services in B.C. It didn't take the media long to see a dynamite story percolating there.

At a news conference after his swearing-in as minister, one reporter asked, "What could people expect from you as minister given your reputation?"

"If people are elderly and they're in need of help, we're probably not doing enough," Vander Zalm responded. "If they're handicapped, I know we're not doing enough. We should be doing a lot more, and I intend to. But if they're employable, if they're able to work and they refuse to work, they'd better start picking up a shovel or I'm going to give them a shovel."

Bingo! Zowie! Talk about headlines! It didn't matter what the premier or any other minister had to say that day. Vander Zalm and his shovel comment became the story.

"And I became the target for all sorts of editorials," he recalls. "They lampooned me, of course, in the cartoons."

It may have been a delicious quote, but it was also a clarion call to battle for his opponents. At one cabinet meeting, a delegation stormed the chamber, screaming for the minister's head. But this protest was a little different. All the demonstrators were armed with shovels.

Vander Zalm's enemies may have expected him to back down or show contrition, but he had other ideas. "I decided to turn that to my favour," he says.

Vander Zalm the cabinet minister suddenly became Vander Zalm the promoter.

"I immediately went out and I got some little shovel cards printed that said, 'This is your good luck shovel. The harder you shovel the luckier you'll get. Happy Shovelling.'"

And there was more. Vander Zalm got some lapel shovel pins made. The first fifty were sterling silver. The next batch were fourteen-karat gold. He also bought every short-handled shovel he could find at every garden centre in the Lower Mainland, and had them engraved, HAPPY SHOVELLING, THE HARDER YOU SHOVEL . . . or THIS IS YOUR GOOD LUCK SHOVEL, THE HARDER YOU SHOVEL THE LUCKIER YOU'LL GET, [SIGNED] BILL VANDER ZALM, MASTER SHOVELLER.

"We sold those packages, the cards, the short-handled shovel and the lapel shovel at every fundraiser in the Lower Mainland, for every type of cause," he laughs. Vander Zalm sometimes played auctioneer and actually raised $400,000 for various charities.

"It became a great thing," he says. "Even those people that had protested wanted me to come to their fundraisers to sell shovel packages."

But it wasn't all fun and games. In 1978, Vander Zalm sued the Victoria *Times Colonist* over an editorial cartoon that he felt crossed the line. The cartoonist, Bob Bierman, depicted the minister gleefully pulling the wings off a fly. The suggestion seemed to be that Vander Zalm enjoyed torturing those laid off within his ministry, as well as British Columbia's less fortunate, due to his new approach to welfare.

"This particular cartoonist got my goat," Vander Zalm says. "He just went on too much, too far, too long. I was initially only seeking an apology. But the guy wouldn't go for that." Initially, the courts agreed with the minister, ruling the cartoon went beyond fair comment. However, the paper appealed and was acquitted.

Most cabinet ministers don't give out shovels. Most cabinet ministers don't sue the media. (Former Ontario premier Bob Rae once advised politicians never to get into an argument with anyone that buys newsprint by the ton.) Then again, as he would prove time and again, Bill Vander Zalm was no ordinary politician.

Even though the shovel shtick garnered a ton of attention for Bill Vander Zalm, in truth he was becoming increasingly frustrated with politics. He was a guy with big, radical ideas, but felt surrounded by too many timid cabinet colleagues.

For example, he wanted to go further and faster in reforming social services toward a more conservative hue. "My colleagues stopped it, and I can understand that," says Vander Zalm, apparently more understanding of his colleagues' concerns today than he ever was then.

As municipal affairs minister, he wanted to go on a major consolidation spree—agencies, commissions, municipal councils—a big-time reduction in the size of government. Vander Zalm shepherded the bill through first and second reading, which, in the passage of any bill, is where the heavy lifting happens. But just as the third and final reading of the bill was set to take place, the Socreds pulled the plug on the legislature by proroguing the House. That bill, and every other one still to be passed, died on the order paper. "That was certainly my biggest disappointment," Vander Zalm recalls. "I tried to bring about some changes at the provincial level, but I was thwarted on several occasions."

Vander Zalm relates these incidents in a soft voice that carries none of the rancour and frustration he no doubt felt at the time. However, when Premier Bennett called an election in 1983, Vander Zalm decided enough was enough. He and his family were all working harder and harder to make his business succeed. He called his colleagues "a bunch of gutless wonders," declined to run again, and went back to his first love, the gardening business.

Over the next few years, Bill Vander Zalm may have been gone, but he certainly wasn't forgotten. Bennett's Socreds were vulnerable, particularly when three cabinet ministers became embroiled in scandals relating to sins of the flesh. Then Bennett announced his retirement from politics in the summer of 1986 and the stampede was on to replace him. No fewer than eleven candidates threw their hats into the ring. After all, the winner would become the premier. What these candidates didn't know— but the pollsters did—was that if a certain Bill Vander Zalm decided he wanted to make a comeback into politics, they were all dead meat.

At first, it appeared as if Vander Zalm had no intention of return-ing. He had just purchased a new theme park in Richmond that he would rename Fantasy Garden World. He looked quite content in the private sector.

However, the notion of his return seemed irresistible. Despite his critics, Vander Zalm was handsome, charismatic, and a successful businessman. He and Lillian, his wife of more than thirty years, and their two sons and two daughters oozed family values, in stark contrast to the scandals plaguing the three ministers.

Even though he was late to the dance (about one month after the other eleven had already announced), Vander Zalm decided to get in anyway. Ironically, the ensuing leadership convention would be memorable not because of anything Vander Zalm himself said, but because of something said about him by one of his opponents, Kim Campbell, who would go on to become Canada's nineteenth prime minister.

"It is fashionable to speak of political leaders in terms of their charisma," Campbell admonished the delegates. "But charisma without substance is a dangerous thing."

Campbell received a standing ovation for her efforts, and some pretty mean glances from the Vander Zalm section of the hall. She also received only fourteen votes. The pollsters were right. The majority of the delegates wanted Vander Zalm, and they got him.

In his speech after Vander Zalm's victory, the outgoing leader, Bill Bennett, assured British Columbians that their new premier was someone who could listen well and work together with others. Kim Campbell was having none of it. She likened her new boss to a ticking time bomb.

Despite having two years left in his term, Vander Zalm wanted to strike while his popularity was hot. Just one month after winning the leadership, he called an election for October 22, 1986. British Columbians rewarded his moxie. They gave him forty-seven out of sixty-nine seats—a very nice, comfortable majority government, thank you very much.

This was the moment Vander Zalm should have absolutely adored. No longer would his ambitious plans be stifled by "gutless" cabinet colleagues. He was the boss.

Funny how politics never quite works out the way you think it should. Today, Vander Zalm thinks he wasted too much time trying to create harmony in a cabinet and caucus full of rivals, some of whom never accepted his victory.

"I waited too long to make the changes," he says. "I spent too much time trying to create a peaceful atmosphere, and bring together the various factions."

Ask Vander Zalm about his greatest regret of this time and you'll get an unexpected answer. He was staunchly pro-life on the abortion question and campaigned against public funding for abortions. It was the cause of his deteriorating relationship with Kim Campbell. But Vander Zalm understood that abortion was within the federal government's jurisdiction and as much as he hated it, there was nothing he could do about it. No, he would save his regrets for something more disturbing—going against his principles.

Since the beginning of Social Credit, the party had had a section of its constitution called the "Christian Principle" clause. Vander Zalm didn't think it was too preachy, but some in the party did and wanted it removed. They told Vander Zalm that Socreds were all living their lives by the principle anyway, so why state it if it offended some members?

"And I went along with that," he says. "And I knew that I had gone contrary to my beliefs. I had really sacrificed something that I thought was very much a part of the constitution, historically, and should have stayed there."

"And do you still feel bothered by that?" I ask him.

"I am still bothered about it," Vander Zalm says, with evident remorse in his voice.

Still, financial affairs, as much as espousing Christian principles, were what brought Vander Zalm back to public life and on that front he enjoyed some success. His devotion to straightening out British Columbia's books was such that he initially kept the finance minister's portfolio for himself. (Six months into his government's term, he gave the job to Mel Couvelier.) About two and a half years in, Vander Zalm received a briefing from Finance Ministry officials and got some amazing news. For the first time in the history of his province, the government of British Columbia was not simply balancing its books, but actually paying down debt.

"I felt so good about that that I went out that night and I think I finished the better part of a bottle of wine with dinner, and it was the one night I didn't go back to work after dinner. I felt really great about that," recalls Vander Zalm, who got together with two staffers from his office and his deputy minister at his suite at the Harbour Towers Hotel in Victoria to celebrate.

"It was really a big deal. For me, it was so meaningful because basically that was the main objective, to get the finances in order. That was the best day."

But, as we all know, the rest of 1989 would turn out to be dramatically different for the man from Fantasy Gardens.

British Columbia is unlike any other province in many ways, including the location of its legislature. If the waters are choppy, you have to spend nearly two hours on a ferry to get from the mainland to Victoria, the capital. Because of that geographic reality, the Vander Zalms soon discovered that protestors were seeking out another location to do their thing. Fantasy Gardens in Richmond became protest central. And instead of the premier bearing the brunt of the noise, the premier's wife, who was running the business in her husband's absence, took it instead—from gay activists, doctors, nurses, truck drivers, and farmers.

"Anything and everything," recalls Bill Vander Zalm. "If there was a protest, it happened at the Gardens."

It was during this time that the Vander Zalms started seriously questioning whether returning to politics was such a good idea. The premier found himself wondering, "What the hell for? What am I doing? I could be with the family or friends or you name it."

But Bill Vander Zalm, like Ronald Reagan (who was ending his stint in the White House around then), saw one of his great strengths as being able to project a calm serenity when it looked as though his world was under attack. Where others might not be able to handle the heat, "I could overcome it very quickly, fortunately," he says.

Politics is a tough game to be in at the best of times, even more so for business people. The potential for conflicts of interest are omnipresent. The premier had significant business holdings. And his wife ran them. Clearly, the premier's antennae weren't sensitive enough to appearances of impropriety. Ultimately, that would cost him his job.

The Vander Zalms decided they'd had enough of the headaches associated with Fantasy Gardens, so they decided to sell. The buyers were Taiwanese, and had never been to British Columbia before. The now-legendary real estate agent who brokered the deal, Faye Leung, insisted the buyers meet the lieutenant-governor because they all came from the same province in China. Vander Zalm arranged it.

The Opposition accused the premier of using his office to influence the sale of his business. Then it set what Vander Zalm now regards as a trap that he naively walked right into.

The Opposition had a candidate in mind to investigate the premier's involvement with the sale of Fantasy Gardens. Vander

Zalm's staff urged the premier not to appoint the Opposition's candidate. But Vander Zalm disregarded their advice—so sure was he of the outcome—and he gave the green light.

"I said, 'Well, there's no problem, I don't care who investigates it,'" Vander Zalm says. "'And whatever that person needs, I'll make it available. I'll be there, Lillian will be there, anybody they want, I'll make sure they're there.'"

Today, a politically wiser and chastened Vander Zalm thinks he went overboard to accommodate the Opposition in an effort to look beyond reproach. "And in retrospect of course it was a great mistake, because I think there were biases displayed in all of that."

What came next was a series of events that led to the political demise of Bill Vander Zalm. In April 1991, much to the premier's shock and dismay, the conflict commissioner, Ted Hughes, reported Vander Zalm *was* in a conflict of interest during the sale of Fantasy Gardens.

"That was the worst day," Vander Zalm now says of his time as premier. "It was so contrary to anything I had believed he'd come down with, that I was devastated. I was totally disgusted, and I announced my resignation within an hour of the report having been presented."

"Did your staff try to convince you not to resign?" I ask.

"My staff was really opposed to me having done what I did, but I carried on anyway," he says. "So I was probably not too smart in ignoring the staff as I did at the time."

"You sound like you've learned a lot," I suggest.

"Yes. It's always a learning experience, and I guess for me even more so because I had so much of it so quickly."

More than a decade has passed since this drama unfolded, so it's easy to forget the intensity with which this was all happening. The media was in a shark-like feeding frenzy. The Opposition could taste blood. And the premier seemed oblivious to the problems he had created for himself. Vander Zalm was the butt of countless jokes on national radio and television programs. Comics were mimicking his signature speaking style, to huge laughs.

I want to ask Vander Zalm, as respectfully as possible, about how he got out of bed every day and made it to the office, when so many Canadians . . . and here he interrupts me:

"See you as a bit of a screwball?" he says. (I'm glad he said it.) "I didn't take the personal attacks against me too personally. I saw it more as a lot of politics. I guess I have extra-thick skin."

Vander Zalm's government was persistently dogged by accusations of mismanagement and scandals, but ironically, Vander Zalm himself was ultimately acquitted of the conflict of interest charges. No matter. His fate had been sealed.

His successor would be as historic as the circumstances surrounding his departure. Rita Johnson took over the premier's job, becoming Canada's first female premier. She lasted seven months in the job, called an election, lost, and dropped out of politics. Last anyone heard, she was splitting her time between Vernon, British Columbia, and somewhere in California.

But, just as Bill Vander Zalm quit and returned to B.C. politics triumphantly fifteen years ago, he tried for a short time to repeat the trick in yet another century, with yet another party—his third. He found an issue that re-energized his political batteries and, for a time, he wanted back into the arena.

In 2000, he borrowed then Minnesota governor Jesse Ventura's bus and hit the campaign trail in a by-election in Delta South. Running as a candidate for Reform BC, Vander Zalm came second, winning one-third of the votes. He took solace in seeing the NDP come in at just 2-percent support, but he was a long way behind the Liberal victor.

Vander Zalm insists he's not some tired, old crank unable to move on after the electorate has already rendered its verdict on him.

He seems genuinely troubled at the state of Canadian democracy and is determined to try to do something about it.

"Politics in Canada and B.C. is probably the worst of any place in the world with the exception I suppose of some Third World countries, where you might get shot," Vander Zalm says. "It's a rotten system we live with."

For a while, Vander Zalm was the leader of Reform BC, a job he didn't really want and yet he understood he was one of the few British Columbians who could give the movement some profile. Then the party agreed to join forces with the province's Progressive Conservatives, Family Coalition and Social Credit parties into a new force called BC Unity, a self-described "free enterprise, populist alternative to the 'Big Money' Liberal élites and the discredited socialism of the NDP." The party ran candidates in half of the province's ridings (although Vander Zalm himself didn't run) but managed to attract only 4 percent of the total vote. The would-be coalition began to fall apart before the September 2001 election, but it might not have mattered anyway. Gordon Campbell's Liberals cruised to one of the easiest victories in history, taking a whopping 58 percent of the votes and seventy-seven out of seventy-nine seats in the B.C. Legislature.

BC Unity's fate evidently disappointed Vander Zalm to such an extent that, for the first time in decades, he decided to take a bit of a break from politics. He still helps behind the scenes, but his main energies seem focused on a myriad of new private enterprises. He is the self-proclaimed lilac king of the province, having started Van's Nurseries, an operation that is growing one hundred thousand lilacs for export. He has a company called Aquabiologic Technologies, which aims to improve water quality using "environmentally responsible science." He is part of two different consortia, trying to build two different theme parks in Hawaii. And he owns another nursery for unusual conifers near Portland, Oregon.

Vander Zalm and I speak when he is only a year away from turning seventy, and yet, despite the beating he took in politics, he says: "I feel and I look forty!" Would he ever run again? "'Never' is a word we don't use," he says. "I have no plans. I won't predict it, but I won't totally close the door either. But I've been there. I've done it all."

I ask whether Lillian, his wife of forty-six years, is happy about his continued involvement in politics, albeit peripherally.

"Happy may be an overstatement," he laughs. "But she knows that I am determined to do something, and if it makes me happy, I guess she will stick with it."

Maybe Bill Vander Zalm actually thinks lightning can strike twice. Stranger things have happened. Robert Bourassa left office utterly discredited, only to lay low for a decade, then return to the premier's office in Quebec City and the job he loved so much. Pierre Trudeau came back less than a year after his political epitaph had apparently been written. Joe Clark lost the PC leadership in 1983, then recaptured it a decade and a half later.

"What I miss the most," Vander Zalm says, "is the fun of being with people, having their respect, and I guess the power that you have as premier. Being able to direct policies for the whole of a province is a bit of a wish come true for anyone that seeks challenges and opportunities. It's a rather unique position, there's no question about that. It's a great honour to attain that position. A great honour, and a great privilege."

HOW DOES A POLITICIAN GO from capturing 50 percent of the votes—and winning a landslide victory—to resigning from politics four years later because the same people who gave him that mandate came to hate his guts?

John Savage didn't spend much time pondering that question in the years after leaving politics. When we met to discuss what he was up to now that politics was behind him, it was apparent that he had moved on to another phase of his very full life. His story exemplifies as well as any in politics how political fortune can change in brutal fashion.

Thirty-five years ago, the Welsh-born Savage was a successful family doctor in the United Kingdom. He wasn't crazy about what was happening to the health care system there, so he, his wife, Margaret, and their six children up and left for Nova Scotia, where they had one more child. He thought emigrating to the Maritimes would give his family the fresh start they wanted. And he liked to live beside the sea.

Savage established a practice for himself in Dartmouth and started doing his thing, including delivering babies. What troubled him was seeing so many pregnant teens coming through the door for help. They didn't want abortions, but they didn't want to be pregnant either. Savage investigated the matter further and discovered there was little, if any, sex education happening in the public school system. At this point, he realized the most basic truism of politics.

"Unless you're where the decisions are made, you can't get a lot done," he said. So in 1978, he ran for a position on the Dartmouth school board, openly advocating formalized sex ed programs, which at that point didn't exist. And he won.

One thing led to another. He became school board chair. He started garnering a reputation beyond the issue of sex education—for example, championing healthier communities as a whole and fighting discriminatory hiring practices. Seven years later, he found himself the mayor of Dartmouth, the province's second-largest city with a population then of 75,000. How badly did he want the job? Badly enough to take a whopping pay cut. As a doctor, Savage earned more than $100,000 a year. For the honour of wearing the mayor's chain of office, he was paid $33,000.

After seven years in the mayor's chair, Savage learned another significant truism of public life—one politician's demise always means another's ascent. In February 1992, the people of Nova Scotia learned that Liberal leader Vince MacLean had not only been receiving his publicly paid salary, but was having that topped up with money from a secret trust fund. The revelation became a cause célèbre that eventually led to MacLean's resignation. It was a serious blow to Liberal fortunes in the province. MacLean had come within five seats of knocking off Premier John Buchanan in the 1988 election and seemed poised to win it all next time out. Instead of preparing to pour all their efforts into the next election campaign, Liberals instead found themselves looking for a new leader.

When you're the mayor of the second-biggest city in the province, with well-known liberal views, and the provincial Liberal leadership opens up, your phone starts to ring. So John Savage spent a month travelling Nova Scotia to see whether there was enough support for his candidacy. There was.

"My interest was piqued," he said.

What came next was perhaps the most unusual leadership convention in Canadian history. For all the wrong reasons.

Nova Scotia Liberals decided they needed to make a big splash to show how much more democratic they were than the tired old Tories, who were in considerable trouble. After winning four elections, John Buchanan accepted an appointment to the Senate and Donald Cameron replaced him at the helm of the Nova Scotia Conservatives.

The Liberals tried something very different. They decided to forgo the old-style delegated convention and instead would have party members choose their new leader by phone. On June 6, 1992, 6,998 Nova Scotia Liberals made history. They picked up their telephones, dialled the number for the candidate of their choice, and promptly blew out the province's phone system. It was a big-time crash and a big-time embarrassment for a party trying to convince people that it was modern and competent.

The next question became: Now what? Try the phone vote again and risk becoming the laughingstock not just of Nova Scotia but of the entire country? Or give up and go back to the traditional convention?

After much debate, the Grits decided to gamble on Ma Bell one more time. This time, 6,999 people called to vote and it worked. On June 20, Dr. John Savage became the new leader of the Nova Scotia Liberal Party, winning a close, two-way fight over Lunenburg West MLA Don Downe by just a few hundred votes.

Savage's timing really couldn't have been better. The Tories had been in power for a decade and a half and people were eager for a change. In addition, the public image of the Conservatives took a thrashing one month before the Liberal leadership vote with the explosion at the Westray coal mine in Pictou County. All twenty-six of those who were working underground at the time were killed. The government's response to the tragedy was widely seen as ineffectual.

When Donald Cameron called an election for May 25, 1993, in hopes of renewing the Tory mandate, the results weren't pretty. Savage's Liberals took more than half the total votes en route to winning forty of fifty-two seats. The Liberals also won twelve of sixteen seats in Halifax–Dartmouth, reducing the Tories to just one survivor in the metropolitan area. Even though Cameron kept his own seat, he quit politics that night, after twenty years in the game.

Meantime, in his victory speech, Savage told Nova Scotians to hold onto their hats. "Today you ordered change and I give you my pledge that there will be change," he said.

It was a mixture of promise, warning, and threat—and it was his best moment in politics. Not a bad way to celebrate his sixty-first birthday, which he did a few days later.

As Nova Scotia's twenty-sixth premier, John Savage didn't just promise to bring change to the province. He threatened to do so with a vengeance. He never thought of himself as a lifer in politics and wasn't much on political niceties. He wanted to hit the ground running and implement major change. The year he took over, the deficit was $600 million, following a $300-million deficit the year before. That needed immediate attention. And the province's patronage system for roadwork was a national joke. Every time power changed hands in an election, two to three thousand employees of the Department of Transportation would be fired, and then replaced by two to three thousand friends of the incoming governing party.

"John Buchanan stacked every department," Savage said. "It's a fair statement to say he existed on a corrupt and patronage-ridden system."

As much as Savage despised the system and wanted to kill it, it was a seventy-five-year tradition in Nova Scotia, and many Liberals were now looking forward to their turn at the trough.

But Savage had other ideas. Instead of repeating the historic cycle of firing all the Tories, he said he would create a new system based on ability and professional experience. "The result," Savage reminisced, "was Liberals, who'd been out of power for fifteen years, were very angry. They were not getting what they expected."

The tension between Savage and the membership quickly mounted. One time, the premier was virtually subpoenaed to meet with party officials to hear their grievances.

"They were going to skin me alive," Savage recalled with an impish smile. "It was very, very uncomfortable. Finally in exasperation I said to these people, 'Look, I told you I was going to do this. I told you in this very room.' And a big tall guy in the back stood up and said, 'You know something, you did. But we didn't fuckin' well believe you!' The whole place broke up."

Savage quickly learned that to make an omelette, you had to break some eggs, and he had cast himself in the role of master chef. Nova Scotia's debt from Confederation to 1978—its accumulated deficits year after year—was $425 million. By the time the Tories left in 1993, they had sent the debt to the stratosphere, to $7.5 billion. Nova Scotians were paying 23 cents of every tax dollar just to service the province's debt payments. (By way of comparison, even during the days of $10-billion deficits in Ontario under the NDP, that province only ever paid as much as 17 cents out of every dollar on debt servicing.) The bond rating agencies Moody's and Standard & Poor's were threatening to downgrade the province's credit rating. Difficult decisions had to be made.

The private sector had already lost thirty-five thousand jobs during the recession. But Savage had made job creation his top priority. Firing thousands of public servants to save money wasn't a viable option. Instead, he reduced all public servants' salaries by 3 percent. The idea was to spread a bit of pain and spare a lot of layoffs. But just as Bob Rae discovered in Ontario with his Social Contract, logic and human nature rarely walk hand in hand. Savage came to understand that by trying to save the jobs of several thousand civil servants, he had in fact offended tens of thousands more.

"I felt despondent at times," Savage recalled. "Particularly when I began to lose the support. The succession of blows were very significant. But we knew we had to make the changes."

And that was just the beginning. Savage's government brought in Nova Scotia's first casino, alienating a significant chunk of the population that still regarded gambling as a vice. Still, the casino brought $25 million a year into the government's coffers. It was a much-needed shot in the arm at a time when the federal government was cutting back on its transfer payments. He told the post-secondary education sector that something had to give. Nova Scotia had thirteen universities for a population of fewer than one million people. (Again, by comparison, Ontario has eighteen universities for a population of eleven million citizens.) It simply couldn't be sustained, so he helped transform the college and university system, closing down two institutions. He also pushed a megacity bill through the legislature long before Toronto went through the same battle. He amalgamated Halifax and Dartmouth, figuring it made little sense to have so much duplication of services for a community of 280,000 people.

"There wasn't a single person at one time in Nova Scotia, who wasn't incensed at the things that we had done," Savage said, without a hint of regret. Given the changes he felt were necessary, he almost came to wear that statement like a badge of honour.

But there was nothing honourable about the public's view of Savage. His popularity had tanked. On election day, his support had been more than 50 percent. Less than four years later, it had tumbled to 19 percent, with no hope of resurrection in sight.

The public hated him. The party was depressed at how its fortunes had deteriorated so quickly.

"I had *personally* accumulated much of the ill will over policies that seemed to stick to me like Velcro," Savage admitted during our interview.

The conventional wisdom around Nova Scotia was that some party elders approached the premier and essentially told him he was through. Savage disputed this widely held account.

"Nobody came to me and said 'You've gotta go,'" he insisted. Rather, Savage met with his top advisers, including his son Michael, the one of his now seven children most interested in politics, and realized the Liberals would stand a better chance in the next election with someone else as leader. And so, four years and two months after winning a landslide victory, John Savage quit politics.

"I don't think we made an unprincipled decision the whole time," Savage recalled proudly. "If we had a weakness, it was a lack of political understanding of how much the people of Nova Scotia could take without throwing us out."

Would Savage have done anything differently? It didn't sound like it.

"The people didn't like us. And they particularly didn't like me," he said. "And if they didn't like me, then that was too bad."

At the age of 65, John Savage found himself out of a job for the first time in his adult life. He had won only one election, so there would be no political pension to fall back on.

"I didn't enter politics at sixty in the belief I'd get a pension out of it," he told me matter-of-factly.

The timing of his departure from politics may have been of his choosing. But had he stayed on as premier, there is little doubt that the electorate would have fired him after the next campaign.

The problem was, he still felt relatively vigorous, with something to contribute. It was also true that he was the most hated man in Nova Scotia, so getting a meaningful new job in the province would certainly be difficult, if not impossible.

"The transition was very painful," Savage admitted. "One minute you're making decisions which impact on all kinds of people. The next minute nobody gives a damn about what you do or who you are. And that's difficult to accept."

It wasn't that Savage didn't have any achievements in which to revel. For the first time in twenty-five years, Nova Scotia had a balanced budget. The unemployment rate dropped from 15 percent when he entered office to just 9 percent at his departure. Forty thousand Nova Scotians who had been without jobs now had them. There was greater autonomy for the province's Aboriginal people. The number of women appointed to provincial agencies, boards, and commissions jumped by almost 20 percent. And he received almost eight hundred letters from people offering their condolences at his reversal of fortune.

But John Savage didn't get much time to indulge in self-pity during his transition out of politics. Shortly after his resignation, he got a phone call from one of his predecessor's former staffers. Gerald McConnell used to be executive assistant to Vince MacLean. But now he was calling Savage in his capacity as chairman and chief executive of a Dartmouth-based gold mining company called Etruscan Resources Inc. He wanted to make Savage an offer he couldn't refuse.

McConnell wanted the former premier to be his company's adviser on health, social, and educational issues in African countries where Etruscan was trying to do business. And so Savage advised Etruscan on the construction of three schools and two health centres in Niger, a desperately poor African nation where life expectancy is only forty-six years. It's close to last on the United Nations' list of terrible places to live.

"They've spent half a million dollars in this country without getting a penny out," said Savage, who had been to Africa a dozen times since his political retirement.

In the summer of 2002, he went to The Gambia, the continent's smallest country, in sub-Saharan West Africa, to try to stop the onslaught of HIV/AIDS, which is killing two million Africans every year. Savage had returned to his oldest roots, teaching sixteen- and seventeen-year-olds how to have safe sex, then having them teach eleven-year-olds the same. It's called peer health education. The hope is that teenagers will have greater success influencing preteens about safe sex than adults will.

"I always wanted to go back to parts of the world less fortunate than ours," Savage said. "You go to Africa and you realize how blessed we are here. They have no health care system or doctors. We owe it to do something for these poor countries."

Savage also took a few trips to Chuvash, a state of 1.3 million Russians, six hundred kilometres east of Moscow on the Volga

River. He was helping with a Canadian International Development Agency (CIDA) project in a place where health care standards are equivalent to the rural Canada of fifty years ago. He would fly to Moscow, then take a fourteen-hour train ride to Chuvash.

"Why don't we fly there?" Savage asked a Russian official on his first trip.

"No one flies inside Russia," came the dour reply. Apparently, a recently privatized Aeroflot doesn't inspire great confidence in the average Russian. Savage was part of a team working to improve the health care system in the small state.

You might say John Savage was the Jimmy Carter of Canadian politics. His post-political career seemed to be much more emotionally fulfilling than his time in office ever was. (Of Carter, Savage said, "I've seen him and I think he's a wonderful guy.") In 2002, the provincial government created a new award, the Order of Nova Scotia, for particularly meritorious service and achievement. Savage was one of ten Canadians to receive the award, further confirming that there is life after politics.

Sadly for John Savage, he and his wife Margaret found themselves in the midst of a battle much tougher than anything political life could throw at them. In July 2001, he was diagnosed with inoperable stomach cancer. He opted for seven months of weekly chemotherapy treatment. Then, on December 31, 2002, Margaret Savage rang in the new year by having her colon removed, in her efforts to fight bowel cancer. The diagnosis of her illness came just one week before Christmas. She died three months later, at home, surrounded by her large family.

Savage's cancer was such that he was given a 4-percent chance of surviving more than twelve months. Fourteen months after that diagnosis, he and I spoke again. He sounded strong, active, and still excited about the future. Shortly thereafter, he learned his cancer was back and had spread to his liver.

"I'm seventy years old," he said. "I'm under no illusions. It's not a nice thing to have. We've just gotta see what the good Lord deals us."

On May 13, 2003 the good Lord dealt Savage his final hand. He succumbed to cancer at age seventy, just a couple of months after the death of his wife, and just three days after Governor General Adrienne Clarkson made him an officer of the Order of Canada.

ONE OF THE THINGS most of us forget when we watch a politician go down for the count is that, away from the headlines, away from the dramatic descent, someone may be suffering intense emotional trauma.

In early 1987, the Ontario government under David Peterson enjoyed only minority government status. But Peterson's Liberals were experiencing the kind of honeymoon that was about to translate into a massive victory at the polls later that year. The party began courting star candidates and found one in Chaviva Hosek, a brilliant Ph.D. from Harvard University and head of the National Action Committee on the Status of Women. Hosek was purely and simply a dream candidate: intelligent, urbane, literate, and ethnic (Czech-born and Jewish). The Liberals parachuted her into a very multicultural midtown Toronto riding, and on election night she was victorious. Premier Peterson immediately put her into his cabinet as minister of housing, a portfolio with enormous responsibilities, given the government's commitment to doing big things on the social housing file.

But in their haste to exploit Hosek's star power, the party brass forgot one crucial detail—she had never been a politician before. She was prominent, commanding more headlines than colleagues with decades more experience, and she was exceedingly well educated, but oh so raw.

Hosek began to make mistakes. Not necessarily on the housing file, where her sharp mind served her well. But at the politics of the job. She began to alienate colleagues, some of whom were no doubt jealous of her meteoric rise. Her lack of any experience in the legislature made her easy pickings during question period. Then she picked a high-profile fight and lost.

She had been feuding with former Toronto mayor John Sewell, who was then chair of the board of the Metro Toronto Housing Authority. She told her friend, Attorney General Ian Scott, that she was going to resolve the feud by firing Sewell.

"You can't do that," Scott told her. "John Sewell's an icon in this city. You won't win."

Hosek did it anyway, and she was practically run over by the outpouring of support for Sewell. Her political judgment, rather than her housing record, became the issue. And so Peterson dumped Hosek from cabinet. Her career as an elected politician, which just twelve months earlier had seemed limitless, had hit the skids.

Her one-time cabinet colleague Greg Sorbara called her the night she was dumped.

"I phoned her just to say how sorry I was and how upset I was," Sorbara recalls. "And the tears on the other end of the phone broke my heart. It was very powerful."

Despite it all, Hosek ran for re-election in 1990, but lost.

"You can't forget about the humanity of the business," Sorbara admonishes us all.

# THE PRICE
# OF BIG IDEAS

Big ideas are so hard to recognize, so fragile, so easy to kill.
Don't forget that, all of you who don't have them.
*—John Elliot Jr., chair of the advertising agency Ogilvy & Mather*

To swear off making mistakes is very easy.
All you have to do is swear off having ideas.
*—Leo Burnett, advertising guru*

DAVID PETERSON TOLD US in an earlier chapter that, truth be told, he just couldn't get too excited about auto insurance rates when historic and urgent discussions about the constitution were dominating his agenda. It's a candid observation, and in Peterson's case, it proved to be a fatal character trait. The electorate punished him just a few months after he had returned to Queen's Park as the conquering hero, having made a unique sacrifice to help garner constitutional peace.

Peterson's story is far more typical than you might think. It's a good Canadian example of something we've seen all over the world. George Bush the elder demonstrates unprecedented boldness, evicts Saddam Hussein from Kuwait, and watches his approval ratings soar into the stratosphere. A year later, he's out on his ear because the American public finds him lacking in sensitivity to their new and distressing economic circumstances. Winston Churchill is an even better example. All he did was lead a beleaguered nation to victory against the most evil regime in the history of the world. The British people thanked and praised him for winning the Second World War, then sent him and his fellow Conservatives on to the Opposition benches in the first post-war election in 1945.

In Canada, we have our own leaders who paid the ultimate political price for chasing bigger ideas than their electors were comfortable with. Later in this chapter, we'll meet two such leaders from Saskatchewan who experienced the thrill of election-night victory, the excitement of influencing history on the run, and then were shown the door for their troubles.

THERE ARE TWO major Canadian political figures of the second half of the twentieth century—one from the East and one from the West—who, in death, have become even more mythical than they were in life.

One is Pierre Elliott Trudeau. That Trudeau occupies such a place in our lives shouldn't be a surprise. He remained, well into his seventies, an important political voice that others ignored at their peril. He was the third-longest-serving prime minister in Canadian history, behind William Lyon Mackenzie King and Sir John A. Macdonald. The outpouring of emotion after his death in Montreal in September 2000 spoke volumes about how Canadians regarded Trudeau.

The other figure whose stature continues to grow posthumously is Tommy Douglas. Canadians have repeatedly told pollsters for years that securing the quality of the country's health care system is their top priority. And Tommy Douglas, as the father of medicare, has had his name invoked countless times as the debate on how to improve the system rages on. Unlike Trudeau, Douglas has not been a recent presence in our lives. He died nearly two decades ago, in

1986. But the legacy that this Baptist preacher created, as premier of Saskatchewan from 1944 to 1961 and the first leader of the New Democratic Party of Canada, endures.

Imagine being fortunate enough to have served at the same cabinet table as Thomas Clement Douglas. Imagine having crossed swords at the constitutional negotiating table with Pierre Elliott Trudeau.

Allan Blakeney has done both.

Allan Emrys Blakeney was born in 1925 to a Conservative family in Bridgewater, Nova Scotia, which will sound surprising to some, since the usual assumption is that he emerged a proud socialist from the wheat fields of Saskatchewan. Not so.

His father, John C. Blakeney, was wounded in the First World War and treated by a nurse in Wales. That soldier and that nurse later married, and gave their first son the middle name Emrys, a Welsh name, after the nurse's brother.

Allan Blakeney recalls his father being utterly disillusioned with R.B. Bennett, and despite being a loyal Conservative, voting against the Tory prime minister in the 1935 election. (He couldn't go so far as to vote for the Liberals, but voted for the short-lived Reconstruction Party of H.H. Stevens.) Five years later all was forgiven, and Allan, fifteen years old, had the pleasure of meeting the new Conservative leader, John Bracken, in Bridgewater. "I can still remember him talking about rural free delivery of mail," Blakeney smiles.

Like his father, Blakeney supported the Conservatives at first, but he started to have doubts. However, his classmates had no doubts about him. In his high school yearbook, they prophesied: "Allan Blakeney will be a lawyer and a politician." They were right on both counts. Blakeney went to Dalhousie University, where his formal conversion to socialism took place. He got interested in the policies of the Co-operative Commonwealth Federation, the forerunner of the NDP, and helped establish a CCF club on campus. Halifax businessman Lloyd Shaw was also influential. He would visit the campus on behalf of the CCF, although he will perhaps be better remembered for being the father of a future NDP leader, Alexa MacDonough.

In the late 1940s, just before Peter Lougheed started playing football for the Edmonton Eskimos, Blakeney was on his way to Oxford University on a Rhodes Scholarship, and played right wing, oddly enough, for the Oxford University hockey team.

"There were two types of players," Blakeney explains. "Good ones, and ones with equipment."

"Which one were you?" I ask.

"What do you think?" he laughs. "They wrote me a letter. They said, 'You're a Canadian. You're expected to play and bring all your own equipment. We have none.'"

Even before Blakeney left for Britain, he knew he would seek elected office some day. He assumed he would launch his political career in Nova Scotia, though "CCF-ers weren't thick on the ground there."

Blakeney returned from Oxford in 1949, then took a trip that would change his life and the course of Canadian history. After spending three months in Edmonton articling at a law firm, he went to Regina, because he had heard about a man named Tommy Douglas running North America's only social democratic government. He intended to stay long enough to study how the CCF governed, then move on. But he ended up getting a series of jobs in the public service that interested him. He was corporate secretary and lawyer for a string of Crown corporations—telephone companies, timber companies, the Industrial Development Fund—that made loans to private businesses, and so on. "I grew up in a small business family, so this made sense to me," he says. His short sojourn to Saskatchewan had now lasted five years, and put him in direct contact with Premier Douglas and his cabinet ministers. Following this, he served as chairman of the Saskatchewan Securities Commission for three years.

And then, just as Blakeney was considering running for the legislative assembly, disaster struck. His wife of seven years, Molly, died in her sleep of a heart attack. There was no warning at all. Blakeney frantically called his family doctor: "She's not moving at all. Please come." But it was already too late. Molly was thirty years old. Blakeney was now a widower with two children, Barbara and Hugh, aged four and two.

Who knows how people get through tragedies such as those. Somehow Blakeney carried on. More than forty years later, in describing that time, Blakeney looks solemnly at the floor and simply says, "That's tough stuff."

A year later, in 1958, Blakeney decided that if he were ever going to take a run at politics, he shouldn't be working in the civil service. Moreover, friends in the public service were bugging him to get into the arena.

So he left the government, joined a law firm in the capital city, and ran for the CCF in the riding of Regina. In those days, the Regina constituency sent four members to the legislature. In the election of 1960, Blakeney came second. His yearbook prophecy was now fact.

Blakeney's personal life also took a major turn for the better. The year before the election, he married a lecturer from the University of Victoria. Policy nerd that he was, he courted the future Mrs. Anne Blakeney by sending her position papers on housing that he had written ("My capacity as a Romeo!" he jokes). The two discovered they had very similar backgrounds: her father was a food broker; his father was in the wholesale fruit business. And both their mothers were nurses. The couple would go on to have two children: David and Margaret.

The 1960 campaign may have been the most important election any province has ever held. Premier Douglas fought it on one issue: province-wide, publicly funded medicare. Douglas had suffered from osteomyelitis (an inflammation of the bone or bone marrow) as a young man and required many operations on his leg. His family couldn't afford to pay for the procedures, but they were lucky. Charitable doctors performed the operations for free. Nevertheless, Douglas is said to have vowed that if ever he got into a position to do something about health care, he would make it as accessible and affordable as public education.

Douglas got his chance in 1960, when his CCF won thirty-eight of the fifty-four seats in the Saskatchewan Legislature. The premier interpreted that as a mandate to bring in medicare. The Medical Care Insurance Act was drafted and introduced into the legislature in the fall of 1961, after which Douglas left provincial politics. He was off to lead a new federal movement, the New Democratic Party. It would be left to his successor as premier, Woodrow Lloyd, to make medicare the law of the province.

Saskatchewan's doctors went berserk, their outrage culminating in a province-wide strike. As the drama was unfolding, there was a second-year law student at the University of Saskatchewan at Saskatoon who was mesmerized by it all. He understood there was something tremendously significant, perhaps unprecedented, about what was happening in the provincial capital. So he and a friend hopped into a Volkswagen and drove to Regina to watch history unfold. When he arrived, he saw as many as five thousand protestors at the legislature, almost hysterical at the possibility that medicare might soon become the law of their province. The demonstrators carried effigies of Woodrow Lloyd and Tommy Douglas that said DOWN WITH DICTATORS. They carried signs reading kod—Keep Our Doctors—since many were leaving Saskatchewan at this time. Allan Blakeney was conducting twice-daily briefings for an unheard-of number of journalists—perhaps as many as one hundred—who had descended on Regina from all over the world to cover the story.

The law student, who supported the CCF's plans, offered to do anything to help Blakeney achieve the government's goals. He wanted a front-row seat at history in the making. So he started by carrying Blakeney's bags. It wasn't glamorous, but he didn't care. He wanted to be where the action was.

His name was Roy John Romanow.

MICHAEL ROMANIV LEFT his native Ukraine for Canada during the worst of the dirty thirties. Two things brought him to Saskatchewan. First, it was Canadian government policy to urge new immigrants to settle in areas that reminded them of home. Romaniv had been a farmer in the old country, and Saskatchewan was supposed to be offering some of the best farmland in the New World. That proved to be a cruel joke in the thirties, so Romaniv became a labourer with Canadian National Railways. The second factor was that two of Michael's uncles were already in Saskatoon, so the province became the logical place to start his new life.

He started that new life with a new name. As was so often the case, an immigration official was unable to spell Romaniv (pronounced *Roma-nyuve*) on Michael's documents, so the name simply became Romanow. A few years after Michael became settled, he sent for his wife, Tekla, and his daughter, Ann. In 1939, Tekla would give birth to a son, Roy.

Ukrainian was Roy Romanow's first language. His parents insisted he speak it at home. Michael knew only about 150 words of English his entire life. Roy attended a Ukrainian school; three times a week he had to take violin lessons to maintain his Ukrainian culture; he attended Greek Catholic church.

"You could go to church, shop, and visit friends and neighbours without speaking one word of either of Canada's official languages," Romanow remembers of his childhood.

Eventually, he would learn English, first on the street from friends, and then in elementary school.

One of the things the two men in the Romanow household loved to do was listen to the radio. And among their favourite things to listen to were the proceedings of the Saskatchewan Legislature, featuring the spellbinding orations of Tommy Douglas. For young Roy, a seed was planted. To be sure, he didn't understand the issues. But he loved the cut and thrust of the debate, and the excitement, the cheering, the heckling.

"It was entertaining as hell," he recalls. By the time he got to university, he was immersed in left wing politics, running for student council, and contemplating a career in politics.

"I always had the political itch," Romanow says. "But I wasn't sure I'd seek elected office." Regardless, he figured having a law degree was a good backup plan, in case disaster struck, which in politics it almost always does. However, in the meantime, there was a doctors' strike to be won.

"These guys went through hell," Romanow says of the CCF government. "I remember going to Woodrow Lloyd's house and you'd have to get through two squad cars at the end of the street because of the death threats on Woodrow."

In the end, it became a war of attrition. By July 1962, the government had broken the back of the doctors' strike, which had lasted three weeks. The CCF introduced medical care insurance to the province, and signed a formal entente with the College of Physicians and Surgeons of Saskatchewan. Allan Blakeney participated in the negotiations leading to that agreement, and was then shuffled to the health portfolio to make it all work.

Blakeney would go on to spend more than a quarter of a century in politics, but he always considered that victory his finest hour in public life.

He wouldn't have long to enjoy it. In 1964, the Lloyd government fell to Ross Thatcher's Liberals. Blakeney would spend the next seven years on the Opposition benches. Roy Romanow would have to get more serious about law as a career. He was fortunate to begin that career with one of the province's largest law firms, Goldenberg Taylor Tallis. George Taylor was *the* labour lawyer in Saskatchewan. He supported the workers in their quest for jobs at the Regina Riot in 1935, and fought against Generalissimo Francisco Franco in the Spanish Civil War. Calvin F. Tallis would go on to an appointment on the Saskatchewan Court of Appeal in 1981 and then, in 1999, become a deputy judge of the Nunavut Court of Justice.

Romanow found the law interesting enough, but one day, his itch for politics got a good scratching from Bob Walker, a one-time attorney general for Tommy Douglas.

"Roy," Romanow recalls Walker saying, "what you should do is enter provincial politics, serve there, get some experience, then enter federal politics. I think you'd do well in federal politics."

Romanow was approached by some party officials from the CCF–NDP (the party wouldn't lose the CCF moniker until the next campaign) to seek a nomination on the west side of Saskatoon. It was working-class. It was multicultural. It was available. And best of all, Romanow already lived there. In October 1966, about 160 people gathered at King George School auditorium to nominate Romanow as the next candidate for the riding of Saskatoon Riversdale. He was unopposed at the nomination.

THE 1967 GENERAL ELECTION turned out to be worse for the NDP. Ross Thatcher's Liberals picked up three more seats and the NDP lost two. But Allan Blakeney held his. And Roy Romanow became one of eight new Young Turks to find a seat in the legislature.

Having lost two elections in a row, Woodrow Lloyd resigned as NDP leader.

The story line for the ensuing leadership convention came right out of a Hollywood script. Allan Blakeney was the obvious choice to replace Lloyd as leader. He had done so much of the heavy lifting during the medicare crisis. His knowledge of the inner workings of government, from the time he had spent both in the civil service and around the cabinet table, was unparalleled. He was the clear choice of the party establishment. You can imagine his surprise when Roy Romanow telephoned with some unusual news.

Romanow and his fellow young rookie MLAs thought they should have a meaningful role to play in the contest. So they agreed Romanow should challenge Blakeney for the leadership. Ten years earlier, Romanow had been carrying Blakeney's bags to meetings. Now he had the chutzpah to tell this almost-legendary figure in the party and the province that at age thirty-one, he was a superior choice to challenge Ross Thatcher in the next election.

"I think he was hurt a little bit," Romanow says of his mentor. "I think he was angered because of the relatively limited experience I had."

Blakeney quickly put his reservations about Romanow's bid behind him and focused on the job at hand, which was to stage a clean leadership contest, then emerge united to battle the Liberals in the next election. The two main contenders met and agreed not to speak ill of each other, which they pretty much kept to.

The convention itself, on July 6, 1970, was a nail-biter. The upstart Romanow led all four contenders on the first ballot by just fifty-six votes out of two thousand cast. The first candidate to drop from the ballot was Romanow's former boss at the law firm,

George Taylor. On the second ballot, Romanow led again, this time by just thirty-three votes. That knocked off Don Mitchell (whose brother Ken is a well-known poet in Saskatchewan; Don would go on to become mayor of Moose Jaw). On the third and final ballot, the master and the student went mano-a-mano. Blakeney took the contest by fifty-four votes, promptly made Romanow his deputy leader, and quickly healed any wounds that had been created in the first place.

The year 1971 offered three provincial elections in Canada, featuring three new leaders who would make significant contributions to their provinces and country. William Davis was elected premier of Ontario. Peter Lougheed in Alberta. And on June 30, 1971, Allan Blakeney became the first NDP premier of Saskatchewan, having one week earlier defeated Ross Thatcher with forty-five out of sixty seats. Roy Romanow became deputy premier and attorney general. The mentor and the student would complement each other's skills to a T. Blakeney was the quintessential technocrat, with an incredible command of policy detail. Romanow was the great communicator. To show how serious Blakeney was about the province's finances, he kept the treasurer's job for himself during the first year of his new government." As Blakeney describes it, "Every government needs a bean counter and a mouthpiece. I was the bean counter. He was the mouthpiece."

The NDP under Allan Blakeney would go on to win two more majority governments, in 1975 and 1978. From 1971 to 1982, the government would introduce eleven budgets. All eleven would be in balance.

"That was our style. It played well with the public," Blakeney says. "There were still many scars from the Depression. People had great fears about debt."

Allan Blakeney had emerged from the shadow of Tommy Douglas as the undisputed political leader of his province. But his battles with Canada's other mythical figure, Pierre Trudeau, were still to come.

Blakeney had spent seven years on the Opposition benches, waiting for his chance to get back into power. Now that he had achieved his goal, he had a lengthy shopping list of policy initiatives he wanted to pursue. Not surprisingly, medicare was still at the top of his list. He set about to eliminate medicare insurance premiums for senior citizens. He also killed "utilization fees"—in effect, a special charge every time an adult or child visited a hospital or doctor. Blakeney considered those fees a tax against the sick and the poor. He went further, reducing the costs of essential drugs, eyeglasses, dentures, hearing aids, braces, and wheelchairs. And, of course, to do it all he came up against the entrenched medical establishment, which tried to re-fight the medicare battles of the 1960s.

Blakeney's government pursued an environmental agenda of sustainable development more than a decade before that buzz phrase became common. He talked about job creation in harmony with the environment.

His inside knowledge of how government worked led to a unique policy development—the Crown Investments Corporation of Saskatchewan, or CIC. Blakeney wanted an agency that would invest the income from other Crown corporations. He saw a day, many years down the road, when Saskatchewan's non-renewable resources—namely mining, oil, and gas—might not provide the tax revenues the province had come to depend on. And so, in 1978, new legislation transformed an old provincial body, the Government Finance Office, giving it control over all Crown corporations under its new name, the CIC. It may have been the most innovative and important change to emerge from his years in power.

Allan Blakeney loved governing. He loved devising policies, administering them, and developing the communications package around them.

*How are we going to tell the folks about this? Are they going to buy it? Will it "play in Peoria"?* These, he recalls, were the questions he asked himself before rolling out a new idea. "No policy is a good policy," he says, "if the public don't like it or can't be persuaded to like it. This is essentially where the buzz from politics comes from. There's practically no other job which allows you to work at the limit of your capacity over a greater part of your day than being a first minister."

One of the most difficult tasks any premier has is deciding who gets into cabinet. If you were going to get into Allan Blakeney's cabinet, you had to listen to a lecture from the premier, not only on how to run your department, but also on how to conduct your personal life. In the days before Gary Hart and Bill Clinton, Blakeney thought he needed to read the troops the riot act as it related to extramarital affairs.

"Fellas," Blakeney told his assembled ministers ("and we were all men at the time"), "we've got some rules around here. You can't be playing around with anyone within government. If you want to play around, go outside the province. Don't do it in the province. It's too rural, too traditional. I'm not telling you how to run your lives, but there should be no dalliance with anybody in the government and particularly anyone in your department. It erodes morale."

Naturally, not everyone followed the first minister's advice. In fact, one of Blakeney's ministers was having an affair with a fairly prominent person in the NDP government, but the premier knew nothing about it. However, the minister's wife found out about it and told him he was either out of the government or out of the marriage.

"He came to me one day and said, 'I'm resigning for personal reasons.'" Blakeney recalls. "I wondered, what the hell are these personal reasons?" The premier asked his chief secretary—"they always know what's up"—and the secret was revealed.

"No one knew about it, and if the media did, it happened in the days when you didn't report it," Blakeney says.

Actually, there were a couple of other cases where Blakeney shuffled cabinet ministers to get them farther away from potential sexual troubles. "I was trying to keep that sort of thing from becoming public property and corrosive of morale," he says. "I don't know if that's true any more, whether anyone cares if someone's having an affair with someone in the next department. But certainly in Saskatchewan in the 1970s, I felt it was quite inappropriate and conveyed quite the wrong impression of what I wanted the government to be.

"By the way," Blakeney smiles, "I don't think I caught all the cases."

Maybe not, but in an era before conflict of interest commissioners, before privacy commissioners, before ministers' expense accounts could be obtained through freedom of information requests, Blakeney ran a relatively clean government and everyone knew it. Sure, there was the odd guy having an affair or drinking too much, but Blakeney had (for the times) an unusually low threshold for shenanigans, particularly as they might relate to taxpayers' dollars. Again, without any formal statutes or codes of conduct in place, Blakeney let it be known that ministers who abused their communications allowances, practised nepotism, or gave contracts that couldn't pass muster would find themselves deep inside the premier's doghouse. In fact, it was Blakeney's deputy premier and attorney general who began to formalize a stricter code of conduct for politicians. Roy Romanow introduced the requirement that all cabinet ministers file conflict of interest forms, the first of several measures nationwide, in a sea of changes relating to politicians' personal conduct.

Romanow also immersed himself in modernizing his province's justice system. He introduced legal aid to Saskatchewan, created a provincial human rights commission, a human rights code, and an ombudsman's office to address citizen complaints. But Romanow's toughest file was filled with potash. Saskatchewan had the largest naturally occurring potash deposits in the world (potash is used in agriculture for fertilizer). But the NDP government wasn't realizing the tax revenues to which it thought the public was entitled. In 1975, Blakeney resolved to ameliorate the province's position by introducing a bill that would allow the government to nationalize up to half the industry, should it choose to. Predictably, the industry responded apoplectically. But with that bill in its back pocket, the province was able to negotiate from a position of strength with American-owned companies. The result was the creation of the Potash Corporation of Saskatchewan, a new Crown corporation that became a major player on the scene, buying some companies and partnering with others to develop Saskatchewan's most precious natural resource. It was part of Romanow's job to bring the issue to a conclusion, which he did with a seventy-two-step process that took more than a year.

"That was a momentous occasion," Romanow remembers. "It was politics at its best. We debated principles and ideologies over months and months."

There were other firsts as well. Never before in a Canadian legislature had an Aboriginal organization convened a meeting or conference, until Allan Blakeney became premier of Saskatchewan. The All Chiefs Policy Convention was held in January 1978 in Regina. Blakeney offered the legislature as a meeting place a few months before, to show his willingness to be open to Aboriginal issues.

Roy Romanow experienced a first as well. In 1979, he became the province's first minister of intergovernmental affairs, a post that would become crucial during constitutional negotiations with Pierre Trudeau two years later.

Former Saskatchewan premier Ross Thatcher once said that if he asked the average Saskatchewan citizen for a list of his or her 100 most pressing problems, the constitution would rank 101st. That may have been true in Thatcher's time, but Pierre Trudeau saw to it that the constitution moved to the top of the agenda in the fall of 1981, and both Allan Blakeney and Roy Romanow had front-row seats to it all. Ironically, they may have gotten too close to the Sun King for their own electoral good.

Two decades later, neither man has many regrets about the agreement the federal government and nine provinces reached. Romanow stayed up into the early hours on the night the so-called kitchen cabinet negotiated the pact: he didn't get to bed till four in the morning. He remembers sleeping poorly when he finally got to bed, not because of fears over Quebec's exclusion, but rather out of the thrill at what had been achieved.

"We were so excited that we were able to patriate and eliminate that last vestige of colonialism," he says. "All the kitchen stuff with [Jean] Chrétien and [Roy] McMurtry was just highly, highly exciting. Patriation and the Charter will be judged by historians as the final step in the achievement of full Canadian sovereignty and confirmation of our national maturity."

Particularly satisfying to Romanow was a new clause in the Canadian Constitution, Section 92 (a), which gave all provinces much greater control of their natural resources. "This was quite a victory," he says. "It was quite an enhancement of provincial power in light of the battles over the years."

"It was a kind of high," Blakeney adds. "There was a sense of satisfaction that it wasn't a total failure. With hindsight of two decades, we were still right to do what we did."

The only major rewriting of history Blakeney allows himself is to wonder how things might have been different had Trudeau simply patriated the constitution against the wishes of all of the provinces save Ontario and New Brunswick, which were on side from the start. "[René] Lévesque wouldn't have been isolated," he muses. "All the provinces would have been shouting. That might have been the better way to handle it." But that option was taken off the table once the Supreme Court of Canada ruled that a substantial degree of provincial consent was needed to conform to the constitutional conventions of Canada. The fear was, unless those conventions were followed, the British Parliament might delay or perhaps even reject the changes.

But, as is so often the case in politics, the highest highs are followed by the lowest lows, and the Blakeney–Romanow tandem would be no exception. The pair returned home from the nation's capital to deliver joint speeches on their historic achievement. Both went to familiar locations: the premier, appropriately enough, spoke in Regina, the provincial capital and his home constituency; Romanow, befitting his second-in-command status, spoke in Saskatoon, the second-largest city, and coincidentally his home turf. Five hundred people heard Romanow's talk—a great crowd—and yet he sensed something troublesome in the air.

"There were no boos," he recalls, "but there was only tepid applause. Very perfunctory. I couldn't figure it out."

It wouldn't take long for Romanow to get the message. While he and Blakeney were revelling in their constitutional accomplishments, the voters were stewing over 22-percent interest rates, high power rates, high insurance rates, and a worsening farm crisis.

"We got no bounce at all from the constitution," Romanow says. "In fact, quite the opposite. The condemnation was high. People thought we were missing their concerns."

If Romanow needed proof of that, he got it big time at a grocery store in Stoughton, in the southeastern part of the province. He was introducing Elaine Driver, the local NDP candidate, around the riding, when things came to a sudden halt.

"What are you doing here?" the store clerk said with a definite edge to her voice.

"We're campaigning," Romanow explained. "This is a democracy."

"Not in my store," the clerk shot back. "Get out."

Then came a rally, where one of Romanow's assistants was targeted.

"What's your name?" the assistant was asked.

"Why do you want to know?" came the guarded response.

"Because, buddy, in ten days, you're gone!"

By now, Romanow could tell "we were just right out of the game."

Less than two weeks after that glorious moment on Parliament Hill when the Queen and Pierre Trudeau signed the new Canadian Constitution, Saskatchewan's NDP government suffered a stunning rebuke at the polls. The Progressive Conservatives, under thirty-seven year old Grant Devine, staged the greatest upset in the province's history. They out-seated the NDP fifty-five to nine on April 26, 1982. It was the twentieth election since Saskatchewan had become a province in 1905, but only the third time the PCs had even hit double digits on the seat count. Between 1934 and 1975, the party captured precisely one seat. Yet here it was humiliating the vaunted Blakeney machine, and so soon after the NDP's dynamic duo had played an important role in the national constitutional drama.

"I could see it coming," Romanow says. "The election was called on a Saturday, and by Tuesday, I knew we were dead ducks. People wouldn't look you in the eye. I thought, 'Holy cripes, what's going on out there?'"

Both men prided themselves on presenting a dynamic combination to the electorate. They felt they were in touch with the average voter and his or her concerns and values, and at the same time possessed a broader vision that enabled them to play a national role.

In the end, both men paid a price for having big ideas.

"Reporters said the government was out of touch," Blakeney recalls. "Well, great. Thank you for that penetrating observation and glimpse into the obvious," he says sarcastically.

The premier tried to analyze the reasons behind the defeat but was never completely satisfied with any explanation he heard. He knew his constituents well enough to realize that they would be mightily offended by any sex scandals in his government. But evidently he didn't realize that his quest to participate in a historic nation-building exercise was alienating him from those same constituents. Eventually, he settled on the notion that in the midst of the worst recession since the Depression, the people of Saskatchewan thought the government had a lot more money than it did, and they wanted it spent on them.

"I was bitterly disappointed the night we not only lost the government, but were annihilated," Blakeney says. "In politics you win many victories you don't deserve and suffer defeats you don't deserve. That's the way it is. Public will is not totally rational."

Somehow, in the face of a Tory onslaught, Blakeney held his own seat by slightly more than a thousand votes and would stay on as Opposition leader. Roy Romanow was not so lucky. He went to his campaign headquarters on election night with two speeches in hand: one in the event that he retained his seat, and another in case his defeat was complete. Losing the government was a foregone conclusion.

Before long Romanow would discover that the rout was on and the second speech was the one he would be giving. He lost his cherished constituency of Riversdale by eleven votes to twenty-eight-year-old PC candidate Jo-Ann Zazelenchuk. To add insult to injury, when Romanow went to Zazelenchuk's headquarters to concede, he saw six loyal NDP supporters (presumably now *former* supporters) whooping it up and enjoying the hospitality of the winning side.

"The sense of rejection that one gets . . ." Romanow says. "This is Riversdale, where I grew up! It really troubled me for a few weeks."

In the ensuing days Romanow packed up his office, filling box after box with memorabilia. A once-promising political career appeared to be coming to a premature end—at least, it was premature in his view. The now former cabinet minister hopped into his Volkswagen, waved goodbye to the Saskatchewan Legislature, and never looked back. He was convinced that would be the last time he'd ever see his province's seat of government again.

Voters can be cruel to losers and both Blakeney and Romanow would taste that sting of defeat in the days and months ahead. Before the election, Blakeney had committed to attending a formal dinner in Regina where many of Saskatchewan's business leaders would be in attendance. He debated whether to attend the event, knowing he would be on the receiving end of some pointed comments. Ultimately he decided to put on his tuxedo and tails. "I said, to hell with it. I'll stare them down." It was Blakeney's way of saying, I'm not through yet.

It was worse for Romanow. He stopped socializing with friends and acquaintances, tried not to appear in public—so convinced was he that people were shooting angry stares at him.

"Guys would actually come up to me at the tennis club and say, 'Glad we got rid of you,'" he says. Romanow retreated to a solitary job at the University of Saskatoon, where he could read and write privately, collect his thoughts, and engage students who may have been more forgiving than his tennis comrades. It turned out to be a great escape.

Allan Blakeney thought about quitting politics after that 1982 election debacle. The only trouble was, the man he wanted to succeed him as leader of the NDP had lost his seat. So Blakeney rolled up his sleeves, moved his boxes from the premier's office to the Opposition leader's office and started planning his comeback.

Blakeney truly thought he could rebuild the coalition that had brought his NDP to power in 1971. He thought the Tories were a terrible government, led by a decent man in Devine, but utterly incompetent in administering the public's business. One of the first things the PCs did was cut taxes, financing that move by borrowing the money and running a deficit. The Tories would never balance a budget during their time in office, incurring staggering debts in the process.

As the next election approached, Blakeney went to see Romanow.

"Roy, you've gotta get back in," he told him. "This is my last election and I want you to be ready to stand as my successor."

Romanow wasn't sure he wanted back in. He was enjoying his life, free from the tough scrutiny of the public eye, and doubted he could ever surpass what he had already experienced in public life. But between Blakeney's prodding and Romanow's own sense that maybe there was still an unwritten chapter to his political career, he decided to go for it.

When Devine went back to the polls on October 20, 1986, the NDP actually captured more votes than the Tories. But because of the way the votes split, the Tories won re-election, thirty-eight seats to twenty-five.

Blakeney was extremely disappointed. He felt he had been responsible for putting the party onto the Opposition benches, and wanted more than anything to get his MLAs back on the govern-ment side. He took some solace in the fact that the caucus had almost tripled in size and that Romanow was back in the fold.

He also knew, given two successive defeats, that his days were numbered. He privately told senior party officials that he would lead the NDP through the first session of the new legislature, but that was it. In the summer of 1987, Allan Blakeney announced he was finished as NDP leader. He urged the party to find a successor at its convention in November. When he retired in the spring of 1988, he had been in politics for twenty-eight years. But there would be no more tomorrows.

Saskatchewan's New Democrats had no difficulty deciding who they wanted to replace Allan Blakeney. Roy Romanow would be acclaimed the new leader at the party's November 1987 convention. One of the first things he realized was how rusty he was in the arena.

"I found it difficult to get back in," Romanow admits. "I'd become comfortable with a life of privacy and inner reflection."

One of the main changes Romanow had to adjust to was television. When he had left politics in 1982, there was no televised coverage of the Saskatchewan Legislature. CNN was just a baby, and CBC Newsworld was still years away. When he returned, the cameras were in the legislature and the twenty-four-hour news cycle was increasingly becoming a reality.

"I felt I was a boxer out of the ring for four years," Romanow says. "When I stepped in against [Grant] Devine, I felt I was whipped all the time."

Romanow decided to hit the hustings fast and hard. In the time between his winning the leadership and the ensuing election, he averaged two hundred kilometres a day of travel, spreading a new gospel for the NDP.

"I was travelling non-stop," Romanow says. "I'm talking four years, labouring in the vineyard."

It was worth it. On October 21, 1991, Roy Romanow brought the NDP all the way back, crushing the Tories by a seat count of fifty-five to ten (Liberal leader Lynda Haverstock also won her seat).

However, when he looked at the province's books, Premier Romanow may have wondered whether it had been worth winning at all. Saskatchewan was in the midst of a huge financial crisis. The Tories' fiscal mismanagement was so profoundly awful that the province had the worst deficit per capita and the worst debt per capita in the country. Only a handful of lending institutions would consider floating more money to the province to help tackle the debt, which was at $15 billion and counting. Romanow and a group of other senior government ministers decided to make a five-year plan to achieve a balanced budget. They considered it a matter of such urgency that they resolved to do whatever it took to solve the fiscal mess.

"If we lost the next election, so be it," Romanow says they agreed at the time. "It had to be done."

Saskatchewan's finance minister, Janice MacKinnon, went to Ottawa for a secret meeting with her federal counterpart, Don Mazankowski. Her message was simple. Saskatchewan had hit the debt wall, and needed some emergency help. Besides, it wouldn't look too good on the Mulroney government in international circles if one of Canada's provinces declared bankruptcy.

While MacKinnon was making the case in Ottawa, Romanow was having trouble with his caucus back home. He tried to impress upon them the need to make some extraordinarily tough decisions on cutting spending, but MLAs just wouldn't budge. Many of them had been part of previous governments that had created those programs, and they weren't about to make big cuts just to make some international financiers happy.

Romanow was concerned the government might not be able to present a budget. So he threatened his own MLAs.

"It was gridlock," he recalls. "So I said to caucus, 'Look, I want you guys to have a cup of coffee, I'm going to the lieutenant-governor's.' I thought I'd scare them into an early election we might lose, because we were unpopular at that time."

Romanow arrived at the office of Sylvia Fedoruk, Saskatchewan's first female lieutenant-governor. He warned the Queen's representative that he might have to ask her to call an election only one year into one of the most lopsided election wins in Saskatchewan history, because of the intransigence of his own caucus.

"She tried to talk me out of it," Romanow recalls. "I wasn't trying to use her, but I wanted caucus to stew over the consequences of that. If there was no capacity to solve the problem, then the people of Saskatchewan deserved a government that could solve the problems."

Apparently caucus got the message. MLAs came together and, with considerable emergency assistance from the federal government, Saskatchewan was able to avert bankruptcy. But the situation was such that by the time Romanow went to bed each night, his head hurt from the tension.

And then there was Charlottetown. Once again, Canadians found themselves embroiled in attempts to achieve constitutional peace between Quebec and the rest of the country. Just as he had a decade earlier, Romanow had a front-row seat on the constitutional file. The Mulroney government was promoting its Charlottetown Accord as the next logical step after the failed Meech Lake Accord. Authorities held referendums in every province. It would take majority "yes" votes in every province for the accord to pass. Proponents never got close. Even the persuasive Romanow couldn't convince his own electors to support the agreement, which failed by eleven points in Saskatchewan.

However, better days were ahead. Perhaps Roy Romanow's best day in politics came in March 1995, when his finance minister— the first female finance minister in Canada to bring down a budget—was able to stand in the legislature and announce that the government of Saskatchewan was introducing a balanced budget.

"It was on schedule and on time," Romanow recalls. "You felt damn good on budget day. And we did it our way, too. Not like the Alberta or Mike Harris way. It was a very proud day for me. It meant we had turned the corner and could start dreaming a little bit."

That night Romanow, MacKinnon, and other senior finance advisers celebrated over dinner together. Then they went to the Department of Finance, which was also enjoying a raucous, joyous party. By the time he was finished with politics, Romanow's governments had balanced six consecutive budgets, the best record of any Canadian province. And rather than turfing Romanow for the tough decisions the government had made, the public rewarded him on June 21, 1995 with a renewed majority.

Meanwhile, Allan Blakeney was entering the next phase of his life. He left Saskatchewan for the first time in decades, joining the faculty of the Osgoode Hall Law School in Toronto from 1988 until 1990. Then he returned home to spend the 1990s at the University of Saskatchewan's School of Law. In 1999, he added to his educational duties, becoming an adjunct professor at the University of Regina. He collected a few directorships along the way (Algoma Steel, Cameco, Crown Life, SaskTel, The Canada Millennium Scholarship Foundation), even though the business community is not noted for being generous with its directorships to former politicians of a socialist hue. He could also take considerable pleasure in the fact that his succession plans had worked out wonderfully well.

Ironically, such was not the case for Roy Romanow. Saskatchewan's twelfth premier felt certain he had one more good campaign in him when he went to the polls on September 16, 1999. As the early returns came in, it looked as though Romanow would win his third consecutive majority government.

But it was not to be. Once again, Romanow would pay the price for his big ideas—his wandering eye to national concerns, perhaps at the expense of more local issues. As the returns from more rural constituencies started to roll in, a different picture emerged. The new Saskatchewan Party captured the largest number of votes (almost 40 percent) but, because of the splits, came second in the seat count behind the NDP, twenty-six to twenty-nine. The Liberals won three seats and held the balance of power. It was the first minority government in Saskatchewan in seventy years.

Romanow kept his party in power by agreeing to a formal coalition with the Liberals. In exchange for cabinet posts, the Grits would keep the NDP in charge. Romanow would refer to the '99 election as his "near-death experience."

"It's less than perfect, but that's life," he says philosophically. "I did the very best I could. That's one thing I can always tell the people of Saskatchewan." This boxer had always entered the ring expecting to win or lose. The '99 campaign was like a tie. It left an unsatisfying taste in the mouth of a heavyweight competitor.

Which is why, exactly one year and one week after the vote, Roy Romanow announced his retirement from politics. Unlike Allan Blakeney, whose bags he had carried in Regina forty years earlier, Romanow retired as premier—but admittedly not at the top of his game. Originally, he had planned to hang around provincial politics for a few years before making the jump to the federal arena. Instead, he stayed for thirty-three years.

At his emotional farewell news conference, Romanow offered up some reasons why he loved public life so much.

"There can be no nobler occupation than one through which you dedicate your life to the betterment of others, and public service is one such noble calling," he said. "I urge all to celebrate and appreciate those who answer that call."

A few weeks later at the NDP's annual convention, Romanow broke down in tears several times as he tried to express his love for his province, its people, and the job he was leaving.

Allan Blakeney always knew being a first minister was important because, he explains, he constantly asked himself this question: "If you screw up, does it really matter? When you're in politics and you're doing something publicly that's going to affect the well-being of all the people of the province, there is so much more of an element of, if you screw up, it does matter," he laughs, as he starts pacing the room energetically. "This is where the real satisfaction comes. If you're premier and it doesn't go well, it does get laid at your door. Very few people in society have the opportunity to use their talents on a flat-out basis for sustained periods of time."

"The hours are enormous," says Romanow. "The pressures are enormous. You're in the public eye all the time."

Romanow admits he has not led a very balanced life. Politics has been his life, or at least his life's work. Leaving politics presented him with an opportunity to put some balance back in his life.

"Anybody who says they're leaving the premier's chair for a better job . . . " Romanow's voice trails off. "There is no better job. There's no life like it, as they say in the army. I'm going to miss it all."

Just two months after Roy Romanow uttered those words during our interview, he was on his way back into the arena. Apparently, there was only so much balance he could stand in his life. As premier, Romanow had urged the federal government to create a royal commission on the future of medicare. The debate across Canada over the country's most cherished national social program had reached new levels of acrimony, "and I did my share to contribute to that acrimony," Romanow admits.

After his retirement from politics, Romanow returned to university life. Then he got a call from Prime Minister Jean Chrétien's right-hand man, Eddie Goldenberg.

"We've been giving a lot of thought to health care," Goldenberg told him, indicating the prime minister was giving serious consideration to striking a royal commission on the issue. "Would you be interested in doing it?"

Naturally, Romanow was interested, but only under certain circumstances. He wanted to know who else would be on this hypothetical commission, how broad its mandate would be, and how much authority he would have. Evidently those questions didn't deter Chrétien, who invited the former premier to Ottawa for a meeting in March 2001 to go over a working paper touching on all of those issues. But after six hours of discussion with federal officials, chaired by then health minister Allan Rock, Romanow wasn't satisfied with the conditions being offered. So he asked his former deputy minister in Saskatchewan to come in and help negotiate a better package. Greg Marchildon, a Ph.D. from the London School of Economics and professor at Johns Hopkins University, spent a weekend trying to improve the agreement. Eventually, he called Romanow.

"This is the best it's going to be," said Marchildon. "It's pretty good. I recommend it, if you want to do it."

The ball was back in Romanow's court. He had done plenty of bitching about health care for years. Now the government was giving him a chance to make what could be a historic contribution to saving medicare. Romanow was happy about the fact that Chrétien was offering to create a full-fledged royal commission (rather than, say, a weaker task force) with an expansive mandate. He worried about the timetable. The government wanted Romanow's one-man commission to report back in just eighteen months. Canada's most influential health care study, by the late judge Emmett Hall, had taken three years.

Romanow's wife, Eleanore, was also torn by the offer. "She favoured me going into university life and calming down," Romanow says. She also wondered about the health of the potential health care commissioner.

"You've done thirty-four years of this," she told him. "How much more can your body take?"

Still, Romanow couldn't resist.

"And once I got into it, my worst fears became real," he says. "I thought, 'Holy gee [he really does talk like this], this is a hugely complex, subtle, political thing.' I got scared and I got motivated."

Unlike the story with most royal commissions, it seems the Canadian public truly bought into Romanow's efforts. The subject matter couldn't have been closer to Canadians' hearts. This was one royal commission people couldn't ignore. And Romanow felt the heat. Two days before our second interview, he received a photograph of legendary politicians Tommy Douglas and M.J. Coldwell in the House of Commons. The accompanying letter reminded Romanow to "be guided by the values and principles of these men."

"From that point of view, you feel a little bit of pressure," admits Romanow, who referred to his health care adventure as exhausting and invigorating. His report was also widely praised by the public as striking most of the right notes in preserving what Canadians loved about medicare, and suggesting improvements for the things they didn't.

Finally, Romanow recalls a moment shared in the basement of Kim Thorson, who was both a protegé of Tommy Douglas's and a fellow cabinet minister in the Blakeney government. It was late in the day and both men were in a blue mood as the political currents of the day swirled against them.

"You know," Thorson said. "We get no respect at all in this job."

"You're not kidding," Romanow responded.

"The pay is lousy," Thorson added.

"Yep," Romanow said.

"There's no security if you're defeated."

"Quite true," Romanow added.

Then Thorson paused. "The only thing worse, Roy, would be to be told by the public we can't do it any more."

Lynda Haverstock (right), former leader of the Saskatchewan Liberal Party. Today, Haverstock is the province's lieutenant-governor. (COURTESY LYNDA HAVERSTOCK.)

John Munro, the once powerful Trudeau cabinet minister from Hamilton, in 1971. In his seventies Munro still wanted to win one more election when he passed away in August 2003. (COURTESY JOHN MUNRO.)

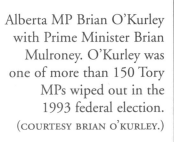

Alberta MP Brian O'Kurley
with Prime Minister Brian
Mulroney. O'Kurley was
one of more than 150 Tory
MPs wiped out in the
1993 federal election.
(COURTESY BRIAN O'KURLEY.)

Just a few months before Premier Bob Rae received an enormous
ovation from delegates at this March 1991 NDP convention,
his government reached a 60-percent approval rating in the polls.
But the recession took the wind out of Ontario's economy and
sent Rae's popularity plummeting. Rae is pictured here
with federal NDP leader Audrey McLaughlin.
(COURTESY JULIEN LEBOURDAIS.)

Ontario Premier David Peterson and New Brunswick
Premier Frank McKenna at the Meech Lake
negotiations in June 1990.
(COURTESY FRANK MCKENNA.)

The author scrums
Premier Peterson on
the way into another
Meech Lake negotiating
session at Ottawa's
Government
Conference Centre,
June 1990. Peterson's
communications
adviser, Mike Tansey,
looks on.
(COURTESY STEVE PAIKIN.)

William Vander Zalm's million-dollar smile helped make the lilac king premier of British Columbia. However, Vander Zalm later resigned amidst a raging BC political firestorm. (COURTESY WILLIAM VANDER ZALM.)

John Savage, the former premier of Nova Scotia, died in 2003, after contributing as much to society in his post-political life as he did while in office. (COURTESY JOHN SAVAGE.)

Allan Blakeney (left) became premier of Saskatchewan in 1971.
Here in 1980 with his mentor, former CCF premier Tommy Douglas,
leader of the first social democratic government in North America.
(COURTESY ALLAN BLAKENEY.)

Roy Romanow succeeded Blakeney as Saskatchewan NDP leader and eventually brought the party back to power. Shortly after retiring as premier, he chaired the most important royal commission in decades—on the future of health care.
(COURTESY ROY ROMANOW.)

Nancy MacBeth when she won the leadership of the Alberta Liberal Party in April of 1998. She became the first woman to lead the Liberals in that province's history.
(COURTESY NANCY MACBETH.)

Joe Clark, moments before losing the
PC leadership to Brian Mulroney at
the 1983 federal Tory convention.
(COURTESY STEVE PAIKIN.)

A father–daughter moment. Former Ontario Liberal
leader Robert Nixon congratulates the new
Liberal MP for Brant, his daughter Jane Stewart.
(COURTESY ROBERT NIXON.)

Some couples play tennis. Others, such as Sharon and John
Carstairs, do politics. Prime Minister Jean Chrétien appointed
Sharon Carstairs to the Senate. She and her husband have
attended dozens of political conventions together.
(COURTESY SHARON CARSTAIRS.)

Tim Murphy and Ontario Liberal leader Lyn McLeod both had their careers
as elected politicians derailed because of the same-sex benefits debate.
(COURTESY TIM MURPHY)

# THE
# OPPOSITE SEX

I will feel equality has arrived when we can elect to office women
who are as incompetent as some of the men who are already there.
—*political activist Maureen Reagan*

LET'S STATE THE OBVIOUS right at the outset. Yes, politics
at every level in Canada is infinitely more accessible to women
today than it was a generation ago. Yes, political parties today
make a much more significant effort to attract women into
public life than they used to. And yes, the careers of some female
politicians take off more quickly than they might otherwise,
because the overwhelming majority of male decision makers
realize it's good politics to have as many women as possible at the
cabinet table.

Having acknowledged all that, let's also get real. Politics is still a
male-dominated game. Politics is still much tougher for women
than for men. Women who had hoped to bring a so-called kinder,
gentler spirit to public life are frequently crushed by the brutal
reality that politics is still a very macho, confrontational enterprise.
There isn't much room for kinder and gentler. And no one learned
that lesson more harshly than a former politician from Alberta
named Nancy MacBeth.

MacBeth's political career started in 1972. Peter Lougheed was premier of Alberta. She was all of twenty-three years old when she was hired to establish a translation service for Alberta's Ministry of Culture. She eventually graduated to the premier's office as his correspondence secretary. In 1976 came another promotion, when she was appointed executive assistant to the minister of municipal affairs, Dick Johnston. Over the years, MacBeth must have done well because Lougheed gave her one of the four jobs on his election advance team for the 1982 campaign. It was to be the most successful of Lougheed's four election triumphs. His Progressive Conservatives took seventy-five of the legislature's seventy-nine seats. Social Credit and the Liberals were wiped out. The New Democrats could snag only two seats. But the highlight of the campaign for MacBeth came toward the end, when she and the premier had a private chat.

"Look," Lougheed told her, "we need people like you in public life. And I hope some day you'll consider it." MacBeth was thirty-four years old at the time and had never before considered running for office. She loved politics, but preferred to make her contribution behind the scenes—at least, until that chat with the premier.

"And then I knew that some day I wanted to do it," she says.

That day came four years later. She had moved on from Lougheed's office to work for Lou Hyndman (he was Alberta treasurer at this point). Hyndman had also announced that he would be stepping down before the 1986 election. Coincidentally, MacBeth had grown up in the treasurer's Edmonton Glenora riding, so she decided to make her first attempt at elective politics there. She called former premier Peter Lougheed to tell him of her decision.

"You told me back in '82 that I was needed in government," she told him. "And I never did forget it." Lougheed was pleased with the news.

MacBeth had also seen first-hand what the life of a backbench MLA was like and thought it would jive nicely with her own lifestyle. She had an eighteen-month-old son, Fraser, and thought that, with a little planning, she would be able to spend plenty of time with him. But, of course, in politics, things almost never work out the way you plan them.

MacBeth's first election was also Premier Don Getty's first general election as the new PC leader. While Getty did take sixty-one of the legislature's eighty-three seats—a solid majority in anyone's books—the mood on election night was less buoyant because Edmontonians turned their backs on the Tories in dramatic fashion. The NDP had its best showing ever, with sixteen seats, while the Liberals got back on the electoral map with four seats. Only four Tories survived in the provincial capital, and MacBeth was one of them.

Still, it was a triumphant night. MacBeth won her riding by more than two thousand votes. But spending more time with Fraser—that wasn't on. MacBeth's expectations of learning the ropes on the backbenches never materialized. Premier Getty put her right into cabinet, as minister of education no less. Being one of the few Tory survivors in Edmonton helped secure the appointment. Being one of just six women in the PC caucus no doubt helped some more.

Politically, her career was taking off, but MacBeth's personal life was in trouble. Her marriage to Stefan Betkowski was falling apart for reasons unrelated to politics, but politics sure didn't help. A year after her election, the two separated and eventually they divorced. (MacBeth is actually the last name of her second husband, Hilliard, who she married in 1990. When she first entered public life, she went by the name Nancy Betkowski.)

The greatest challenge the new education minister now faced was getting a new Schools Act through the Alberta Legislature. She inherited a bill that nobody liked, so she spent the next two years consulting all the right people and redrafting the proposed legislation.

On one occasion, MacBeth was scheduled to meet with a group of women to address their concerns.

"We want to talk to *you*," they said. "We don't want any of your team here that's writing this bill. We want you in, with us, and we want to tell you something."

"Okay," MacBeth said. "Let's do it."

The group wanted to talk to the minister about a phrase in the bill they despised: "non-educable children." Before the meeting, MacBeth (naively by her own admission) thought there were such children. She was about to get a lecture from some mothers who found the term offensive and wanted to change her mind.

"From the moment that my baby was born, I knew there was something wrong," one of the mothers told her. "And from the moment he was born I've been fighting to get him the things he needed to make his life the best it can be. He may not get his Grade 12 diploma, but he has progressed.

"It seems to me that once that kid gets into school, he shouldn't have to fight any more. There should be a system in place there that's going to be his advocate."

MacBeth emerged from the meeting with a re-dedicated sense of purpose. The previous School Act ironically mentioned the word "student" only twice, an odd situation considering students are supposed to be at the centre of everything the Ministry of Education does. The new law would proudly proclaim that its purpose would be to educate all of Alberta's children, no matter what their needs.

MacBeth completely immersed herself in the task and her efforts paid off. The new School Act passed the Alberta Legislature unanimously.

"It was like walking out into the sunshine," she says. "You've been in the closed dark room for a whole lot of time and thinking, is this ever going to resolve? Then when it happens, there's a reason why you go through all of these steps. That is the most rewarding part."

MacBeth had lived the education file for two years, knew all the major players, had an instinctive feel for what needed doing, and finally understood how the system worked. Then Don Getty called her into his office.

"I want you to take the Ministry of Health," the premier told her. Alberta had just come through a nasty nurses' strike. The previous minister had been eaten alive by the issue, so Getty wanted a different hand on the tiller to move the government's agenda to the next stage.

MacBeth's response? "Oh shit," she recalls saying to herself.

It wasn't just that health was considered a killer portfolio. MacBeth had come to love education; she didn't want to leave.

"We're not going to make the announcement public till tomorrow," Getty said, "so you've just got to continue on, as if you're still the minister of education."

Easier said than done. MacBeth was in the midst of giving what would turn out to be her last speech as minister when she simply became overcome by emotion. She started to cry, in front of a group of northeast Alberta school trustees at Fort Saskatchewan. "I really love this job," she told the stunned audience, who had no clue as to why the minister was having an emotional meltdown in front of them. The next day, when Getty announced the shuffle, everything made sense, and several trustees sent MacBeth letters thanking her for a job well done.

But if Nancy MacBeth thought her promotion to the biggest-spending ministry in the Alberta government would take her to the next level in politics, she was sadly mistaken.

Just as a populist, neo-conservative element took over the Ontario PC party in the 1990s, the same thing was happening in

Alberta. When Don Getty announced his resignation as premier, the moderate conservatives and the neo-cons had it out for control of Alberta's PC party. MacBeth described it as a fork in the road. She was concerned the party was jumping on the wrong tines. Ralph Klein, who believe it or not was once considered a Liberal, became the darling of the neo-cons. MacBeth became the champion of the more traditional Lougheed-style progressive conservatives. Klein was pushing tax cuts, deficit reduction, and big-time spending cuts. MacBeth was pledging to balance the books by holding the line on health and education spending, while also promising a system-wide reorganization of the health care system. That meant telling many fellow caucus members no, we won't be building that hospital in your riding, because health care is becoming more community-based, less hospital-focused. Naturally, all those MLAs gravitated to Klein's team. Still, MacBeth thought her plan was plenty tough enough, and her mantra was to protect programs Albertans "need to have, not that are nice to have." She seemed to capture the early momentum in the campaign, particularly after Klein appeared not to understand the difference between annual budget *deficits* and accumulated *debt* during the first leaders' debate in Grande Prairie.

In Ontario, the 1990 leadership fight between the progressives and the conservatives never got terribly ugly. After all, the contest between North Bay's Mike Harris and London's Dianne Cunningham was a battle for the right to lead a party that was in third place. But in Alberta, Ralph Klein and Nancy Betkowski were vying to become premier. Neither one had ever lost an election. The job, the pressure to stay perfect, plus their irreconcilable visions for where their province ought to go, made for a very nasty tussle.

After the first round of voting, MacBeth found herself atop the leader board, just one slim vote ahead of Klein. The other candidates dropped off the ballot and endorsed MacBeth. But there would be one week until the second ballot—and no rules against signing up new members, or against hardball politics.

"It was a blood sport," MacBeth now admits. Klein played it; MacBeth wouldn't. At one point, Klein actually said, "Let's get it on, Nancy!" in a bit of boorish machismo. Ask yourself if you can imagine one male candidate saying that to another male candidate. It was Klein playing the gender card, much to the delight of his core support and to the embarrassment of everyone else.

On December 6, 1992, Ralph Klein emerged victorious on the second ballot, taking the leadership by fourteen thousand votes.

"Suddenly I lost something that was really big," MacBeth says. "To lose that leadership and know where the health care system was going to go as a result . . . there is no justice in this world. I really thought it was one of the worst things that had ever happened to me and the province."

In fact, MacBeth went into a deep depression, something common to many politicians who lose a particularly personal battle. "I think depression is probably a very accurate term," she says. "I didn't go on medication for it, but I certainly felt that the spirit had gone out of me."

The Alberta Conservatives were a badly split organization because of the brutality of the leadership campaign. All the traditional cleavages—Edmonton vs. Calgary, men vs. women, north vs. south, moderate conservatives vs. neo-cons—emerged. And yet Klein was not terribly gracious in victory. He declined to make the courtesy phone call to his opponent to begin the process of patching things up. Finally, several days after winning the job (and having been shamed into reaching out by outgoing leader Don Getty), Klein called MacBeth. They agreed to meet.

The incoming premier said he would do his part to end the family feud, so he offered MacBeth the treasurer's job.

"I think for a treasurer, you really need someone that's your agent," MacBeth recalls telling Klein. "I really think you need an alter ego in treasurer." Clearly, that wasn't her. She had another idea. Klein was a "great people person." MacBeth had shown that her strength was managing government. How about deputy premier? "You do what you do and I'll do what I do, and we can work together that way," she explained. Trouble was, Klein had already promised that job to Ken Kowalski and Peter Elzinga, two of his most ardent backers in the leadership fight. Klein came back with another offer: Ministry of Federal and Intergovernmental Affairs.

"Well, where am I on the priority list?" MacBeth wondered. If she couldn't have a major ministry, she at least wanted some seniority in cabinet.

"Sixth or seventh," was Klein's response.

And the other leadership contenders who had backed MacBeth? Shut out of cabinet altogether.

MacBeth did want one other thing from Klein, not so much for herself, but for her husband and son. The sexual innuendo of the "Let's get it on!" comment still stung and made MacBeth's family wonder how she could work for a man who would utter such a sexist, undignified phrase, even in the heat of political battle. The premier was most apologetic.

"As soon as the words were out of my mouth, I knew it was a mistake," he told her. Would Klein mind dropping a quick line to MacBeth's family, reiterating that?

"Consider it done," Klein told her.

It was the last time the two rivals would ever meet privately.

MacBeth left the meeting promising Klein she would think about the premier's job offer, all the while figuring, reluctantly, that she would have to take it. She told the premier she was taking her family on a skiing vacation for a few days, but here's my phone number, let's talk soon.

The next day, MacBeth picked up a newspaper and read that she had gone off to pout over her loss and no one in the premier's office knew where she was. It seemed like another in an endless litany of cheap shots.

"They were poor winners," she says. "They were kicking sand at the person that had lost."

She began to wonder how she would actually function in Klein's cabinet, with all of her opponents in senior positions.

"Every time I got passionate about something that we were trying to do as a government, and there was any kind of disagreement, I'd have them all saying, 'Hey, don't forget lady, you lost. Don't push your luck,'" MacBeth figured.

So when she and Klein talked again, this time by phone, MacBeth stunned the premier by declining his offer.

"What's it going to take to get you into the cabinet?" Klein asked her.

"Well, you've made your decision and I've made mine," MacBeth told him. "I will support you as a member of your caucus, but not as a member of your cabinet."

Klein was upset, so much so that his "consider it done" letter of apology never materialized. Before long, MacBeth decided that not only could she not serve with Klein in cabinet, but she couldn't even stomach being in his caucus. She had been a Tory for more than twenty years, but enough was enough. She declined to seek re-election, and dropped out of politics.

"It got to the point where I said, maybe this isn't where I'm meant to be," MacBeth recalls.

MacBeth became a health care consultant, took a job in the Northwest Territories, and closed the books on a career filled with "what-ifs."

But, as Yogi Berra once said, it's never over till it's over. And for Nancy MacBeth, it wasn't over yet.

In 1994, after Laurence Decore stepped down as Liberal leader of Alberta, some party officials approached MacBeth to run for the job. It was tempting. The Liberals were in reasonably good shape, having enjoyed their best election showing in the 1993 campaign. (That had been Klein's first campaign as premier and, despite predictions of a major Tory demise, his Conservatives held on to power. However, with only fifty-one seats, it was their worst showing in more than twenty years. The Liberals under Decore, the popular former mayor of Edmonton, took thirty-two seats. In any other election, that would have been considered a triumph, but it was actually a disappointment for the Liberals, who harboured hopes of ending the Tory dynasty.)

But MacBeth had a sense that going for this job at this time just wasn't right. It smacked too much of getting even with Klein and not enough of the positive things she hoped to do for her province. So she took a pass.

Three years later, opportunity knocked again. MacBeth's phone kept ringing and ringing. The Liberals were again looking for a leader, because this time Grant Mitchell was resigning. MacBeth tried explaining it to her thirteen-year-old son.

"The reason so many people are phoning me, Fraser, is because those people want me to run for the leadership of the Alberta Liberal Party," she recalls telling him.

Without a moment's hesitation Fraser replied, "Mom, do it."

"Fraser, I am surprised at you," MacBeth said. "You know what it's like. What happens if we lose?"

"So what, Mom? We've been through that. But I know you really like it. And it matters."

And so MacBeth dived back in. She took the Liberal leadership over four other candidates on the first ballot on April 18, 1998, and in doing so, became the first woman to lead the Alberta Liberals. (She was not the first woman to lead a major party in Alberta, that having been accomplished by the NDP's Pam Barrett a year and a half earlier.)

Now that they were in different parties, MacBeth and Klein felt free to indulge in the animosity that had become a hallmark of their relationship. They didn't stop talking to one another, although MacBeth made sure others were always present. She says she would have been insane to have a private meeting with Klein, given the way the last one had turned out. For his part, Klein continued to mock his opponent, again in a way that he wouldn't have if his opponent had been male. MacBeth's change of name and party were easy targets. In reference to her divorce, Klein spoke of MacBeth's "evil twin sister Nancy Betkowski," who, the premier claimed, said different things from Nancy MacBeth.

At first devastated, she began to develop a new understanding of her PC leadership loss to Klein. She came to think of it as one of the best things that had ever happened to her. It made her realize there are forces in the universe greater than her will.

"If I stayed stuck in the anger and the resentment, I would have been even sicker than I was," MacBeth says. "I am much stronger now as a result of that loss. The personal attacks they used to melt me with—they're not working any more, because I am feeling a whole lot stronger for them."

Two months after becoming Liberal leader, MacBeth won a by-election in Grant Mitchell's old Edmonton McClung riding. After a six-year hiatus from politics, she was now officially back in.

MacBeth spent the following three years preparing to do battle with Klein again. There were some victories. The Alberta Liberals were almost $300,000 in debt when MacBeth took over; through hard work and aggressive fundraising, she led a major effort to eliminate the debt.

For many, being in opposition can be a soul-destroying venture. Your job almost requires you to be critical and negative twenty-four hours a day. Seldom does a politician run for office hoping to be leader of the Opposition. And yet MacBeth found plenty she liked about the job.

As a cabinet minister, she had found herself in the crosshairs of both the Opposition and the media. She had competed with cabinet colleagues for budget dollars and ice time. When she was health minister, many backbenchers grew to dislike her because, in an era of increasingly decentralized health care, she refused to build a new hospital in every riding. And, of course, there was always the fear of screwing up and making the premier look bad.

"One of the beauties of being in opposition was to stand there with a caucus, albeit small—but very supportive—all around me, and be able to direct the question and confront," MacBeth says. "There was something so honest about it. And that was good."

Every Opposition leader loves to have one incredibly contentious issue that it can use to throttle a government, and on that score, MacBeth got lucky. Premier Klein dropped two whoppers in her lap: deregulating Alberta's electricity market; and introducing the controversial Health Care Protection Act, better known as Bill 11, the private hospitals bill. Both turned into messy, public relations problems for the provincial government. However, on both files, the public seemed to believe that Klein would somehow figure out a way to make it all turn out right. Day in and day out, MacBeth hammered away at the government's shortcomings on both issues, but the government sustained no long-term damage on either.

"Every single day all I have heard from the MacBeth Liberals is, 'The sky is falling. The sky is falling,'" Klein observed. "Where is her head?"

And he kicked the rhetoric up a notch from there: "I whupped her once and I'll do it again," Klein boasted to his delighted supporters.

On March 12, 2001, Albertans went to the polls to render their judgment on Ralph Klein's time as premier, and Nancy MacBeth's fitness to take his place. For MacBeth, the judgment was harsh. Buoyed by his sunny personality, lower unemployment and tax rates, and more than $7 billion in unanticipated oil and gas revenues, Klein cruised to one of the most lopsided victories in Alberta history. He garnered 62 percent of the votes, good for seventy-four seats. (In 1982, Peter Lougheed had captured 63 percent of the votes and seventy-five seats, still the best numbers in Alberta history.) The Liberals were blown out of the water in MacBeth's backyard, Edmonton, and were reduced to seven seats overall. The New Democrats won two.

"Welcome to Ralph's world!" Klein beamed on election night; given the numbers, who could argue with him?

The turnout was one of the lowest in decades, but the result was clear. The majority wanted Klein, and they didn't want MacBeth, who lost her own seat by more than a thousand votes.

It was the first election MacBeth had ever lost.

It also re-ignited the now-familiar debate as to whether a woman leader can win—a debate that Canadians engaged in after Kim Campbell, Ontario's Lyn McLeod, British Columbia's Rita Johnston, and others lost elections. On election night in McClung riding, one Liberal campaign worker told reporter Darcy Henton of Canadian Press, "They are not ready for a lady leader and they won't admit it."

"In 1992," MacBeth remembers, "I got the question on average at least once a week—do you think Alberta is ready for a female premier?" MacBeth's answer was always the same: the question, she would say, wasn't should a man or woman be premier, but whether Klein or MacBeth should be premier. "As leader of the Liberal Party and leader of the official Opposition, I never got the question," she says. Having said that, being a female leader anywhere in Canada is still somewhat of a novelty, and until a woman leader wins a second election, the debate will endure. (Catherine Callbeck was victorious in Prince Edward Island in 1993 and remains the first and only woman first minister to win an election in Canadian history. However, she only lasted one term, becoming so unpopular so quickly that she declined to run for re-election. She was appointed to the Senate by Prime Minister Chrétien in 1997.)

Meanwhile, MacBeth and her husband had built a new home in MacBeth's new McClung constituency. They hadn't lived there for very long and now the majority of her new neighbours were essentially saying they didn't want her representing them any more. It was something that crossed Hilliard MacBeth's mind as he and his wife drove home on election night.

"Oh, goodness, I can't stand our neighbourhood!" he blurted out in frustration.

The next morning, snow fell like crazy in Edmonton. When Nancy MacBeth looked out the window at her driveway: one of her neighbours was clearing it with a snow blower.

"This is a wonderful neighbourhood," she said to herself. At that moment, she came to understand one of life's great lessons—that politics isn't personal. "Too many people take it personally, whether it's to exalt themselves or to put themselves down," she says. "And I think it's the biggest lesson I learned. Don't take it personally."

Two days later, MacBeth resigned as Liberal leader. Her political career was now over.

A year and a half after that election, I spoke to Nancy MacBeth again to understand, with the benefit of much more hindsight, what other lessons she had learned from her time as Liberal leader.

"I guess the insight is this question: 'Am I supposed to be there?'" MacBeth says, referring to public life.

"Do you think you have an answer to that now?" I ask.

"Yes, a really clear answer," she says.

"What's the answer?"

"The answer is, 'No, you're not supposed to be there. Get on and do something else!'"

MacBeth knew on election night that she had led her party to one of the worst thrashings in Alberta history, but she was strangely philosophical and at peace with it all. The clarity of the results on election night meant that she would never have to experience a future filled with what-ifs.

"We gave the choice to Albertans and they made their choice and that was the Albertans' right to do, and now I can accept that. I couldn't accept that ten years ago," she says, referring to her 1992 leadership contest with Klein.

How much of MacBeth's return to politics was rooted in her desire for revenge on Klein?

"Earlier on, after the leadership, it was *definitely* about that," she confesses. "But I'm glad I made it through and now I don't feel any unfinished business whatsoever. I don't feel any continuing concern about Ralph Klein."

It's traditional for politicians to say that the voters are never wrong. Even those on the receiving end of some of the most crushing defeats in history have felt compelled to say it (John Turner in 1984 springs to mind). Nancy MacBeth is no longer a politician, and thus the following very candid remark about the electorate is now permissible.

"I think they can be easily duped," she says, not in a mean-spirited way, perhaps referring to $2 billion worth of electricity rebates Klein gave Albertans six months before election day.

"I know that I will never run in an election again. I know you're supposed to say 'never say never.' But I know that I won't run again. I feel like I'm finally free of it after thirty years. I loved it and I'll always follow it, but now I can move on," she says.

When I ask MacBeth what she's doing now, she bursts out laughing. "I knew this question was coming!" She seems a tad embarrassed to reveal that, at age fifty-four, she's essentially dropped out of the workforce and is simply enjoying her private life for the first time in decades. She's doing volunteer work. She's learning how to play bridge. She's travelling more with her husband and seeing more of her son before he goes off to university next year. But her favourite passion at the moment is riding dressage on her new horse, Mickey, whom she keeps at a stable less than fifteen minutes from her home. She rides virtually every morning.

"I am amazed at how happy I am to be doing something different," MacBeth says. "It's not to put down politics. I loved every minute of it. But I'm really glad to be free of it."

# THE MOUNTAIN CLIMBER

Getting to the summit is optional, getting down is mandatory.
—*Ed Viesturs, mountaineer*

Anyone who's spent any time trying to get elected, and then tried to climb the greasy poll that is partisan politics, will know that the analogy of political life to mountain climbing is spot-on. Many would-be politicians start their journey at the bottom and, as time goes by, make their way up through a treacherous set of obstacles until precious few of them feel the exhilaration of reaching the mountaintop.

This chapter is about a man who made it to the top of the mountain well before he had any business getting there, only to fall so precipitously that he spent more than two decades in an ultimately futile attempt to get back. He left politics for a while, but realized the private sector held none of the appeal or range of issues he cared about, and thus a comeback was soon afoot.

But Canadian politics is not a Walt Disney movie. A storybook finish wasn't in the cards.

This is the story of Canada's sixteenth prime minister, Joe Clark.

IT'S A FRIGID FEBRUARY DAY in Canada's capital city. The sky is a perfect blue, which does compensate for the fact that it's minus twenty degrees. After the obligatory walk through the metal detector and some more questions from other security officials— yes, things are a lot more tense on Parliament Hill since September 11, 2001—I am on my way, six storeys up, to an appointment with a man whose political experiences may be the most singularly distinctive in Canadian history.

It's hard to think of another politician who tasted electoral success so quickly, only to lose it in the blink of an eye, who was the target of such harsh ridicule (most of it from people who were supposed to be his supporters), and yet ended his career widely respected in Canada, even admired, for his contributions to public life.

Such is the paradox of Charles Joseph Clark.

Clark's political roots go back to an Alberta provincial election in 1955, when as a Grade 10 student he banged some signs into the ground for the Liberal Conservative candidate Ross Ellis, the mayor of High River, who was running against the Social Credit minister of education. Just to prove all politics is local, even though Ernest Manning's Socreds won a healthy majority government (thirty-seven seats to just twenty-four for the seven opposition parties), the mayor became the only Liberal Conservative MLA in the legislature. He upset the Socred cabinet minister, whose government may have been popular province-wide, but wasn't in Clark's home community of High River. People were upset because the government was extending Highway 2 but missing High River, a lovely community forty-five kilometres south of Calgary. (In fact, the columnist Allan Fotheringham, "in the only kind word that he ever said about me, said the view from my parents' back step was the most spectacular in Canada," Clark jokes.)

Not only is it fun to work on a winning campaign, but it's good to be the guy in the spotlight, which Clark was at a public-speaking contest held by the Rotary Club in 1956. His family published three weekly newspapers in southern Alberta, and so the topic for his speech—the first printing press in Western Canada—was a natural. It also didn't hurt that ten doors down from the Clarks lived the late William Ormond (better known as "W.O.") Mitchell, one of the country's foremost authors and playwrights, who helped Clark with his speech. And yes, Clark won the contest.

Another event that same year turned out to be extremely influential in bringing Joe Clark closer to politics. His grandfather's older brother, Hugh Clark, born the same year as Canada, was a member of the Ontario Legislature in the twentieth century's first decade. In 1911, he moved to the federal scene, and served another decade in Parliament, even becoming parliamentary secretary to the minister of foreign affairs for a couple of years. (Seven decades later, his more famous great-nephew would become minister of external affairs, completing a family circle of sorts.)

In any event, Joe Clark visited Parliament Hill in 1956 and on the strength of family ties with his great uncle, plus a phone call from a businessman in High River who knew the leader of Her Majesty's Loyal Opposition, the young lad suddenly found himself in conversation with Colonel George Drew, the Conservative leader, who at the time was minutes away from participating in one of the most raucous and important question periods in Canadian history: the pipeline debate.

"What astounded me," Clark recalls, "was that the leader of the Opposition usually sees nobody a few minutes before question period, because you're psyching yourself up, and particularly during the days of the pipeline debate."

But Drew did see the now self-described "hick kid from somewhere out West" and they did speak. And Clark was so impressed, he went right from that conversation to get in line to watch question period. The lines were so long that by the time he was able to get in, the pipeline debate was over. But his interest in politics was piqued.

Clark was getting considerable exposure not only to politics but to the notion of public service. In those days in Alberta, newspaper owners (his father and grandfather) and teachers (his mother) were regarded as quasi-public servants. When big names came to High River, a courtesy call to the Clark homestead was a typical item on the itinerary. When people had problems that needed solving, they were just as likely to visit their local newspaper proprietor as they were their local politicians.

"And so I grew up in that tradition," Clark explains. "I had a sense of public obligation, public service, from the very beginning."

From as far back as he can remember, the Clarks were a partisan Tory family (although, interestingly, not his mother, who was a Canadian Co-operation Federation supporter in university, then one of a tiny handful of Liberals in High River). In 1957, the year John Diefenbaker upset the Grits and returned the Tories to power for the first time in more than twenty years, the news was greeted with such delight in the Clark family that it almost caused some serious casualties. Clark and his father were driving to the High River Memorial Centre, where the votes in the '57 campaign were being counted.

"My father, who was a very careful driver most of the time, was driving, and the radio was on. The news came in that Doug Fisher had defeated C.D. Howe," Clark says, referring to the maverick CCF-er who staged a shocking upset of the Liberals' powerful minister-for-everything. "My father took both his hands off the wheel and clapped his hands. We swerved and nearly hit a tree."

Diefenbaker's 1957 minority government was just a prelude to the smashing majority government he would win nine months later, a victory that emboldened Conservatives in Alberta—who had never formed a government—to dream big. In fact, Progressive Conservative leader Cam Kirby and his driver, valet, gofer, press secretary, and adviser (all of whom happened to be Joe Clark) campaigned their backsides off and managed to move the Tory vote from 9 percent in the '55 campaign to 24 percent four years later. Unfortunately, they also went from three seats to just one. Ernest Manning won sixty-one of sixty-five seats, keeping the Social Credit dynasty alive.

Clark's recollections of that election make him smile. The Tories thought they were doing so well that the leader and his chauffeur, during one of those very long drives from one event to another, began considering who would make it into the first Progressive Conservative cabinet of Alberta, an event that wouldn't actually happen for more than another decade. Clark also remembers that campaign being the first time he ever drove a car with an automatic transmission and power brakes.

"I got through most of southern Alberta but . . ." Clark pauses and laughs, "there weren't many red lights then. There was a red light in Medicine Hat. So I touched the brakes and nearly put Cam Kirby through the windshield."

But Conservative fortunes would improve in Alberta. Clark's father, Charles, would nominate a Calgary lawyer named Peter Lougheed at the party's leadership convention in 1965. Joe Clark, as national president of the PC Student Federation, eventually became part of Lougheed's inner circle of a dozen or so advisers. (For the record, Clark himself, his father, and grandfather were all named Charles. But the youngest Clark didn't fancy going through life as Charles III, and thus "Joe" was born.)

Joe Clark was not only doing politics at this time, but teaching it at the University of Alberta, which is another improbable story in itself. Clark was a political science student in Professor Bill Dawson's class. Dawson came from an academic family. His father,

R. MacGregor Dawson, wrote *The Government of Canada,* one of
the staples of every Canadian studies reading list back then. One
day, Bill Dawson took one of his students aside.

"Mr. Clark," he told him, "you have no natural aptitude for this
subject. I would suggest you drop out."

"No, Professor Dawson, I'm not going to drop out," Clark boldly
responded.

Sure enough, Clark finished the course, did well, and when Bill
Dawson got lured away to the University of Western Ontario rather
suddenly, guess who got hired to teach the course?

But back to Alberta politics and the election of 1967. Peter
Lougheed would eventually become one of the most successful
politicians in Canadian history. He would win four successive
majority governments, and, in an electoral achievement perhaps
unparalleled anywhere in the western world, he wouldn't lose a
single seat in any of those elections. But the Lougheed juggernaut
hadn't quite arrived by the spring of 1967. Social Credit still had
some muscle left. Clark was in charge of finding candidates in all of
Alberta's sixty-five ridings, but could fill only three-quarters of
them. Then an already difficult job became even harder thanks to a
candidate named Fred Peacock, who was a prominent businessman
and was in a tough fight against Arthur Dixon, the Speaker of the
legislature, in Calgary South. Peacock actually became the first
politician in Alberta history to commission a poll and when he saw
the numbers, his political life passed before his eyes.

"This is the worst riding I have ever seen," his pollster, Ben Crow,
told him.

So Peacock quit the race. Two days before election day. Clark
did the only thing he could. He checked out the circulation list for
his family's newspaper, the *High River Times.* It had fifty-six names
on it. He called them all, begging them to come to a meeting. Fifty
of them did so, thereby constituting an official meeting of the

Calgary South PC Association. Clark got himself nominated as the candidate.

"And I remember talking to Ben Crow and saying, 'Ben, is this really impossible?' And he looked at me and he said, 'Well, there was the virgin birth.'"

Certainly Clark's mother, Grace, was concerned about her son's prospects.

"My mother was convinced I would be shattered by the experience and so badly beaten," Clark recalls. "So she drove up from High River, and was in the headquarters all the time, as much as anything else, to look after her son in the event that he needed that when he really got pasted. She was a pessimist about those things."

Clark actually has very fond memories of this time in 1967. The Tory campaign had energized hundreds of young people around Alberta, who were running through the streets singing Bobby Gimby's "Ca-na-da" centennial theme song.

Nevertheless, five weeks before Canada's one hundredth birthday, Peter Lougheed's Tories won 26 percent of the votes, which sounds good, except that it translated into only six seats. Joe Clark's wasn't one of them. But he did come within 240 votes of defeating the Speaker. Had Lougheed won eight seats, Clark would have been in.

"I had a telegram prepared for Ben Crow saying, 'Come to Bethlehem and see!'" Clark smiles. "But I didn't get a chance to send it."

If Joe Clark had wanted to stay in Alberta and lick his wounds from his 1967 provincial election loss, he wasn't about to have the luxury of doing so. Almost immediately, he immersed himself in the race for a new national Progressive Conservative leader to replace the deposed John Diefenbaker. Clark was backing the pride of Kamloops, Davie Fulton, a former justice minister and veteran of more than two decades in the House of Commons, for whom Clark was a special assistant. And there were others on

Team Fulton who would become extraordinarily influential in not only Clark's life, but the life of the party and the country—friends such as Lowell Murray, Michel Cogger, and Brian Mulroney. But Fulton lost to the premier of Nova Scotia, Robert Stanfield.

After the convention, Clark agreed to become executive assistant to Stanfield, just in time to watch the new Tory leader get run over by Trudeaumania in 1968. In fact, if you hadn't known how the 1970s would end, you would've sworn that Clark was making a monumentally stupid career decision by staying in Ottawa. After all, in 1971 his old friend Peter Lougheed stunned Albertans by ending the thirty-six-year Social Credit dynasty. Had Clark returned to Alberta, he certainly would have been a senior minister in Lougheed's government.

But Clark made a different decision. He determined to make his future in a city where the Liberals were the natural governing party, and where Tories, in the twentieth century at least, had a long, inglorious history of never being satisfied with their leader and being perpetually in opposition. On the face of it, it seemed an inexplicable move.

But several things happened that suggested to Clark that the nation's capital was where he ought to be. In early 1957, after Diefenbaker had won the PC party leadership but before he became prime minister, he travelled to High River. Joe Clark was president of his school's student council. His father convinced him that, as such, he was a public official of some stature in the town and therefore should attend the event being held for Dief. There, Clark heard for the first time the Opposition leader's cry for a new vision for one Canada. But it was what happened after the address that truly inspired Clark.

"Dief actually came to the back of the room," Clark says, "and sat down beside me and said, 'What are you going to do, young man?' I was impressed by the fact that he would ask me. And he sat there for about five minutes and talked to me about Prince Albert and Parliament, and how we needed to get young men like me involved in the public life of the country." (Incidentally, knowing how influential Dief's gesture was to him, Clark makes it a point of doing the same whenever he encounters young people.)

Fast-forward to the following year. It's 1958 and Diefenbaker's Conservatives have just won the biggest majority government in Canadian history. Clark remembers being an eighteen-year-old tourist in Ottawa on a late-spring/early-summer day. He's standing outside the West Block of Parliament. Suddenly, National Resources Minister Alvin Hamilton walks by, stops, and for no particular reason, begins to strike up a conversation with the teenager. Then a moment later, Hamilton's Ellen Fairclough, Canada's first female cabinet minister, does likewise. And then Davie Fulton joins the group. Almost half a century later, Clark is still visibly moved describing this encounter.

"I was just some Canadian kid there, and here were these people whom I had thought of as sort of luminaries," he says. "They came to say hello to me. It's a recurring theme in Canada. But seeing these people, about whom I'd heard, and have them pay attention to me . . . " Clark still marvels at the scene, as his voice trails off.

These important events involving national politicians, combined with five years of effort to make Robert Stanfield prime minister, oriented Clark to a future on Parliament Hill as opposed to Edmonton.

"People keep quoting me as having said when I was three months old that I was going to be prime minister," Clark says. "I have no recollection of any of that. I don't remember having made those claims or even holding those aspirations. Frankly, I was intrigued by politics. And I knew that once you got here, possibilities opened." And so, at age thirty-three, Clark resolved that it was time to put his name on a ballot again, this time running for Parliament in the 1972 election.

The next challenge was to find a riding, and on that front there were three options. Doug Harkness, the former Diefenbaker cabinet minister, was retiring after winning nine successive elections. His Calgary Centre riding seemed a completely safe bet. But two other nearby seats, both held by Liberal rookies—cabinet minister Patrick Mahoney in Calgary South and Allen Sulatycky (later associate chief justice of the Court of Queen's Bench of Alberta) in Rocky Mountain—were vulnerable for the Grits. Both MPs won on the strength of Trudeaumania, which had fizzled badly by 1972. Clark thought both MPs could be defeated (and in fact, they both were).

Which to choose? Clark proceeds to explain in our interview, but does so very carefully, knowing that what he's about to say could be misinterpreted and thus not play well to the folks back in southern Alberta. He starts by talking about his family's roots in rural southern Alberta, where two different kinds of public leaders emerged: those who served modestly and those who were outspoken. Clark held a special admiration for the outspoken mavericks such as Jack Horner, an MP in southern Alberta for twenty-one years who crossed the floor to the Liberals for a cabinet job, then was defeated in the 1979 election.

"They could run a ranch, they could fix the tractor, things that I wasn't very good at," Clark says. "In a punch-up, at a country dance hall, they would be last out, I would be first out. I'm making that seem almost too caricaturist. They genuinely represented a strength of the province, but it wasn't my strength."

Instead, Clark hoped to offer his part of the country something different. He tries hard not to say that a man with a bachelor's and master's degree in political science, who taught the subject, and who studied law at two first-class Canadian universities and became bilingual, isn't your typical rural Albertan. But he wasn't. All the more reason, he thought, not to run in Calgary.

"I wanted rural Alberta to be seen as more than the maverick strain that Jack had come to represent," Clark says. "The deciding factors were, I thought I could make more of a difference as a member of Parliament for a rural constituency. And secondly, I wanted to demonstrate that there was another side to rural Alberta, in Alberta. So I sought the nomination in Rocky Mountain. It wasn't High River, but it was as close as you can get."

And this time, Clark won. By more than 5,000 votes. Pierre Trudeau barely held on to the prime minister's job, winning a squeaker over Robert Stanfield's Conservatives 109 to 107 seats. The popular vote was just as close. The Liberals eked out 0.8 percent more votes than the Tories. The NDP held the balance of power in Trudeau's only minority government.

While some Conservatives might have taken satisfaction in coming so close to knocking off Trudeau, the reality was that the Liberals were staying in power, and Stanfield had just lost his second consecutive election. The Tory faithful then became downright ornery; less than two years later, voters went back to the polls and gave Trudeau back his majority government. Robert Stanfield was finished. But in Rocky Mountain, Joe Clark was consolidating his base. Even though the PCs lost twelve seats, Clark won his by a greater margin—almost ten thousand votes in 1974.

True, he was still a relative newcomer to the House of Commons and only thirty-five years old, and yet Joe Clark started to think about the party leadership. Three things happened that ultimately convinced him to go for it.

He first talked to Peter Lougheed to sound out whether the Alberta premier had any federal intentions. Lougheed was staying put.

Then he talked to Harvie Andre, who like Clark was an MP from the Class of '72. Andre had won Doug Harkness's old seat and he in turn asked the former MP for his thoughts on whether Clark should go for it. When told who else was running, Harkness said, "Hell, if these guys are going to run for leadership, he should. He's as good as any of them."

In fact, the cast of characters trying to replace Robert Stanfield was almost a stampede. No fewer than twelve candidates entered the race, ten of them members of the PC caucus.

Finally, there was Flora MacDonald, who like Clark was known as a "red Tory." Clark thought he might support her candidacy for leader. "But as I talked to more people, I came to the view that Flora couldn't win," he says, in a prediction that turned out to be brutally true for the MP from Kingston. (In the end, MacDonald and Clark made a deal. Each would agree to support whomever ranked higher after the first ballot.)

With that combination of events, the Clark leadership campaign was afoot. What surprises me as Clark retells the narrative of this time is that he says he actually thought he could win the contest. He wasn't running to put on a good show or secure his place in the party or be kingmaker.

The conventional wisdom in 1976 was that two Quebecers were the odds-on favourites to win: former Quebec attorney general and judge Claude Wagner, the rookie MP from Saint-Hyacinthe; and Brian Mulroney, then a PC party backroom boy, and himself only three months older than Clark. In fact, they occupied the top two spots on the first ballot after the votes were counted. (For the record, the candidates were: Wagner, Mulroney, Clark, MacDonald, Sinclair Stevens, George Hees, Paul Hellyer, Heward Grafftey, Pat Nowlan, Jim Gillies, Jack Horner, and John Fraser.)

"But we thought there was an outside chance that a candidate like me could come up the middle and would win," Clark now says, referring to the strategy that is always advanced by dark horses, but almost never comes to pass. Apparently, he managed to convince his father that was the case because the two men spoke on the phone a few days before the convention.

"Some people I talk to around here seem to think you've got a chance," Charles Clark told his son from High River.

"I think I've got a chance, Dad," Clark responded.

"Well, I'd better get down there," the senior Clark said. Despite suffering from a heart condition that would take his life a few years later, Charles Clark made his way to Ottawa to watch his son make history. And just as in 1967 for the provincial campaign, Clark's mother, Grace, also attended, convinced she would have to help her son deal with the awful pain of losing.

Clark's confidence going into the convention is somewhat surprising, since few tabbed him as the likely victor (particularly after he came third on the first ballot). Nowadays, big pots of money are crucial to winning leadership conventions. But in 1976, Clark was nowhere near the biggest spender. Brian Mulroney conducted one of the most lavish operations ever. Wagner had a well-oiled financial machine. Flora MacDonald's people secured the use of a helicopter for their candidate.

In fact, Clark's people were afraid of being shown up by the MacDonald chopper. They resolved to get some air power of their own, lest they be embarrassed for running a sub-par operation. So they secured the services of a private-plane pilot who was going to take Clark and his wife, Maureen McTeer, on a southwestern Ontario swing, from Chatham to Wiarton and eventually Owen Sound, to meet delegates. The couple drove to Chatham in a blinding snowstorm and began to wait for their air escort.

"Suddenly, there was this flurry down at the end of the runway," Clark remembers. "Some novice ran his plane into a snowbank." Four guys playing poker at the airport interrupted their game long enough to help Clark and the pilot pull the plane out of the embankment.

"I didn't know how else to stop the thing," the pilot told Clark.

As for money, by the end of the campaign Clark was violating the prime directive of political campaigns, which is, don't go into personal debt—some candidates never recover. Over the last few days of the 1976 leadership, Clark was paying for the campaign's expenses with his own personal credit card. It would have been worse had the campaign not been able to rely on so many students, who sacrificed their academic years to work for free and experience the camaraderie of a leadership event; or family friends and acquaintances, who turned their homes into makeshift hotels night after night.

Clark's secret weapon during the campaign was his wife. Maureen McTeer, thirteen years her husband's junior, loved politics as much as Clark did. Her family was from eastern Ontario and organized the area with a vengeance to support Clark's leadership bid. Typically in politics, the spouse feels the slings and arrows aimed at the candidate much more acutely than the candidate, and in McTeer's case, it was literally so. In what may (or may not) have been over-exuberance on the part of a hand shaker, McTeer broke her wrist while glad-handing in a crush of delegates. As the convention neared, she was taking painkilling injections just to get through the day. (Clark says his wife has actually had this happen to her three or four times over the years. Who says politics isn't a body contact sport?)

In any event, as delegates gathered in Ottawa in February 1976 to choose a new leader, objectively speaking Clark's chances didn't appear all that promising. Compared with Wagner's and Mulroney's efforts, his campaign seemed badly underfunded. Given that the Tories were constantly getting clobbered in Quebec at election time, being a westerner hardly seemed an asset. Fellow red Tory Flora MacDonald seemed to have much of the media buzz going her way. Some PC caucus mates such as Jake Epp and Walter Baker, philo-sophically sympatico with Clark, weren't supporting him. Even his mother was convinced he was going to lose.

Except this time, he didn't. Clark placed third on the first ballot, behind the two Quebec candidates, but hung in there long enough to watch support for the top two candidates fail to take off. Clark became the compromise candidate and slid up the middle to win.

Several things had happened, some predictable, some completely bizarre, to enable Clark to win. First, enough Tories respected his aggressive style in the House of Commons and crossed their fingers that he had potential for growth. Second, supporters of the two Quebec candidates simply couldn't abide seeing the other win, thus Clark was a safe alternative. Third, this was the Progressive Conservative Party of the 1970s and too many delegates still weren't ready for a francophone leader. Fourth, newspaper columnist Paul Hellyer, one of just two candidates without a parliamentary seat (Mulroney was the other) gave a disastrous, mean-spirited speech the night before the vote. His support evaporated and much of it went to Clark. And fifth (and this one comes under the category of bizarre), York–Simcoe MP Sinclair Stevens, a right-wing conservative businessman whom everyone thought would support Wagner or Mulroney, dropped off the ballot, walked right past the boy from Baie-Comeau's box, and to everyone's astonishment (particularly Mulroney and Wagner) endorsed Clark.

The Wagner campaign team hit the roof. They had given Stevens $10,000 for his campaign expenses, plus the use of a private jet, in the not-so-subtle hope that Stevens would move to them after his campaign faltered. But Stevens was never satisfied that Wagner's economic views were conservative enough.

His next option was the other Quebec candidate.

"Mulroney had alienated a lot of people with his glitzy approach to things," Stevens told me earlier this year. "And he hadn't been in Parliament before. It was too much of a gamble to go with him. But Clark was fascinating to me."

In Clark, Stevens saw a political pro, someone who had spent much of his life in elected office or in the party organization. Stevens was comfortable with Clark's economic policies. He also thought the PC party needed to identify with Western Canada more forcefully, since the previous leader, Robert Stanfield, was a Maritimer. (Stanfield later told Stevens "Good choice," after he endorsed Clark.)

Stevens's move to Clark created a momentum that drew other candidates, including Flora MacDonald and John Fraser. Eventually, Clark won on the fourth ballot over Wagner by just 65 votes out of more than 2,300 cast.

Joe Clark was thirty-six years old and leader of the Progressive Conservative Party of Canada.

"Didn't you at any time think you were too young for the job?" I ask him.

"Yeah, I did," Clark admits. "But I had pockets of support everywhere. For example, I had a year of law at Dalhousie, and the support I got from the people who were at Dalhousie was just astounding to me. [The leadership campaign was] sort of an adventure to people of our generation."

In fact, there was a group of young Tory hotshots who couldn't wait to get back at the Trudeau government. Manitoba's Jake Epp; Ron Atkey, Flora MacDonald, Sinclair Stevens, Walter Baker, and Perrin Beatty from Ontario; John Fraser from British Columbia; and fellow Albertans Harvie Andre and Don Mazankowski were all destined to become cabinet ministers. Sean O'Sullivan, who was elected in Hamilton–Wentworth at age twenty, was still there, having not yet left politics for the priesthood. Add to the mix Newfoundland's James McGrath, and Elmer MacKay from Nova Scotia (yes, father of the current Tory leader Peter MacKay), not to forget Erik Nielsen from Yukon, and Clark was able to present a pretty effective Opposition to the country.

Clark also had another valuable tool going for him: television. In 1977, cameras were installed in the House of Commons. Where Robert Stanfield's low-key style may have been acceptable in a different time, Clark's sharper, punchier, more aggressive tone was tailor-made for sound bites on the evening news. In fact, the running joke was that Clark could declare his thoughts in thirty-second sound bites, while Stanfield often included thirty-second *pauses* in his remarks.

"When you're the first one on television and you're fairly good on the attack, you're running against the prime minister of whom people have had enough, the novelty of seeing this unpopular prime minister under attack all the time unquestionably helped me," Clark says.

However, Clark's advantages on television were offset by other deeply held concerns the public held about him. Despite his two decades of experience in politics, he was still a very young man. No Canadian had ever been elected prime minister in his thirties. Furthermore, politics—like life—is a deeply unfair business when it comes to other things the camera picks up. Millions of trees have probably died for the noble purpose of telling Canadians that Clark had too little chin, too many jowls, an awkward gait, and unusual hand gesticulations when he spoke. Trudeau may have been despised in huge pockets of the country, but he was still more comfortable in his own skin than Clark, more elegant than Clark, more mature than Clark, more of an intellect than Clark, and much better in French than Clark, despite the PC leader's perhaps unprecedented efforts for a Western Canadian politician to learn Canada's other official language.

The mass media were ruthless in the way they covered Clark. He may have spent two decades in Conservative party circles, but that didn't spare him from the "Joe Who?" headlines and jokes that pervaded newspapers and magazines.

However, Clark had more than three years to get his top three priorities in place. He wanted to bring a greater degree of unity to the Conservative party, an achievement that had eluded all his predecessors, with the possible exception of Sir John A. Macdonald. He also wanted to chip away at Trudeau's popularity by pursuing an aggressive strategy in the House and presenting the Tories as sharp on the attack and a potential government in waiting. And finally, he needed to pull together a platform to take to the country when Trudeau went back to the polls for the fourth time. He did that, in part, by convening a major policy conference in Kingston, to which many political and academic leaders were invited to speak. On all three fronts, Clark made progress.

The prime minister went deep into his third mandate—just two months short of the five full years permitted by law—before calling an election for May 22, 1979, a grand consultation with the people that the Liberals felt confident about winning.

"The Liberals so absolutely expected to win that they were taking us for granted," Clark recalls. "I remember getting on a plane once, well before the election was called, late at night in Montreal, and Jeanne Sauvé [then communications minister] was on the plane. I was back in coach and she was up in first class. And she came back to see me. And she said, 'You know, I really admire your tenacity, because everyone knows you haven't got a chance of winning. You've worked very hard. Those of us who are in government admire that tenacity.'"

Clark accepted the comments as gracefully as he could. He then showed Canadians in "Encounter '79," the leaders' debate, that he was no pushover. Seven million people watched as Trudeau tried to portray him as a lightweight who would hand over the keys of everything to the provinces to get national peace. But it didn't work. Clark held his own, except for the odd time he that he laughed at Trudeau, which in truth did not appear prime ministerial, but rather goofy.

Today, in what must have seemed an unlikely boast at the time, Clark claims he thought the '79 election would be his.

"We knew we were going to beat them," Clark says so matter-of-factly. "And we proved that Western Canadian leaders can win Ontario."

If there was disbelief among Liberals that they actually lost that 1979 election to Clark, it's somewhat understandable. They felt that the whole campaign would come down to leadership, and that when it did, the Liberals would win in a slam dunk. Their television ads screamed "A Leader Must Be a Leader." The Liberals took 40 percent of the total vote, compared to just 36 percent for the Conservatives. And yet, despite capturing half a million more votes than the PCs, the Liberals found themselves on the short end of the seat count, 114 to 136. Just as in 1972, the NDP would hold the balance of power in a minority Parliament. Just a few weeks away from his fortieth birthday, Joe Clark had become the youngest prime minister in Canadian history. John Diefenbaker joked that Canada had celebrated the Year of the Child by electing Joe Clark prime minister. Brian Mulroney, Clark's 1976 leadership rival, was a commentator on television that night. He predicted Clark would be prime minister for a good long time.

In hindsight, Clark's victory still seems improbable. But he got some unlikely help from Trudeau, who at times appeared tired and disengaged. The PM even speculated to CBC-TV reporter Mark Phillips that, if he came a close second to Clark in the seat count, he would still try to retain power. It was an ill-advised comment that seemed to confirm Canadians' darkest fears about Trudeau's arrogance.

The Tories were over the moon that they had been able to defeat Trudeau. Their Ontario organization, so ably led by Premier William Davis, came through big time, helping capture fifty-seven seats for the PCs, compared to just thirty-two for the Grits. Western Canada embraced Clark in significant fashion. In British Columbia,

Alberta, Saskatchewan, and Manitoba combined, the Liberals only won three of a possible seventy-seven seats. However, those thrilling numbers for the Tories were muted by the party's failure to penetrate fortress Quebec. The Conservatives won just two out of seventy-five seats there. Trudeau was still *le roi,* with sixty-seven seats in his home province.

Of course, for Clark and his fellow Tories, the sheer delight of defeating an icon of Canadian politics wouldn't last long. It has become fashionable, in the two decades since the PCs' 1979 upset, to excoriate Clark and his inner circle with a viciousness that borders on cruelty because of what came next. In a series of events that have been well documented over the years, Clark's government would soon be referred to as "The Blue Blip." He came into office pledging to govern as though he had a majority, so sure was Clark that the public would warm to his agenda and had grown weary of Trudeau, who had announced his retirement from politics. That may have sounded arrogant, but Dalton Camp called it a miscalculation of innocence rather than arrogance.

"How long did you think you'd be prime minister for?" I ask Clark today in his Centre Block office.

"We thought it would last longer than ten months," he says, "but we anticipated that it would not be a full term. That was part of the reason that we were so determined to get on with what we had promised."

Ironically, whatever shine there was on Clark's government began to tarnish rather quickly precisely because of one very prominent promise he didn't keep. In an effort to attract votes from the Jewish community in two midtown Toronto ridings (Eglinton and St. Paul's), Clark vowed to move Canada's Israeli embassy from Tel Aviv to Jerusalem.

It was a commitment made in haste. Arab nations threatened to boycott Canada. Forecasters estimated the country would lose tens of thousands of jobs. U.S. President Jimmy Carter had made the same promise, but let it slide. Eventually Clark would do the same, alienating the very community whose votes he had hoped to secure. Interestingly, Eglinton riding (now called Eglinton–Lawrence) has not sent a Tory MP to Ottawa since Clark's embassy about-face. St. Paul's has voted Liberal four times in the six elections since.

However, first and foremost, Clark had promised to bring some fiscal sanity to the way the federal government was spending money. Nowadays, Canadians are accustomed to seeing balanced budgets, even big surpluses. When John Manley delivered the budget address in February 2003, it was the sixth consecutive balanced budget from a Canadian government.

In 1979, though, balancing the budget was still seen as an impossible pipe dream. Clark and his finance minister, John Crosbie, were clear that some deficit financing would continue because the Canadian economy was so sluggish, but they planned to try to get closer to realizing that dream of eliminating the deficit with a tough budget, featuring both the carrot (mortgage deductibility) and the stick (a whopping gas tax increase).

"All of those things that had been key parts of the campaign, we moved up," Clark says. "We wanted to demonstrate ourselves as a government that kept its word."

Clark also demonstrated a willingness to go the extra mile to gain support in Quebec, where he had earned only 13.5 percent of the vote in 1979. He insisted on simultaneous translation for all cabinet and treasury board meetings, even though just one of his ministers (Roch La Salle) spoke French as his first language. All ministers, even unilingual anglophones, were urged to drop a few words of French into their speeches in hopes of getting some coverage from the Quebec media.

At one point during his prime ministership, a Supreme Court vacancy presented itself. The appointment had to come from

Quebec. The federal Justice Department, as it always had, sent a list to Clark with three potential candidates on it. Clark then did something unprecedented. He telephoned the premier of Quebec.

"I want to know," Clark asked René Lévesque "if there is any one of them who is unacceptable to the government of Quebec."

"Why are you calling me?" Lévesque responded.

"You're the premier of Quebec," Clark answered.

"No one's ever called the premier of Quebec on these matters before," a surprised Lévesque said.

"Well, I am," Clark said. "It's my appointment, but it's a judge from your province."

Lévesque asked for a day to think about it. The next morning, he called Clark back with the news that he had consulted his ministers, and the government of Quebec had no objection to any of the names on the list. Soon after, in September 1979, Julien Chouinard was appointed to the Supreme Court of Canada, where he remained until his death in 1987.

It would be more than ten years—1990—before the Meech Lake Accord included a provision requiring that the prime minister consult with a province's premier in appointing judges from that province. Clark was already doing it.

"Things had become so tense in the country, that simple actions went a long way towards what we later came to call reconciliation," Clark now says. "I think we could have put most of the divisions of the 1980s behind us."

It's an intriguing observation. What if the constitutional wars of the 1980s, what if the showdowns between Trudeau and Lévesque, had been avoided? Skeptics will say Lévesque was playing Clark like a fiddle, setting him up for a future confrontation in which the federal government, not the separatist one, is bested. Maybe.

"Another way of looking at it is that the fact that we lost allowed the sort of footloose government to come in and do things that in our more sober moments I don't think we would have tried," he says.

Tory supporters may bemoan the what-might-have-beens. But the reality was, the Liberals skilfully portrayed the Clark government as, among other things, out of touch with the needs of Ontario and Quebec motorists, millions of whom were about to get whacked in the pocketbook. It didn't hurt Grit fortunes that Bill Davis's Ontario machine, which had been so helpful to Clark in 1979, was predictably not very enamoured with an eighteen-cent-per-gallon gas tax. So the Opposition orchestrated a non-confidence vote on the Crosbie budget, the Tories weren't prepared for it, and with that, the Clark government died on December 13, 1979.

"The regret I have today is that we were not more savvy on the budget vote," Clark admits. If the Tories were confused, it was perhaps understandable. They saw a leaderless Liberal Party bringing down a nascent government, which overestimated its popularity in the country. There were also more than a dozen Liberal MPs who wouldn't qualify for parliamentary pensions if they went back to the polls and lost. Would they risk losing the cash-for-life lottery by pulling the plug on Clark's government?

Apparently, yes.

"We were all too optimistic about how the Liberals were organized," Clark says.

THEY DON'T CALL the Liberals the natural governing party for nothing. Backroom boys Keith Davey and Jim Coutts dragged Trudeau out of retirement. The rematch was set for February 18, 1980, and it didn't go well for Clark. Four percent of the votes shifted from the Tories to the Liberals, and that was all it took to bring Trudeau back to power with a majority government. As impossible as this sounds, Clark's Tories did even worse in Quebec, despite his efforts to reach out to that province. The PCs lost half their Quebec caucus. They went from two seats to just one (Roch La Salle won Joliette by 389 votes; Heward Grafftey lost the only other PC seat, Brome–Missisquoi, by more than 4,600 votes). The Ontario vote was the complete opposite of 1979 (Liberals fifty-two, PCs thirty-eight seats).

Even with the majority, the Liberals had to be somewhat disappointed because the election results demonstrated just how badly split the country was. Trudeau managed to win just two seats west of Ontario, and they were both in Manitoba. He was shut out of Saskatchewan, shut out of Alberta, and shut out of British Columbia. If Clark had hoped to bring reconciliation to the country, Trudeau's win cemented serious regional cleavages from which the country has yet to recover. However, after less than a year, Joe Clark was Opposition leader again, and in many respects was seen as damaged goods by the electorate and his party. He was now the youngest ex-prime minister in Canadian history.

Today, Clark sits pensively as he considers the reasons why too many Canadians were disinclined to endorse the results of the 1979 election. Many theories have been put forward by pundits over the years. Here's a new one that Clark thinks deserves some consideration.

"I think that it is almost impossible to become prime minister if you spend a long time in opposition," he says. "There's a fundamental division in the roles. Half of the role is to find fault, and it becomes the defining half of the role that can get you onto the news at night. And yet when people turn to a party for office, they look for someone who will be more than a critic. And the 'opposition versus alternative' dilemma is profound."

The next three years of Clark's political career were as vicious as anything any party leader has had to endure. Think of what Stockwell Day went through in 2001 and multiply it by a factor of twenty. No matter what he did, Clark simply could not overcome the image he had among too many of his fellow Tories that he was a loser, that he had been given a once-in-a-lifetime chance to govern in 1979 and simply blown it. Conservatives gathered in Winnipeg in January 1983 to render their verdict on Clark's leadership and, according to Clark himself, he was found wanting. True, 66.9 percent of delegates endorsed his leadership, but Clark feared that wasn't enough and the internecine warfare would continue (and the Liberals would exploit it) unless he did something dramatic. And so he did.

"I was mad. I was really angry at that vote," Clark says. "I also felt that various forces were less than straightforward in what they were doing."

After the results were made public, Clark huddled with some close advisers to consider his next move. His former cabinet colleague Sinclair Stevens spent half an hour with him trying to convince him not to step down.

"Championship boxers in the ring don't voluntarily throw their belt away," Stevens told him. "If you really want to be the leader, take them on. In anybody's book, [66.9 percent] is a substantial mandate."

But Clark's mind was made up. He'd set a target of support he was determined to hit and even though he'd just missed it, it was enough, he believed, to force his hand.

He quit the leadership, calling a convention for June 1983 in Ottawa, where Tories could, once and for all, make up their minds. If party members chose Clark again, his critics would finally have to shut up. If they didn't choose him, they would have no reason to keep their knives out.

Politics is often more formally described as political science. That's a completely inappropriate description. Politics is an art, and Clark knew it heading into the convention.

"This is not about science," he says. "You have a sense about what your party is going to do or not, and my sense was that after the vote in Winnipeg, my party had sort of stood with me because it felt it *had* to." Clark clearly wanted more. He wanted party members behind him because he hoped they believed in him. Problem was, they didn't.

Shortly after the Winnipeg vote, Clark met late one night at his Opposition leader's residence with some of his closest caucus supporters, such as Jake Epp, Perrin Beatty, Don Mazankowski, and Sinc Stevens. They tried to convince him at least to hang on to the Opposition leader's job in Parliament. But Clark wouldn't hear of it. He feared it would look as if he were going back on his word. He had put his job on the line and he was determined to recapture it with no strings attached.

In some sense, that may have been a turning point in Clark's fortunes. Stevens and Epp shared a taxi back to the Hôtel Château Laurier.

"Jake, I've done all that could be expected of me," Stevens told his fellow MP. "If he's determined to do this, then I'm a free agent." Stevens became the first cabinet minister from The Blue Blip to leave Clark and endorse Mulroney, a move that may have breathed a little life into Mulroney's campaign and similarly damaged Clark's.

During the run-up to the convention, the cable-TV magnate Ted Rogers held a fundraiser, at his Forest Hill home in Toronto, for Clark. I watched Clark at that event and couldn't help but note the irony of how he worked the room. He was absolutely on his game. He knew every issue cold. He was charming. He was funny. He wasn't at all the awkward, goofy caricature the media had made him out to be. Tories chose him to be their leader when he was raw and young and in truth not quite ready for the job. Now, in 1983, he was so much more qualified to be prime minister, but too many Conservatives had written him off. He wouldn't get the chance.

"I bore in mind that I had also had the extraordinary privilege of that sharp, sharp learning curve that not many people have had the chance to try once," he says.

The June 1983 convention was one of the most thrilling in Canadian history. Clark led on every ballot except the one that counted. He took a slim twenty-two-vote lead over Mulroney onto the fourth ballot.

"We thought we could win the leadership convention right up until we lost," Clark says. Mulroney won comfortably, by 259 votes.

In my many encounters with Joe Clark over the years, I have asked him to talk about his very complicated relationship with the man who not only defeated him in June 1983, but whose supporters had worked very hard to undermine his leadership before that. Much to my dismay, Clark has never indulged in any bitter or spiteful comments about Mulroney, on or off the record. He has been unfailingly classy in refusing to settle whatever scores he must have with Mulroney and his minions. I bumped into Clark on the floor of the Ottawa convention. He was taking an impromptu walk toward Mulroney's section of the arena after the fourth-ballot voting had taken place, but before the results had been announced. It was clear to everyone in the hall that even though he was in second place, Mulroney was about to win. John Crosbie was dropping off the ballot, and his delegates (everyone surmised) were going to break overwhelmingly for Mulroney (which they did).

"Are you coming to concede?" I asked Clark.

"No, not at all," he said to me amid a crush of supporters. "I want to tell Brian that whoever wins this ballot, this party must come together and support its leader."

And Clark did just that. When Mulroney's name was uttered by Clark during his concession speech, some of the outgoing leader's staunchest supporters began to boo. Clark cut it off right away. Mulroney, his occasional friend and more frequent rival for two decades, had just taken the job Clark loved and believed in his bones he was most qualified to have. And Clark cut it off. He knew first-hand what the failure to support the party's leader could lead to.

A chant started to rise up from the crowd. "U-ni-ty! U-ni-ty! U-ni-ty!" Tories have preached that before. Except this time, it sounded as if they finally meant it. And despite his pain, Clark was going to ensure it happened.

"I won't pretend that losing . . . losing was very hard. Losing the convention was very hard. The year before was tough. It wasn't fun then."

Clark would learn the hard way about the cumulative effect of so many political blows. After the convention, Clark and McTeer went on vacation for the remainder of June, all of July, and some of August. When they returned to Ottawa, the former leader started having trouble breathing.

"And I remember gasping, telling my doctor I couldn't breathe," Clark recalls.

"If you can't breathe, how are you talking to me?" his doctor responded. "There's nothing wrong with you. It's trauma."

"Come on," Clark said in disbelief, "my trauma was six or seven weeks ago."

"Sometimes it takes that long," the doctor insisted.

Clark spent another week gasping for breath. Eventually, the condition just went away.

I'm hoping that nearly twenty years after that dramatic afternoon in an Ottawa hockey arena, Joe Clark will be more forthcoming about his relationship with the man who defeated him. And he is.

He starts by telling me that he's not sure how deeply involved Mulroney was in his demise. He says it like a man who doesn't want to know.

"There were forces working at my leadership that Brian and his supporters might have encouraged, but they were there well before he came along," he says, referring to the hard right wing of the party. "They were particularly unforgiving after the defeat in 1980, and Brian and Brian's people took advantage of it. I can't hold it against him for being alert, or too sensitive, about his taking advantage of that. He had ambition of his own.

"So it was only personal, and in public life you just have to get over that."

For his part, Mulroney told me in an interview in 2001 that he's innocent of the allegations journalists have made against him in relation to Clark's demise. While Clark was in Winnipeg taking the temperature of the party, Mulroney says he was in Florida, going over plans to close down the Iron Ore Company of Canada's mines in Schefferville, Quebec—in Mulroney's view, that would have been an odd activity for someone who was planning to start mining for votes. It's also worth noting that newspaper baron Conrad Black, in his book *A Life in Progress,* wrote that while he was in Florida, Mulroney visited him and the two did discuss the PC leadership, and whether Black could convince his well-heeled Toronto friends (for example, the Bassetts, the Eatons, and Hal Jackman) to leave Clark and support him. However, even Clark acknowledges that his Winnipeg showing would have been better had Bill Davis's Ontario organization gone to bat for him (although the premier himself publicly endorsed Clark's leadership).

"Whatever was being done by Brian or people working with him, was being done very skilfully," Clark says. "There weren't many smoking guns."

And how is Clark's relationship with Mulroney today, twenty years after their leadership rematch in Ottawa?

"We will never be fully frank with one another," Clark admits. "There will always be a guardedness to our relations."

With Clark now determined not to do a Diefenbaker and, instead, play the loyal second in command, the Conservatives got their act together as never before. Mulroney also had two things going for him that Clark never did. First, because Mulroney took over the party when he did, his time as Opposition leader was relatively brief. And second, Canadians were thoroughly disgusted with the Liberals by the time the 1984 general election came around, partly out of exhaustion with Pierre Trudeau, and partly because his replacement, John Turner, was so stunningly ineffective.

In hindsight, the Clark-to-Mulroney transition went surprisingly smoothly. The potential for hurt feelings and bruised egos took a back seat to the need for Tories to present (finally) a unified, coherent force ready to govern.

There were, however, some glitches along the way. In the 1984 election, Mulroney ran in his home province. But he first got into the House just two months after winning the convention by taking a by-election in Central Nova, a riding temporarily vacated by Elmer MacKay. The new leader and the former leader were campaigning together in Nova Scotia when one of those awkward moments happened.

"The leader sits on the right-hand side of the driver," Clark says, referring to standard protocol. "We both made for that spot. And he sort of looked at me and I looked at him and I realized, oops, I sit on the other side of the car. So I went around. But we got over those and in good humour." Mulroney also contributed to the fence mending by giving Clark's caucus supporters prominent roles to play; for example, Clark's deputy leader, Erik Nielsen, would assume the same role under Mulroney.

"So we both worked at it," Clark says.

Having said that, he reveals that an exit strategy was presented to him, in case things didn't work out.

"I was approached by two or three people who very sincerely said, 'Look, we understand that if you wanted to do something else, here are some opportunities you might want to pursue,'" Clark says.

But Clark, as we know, wasn't finished with politics. "There were things I still wanted to do," he says. "I thought there were things that I could do and I was reasonably sure that I would have an opportunity to do them. And I got them."

But before he got them, Clark's ego would have to sustain another series of blows. When John Turner called the election for September 4, 1984, the Conservative campaign strategists did have one unusual problem: what to do with Joe Clark. Yes, he was a former prime minister and had a huge hand in bringing the party together after the 1983 leadership convention, and as such, should merit a high profile role during the election campaign. However, too many Conservatives still saw Clark as the guy who blew their last chance at power. They wanted to give him a respectable role, but didn't want him featured in any way. Brian Mulroney was now the guy. He looked and acted like a winner and, most important, had no association with the 1980 defeat.

So Joe Clark spent that entire 1984 campaign in the remotest parts of Canada. The only cameras near him would have been those owned by tourists snapping souvenir shots with their pocket cameras. He was never once in Toronto. Perhaps predictably, Clark has a charitable interpretation of his role in the campaign.

"I campaigned in the rural areas. But it was in the rural areas where the suspicions about Brian were within our party," says Clark, who tried to convince people that, even if they saw Mulroney as too Montreal, too French, and too slick, not to worry. "I work with him. I know him. Trust me," he told them. "And so it worked."

Did it ever. With a new leader, a new spirit of unity, and a poorly executed campaign by John Turner, the PCs romped to victory in the 1984 election, electing 211 MPs, the most ever. Was there even a tiny part of Joe Clark on election night that thought, if only I'd won the leadership contest the year before, this could have been my victory? That the Liberals were so inept, even I could have led the party to this? Apparently not.

"I knew that couldn't be," Clark says. "I wouldn't have won that many seats. I got that out of my system." In fact, it was just the second time since 1887 that the PCs had won a majority of the seats in Quebec (1958 was the other), a feat that unquestionably couldn't have been accomplished without Mulroney at the helm.

If Clark was at all jealous that Mulroney was able to accomplish what had eluded him, he kept it to himself. He continued to play the role of a loyal soldier. And to his credit, Mulroney enabled Clark to enjoy a successful second act in politics, something most politicians never get. Clark served as external affairs minister for almost seven years, but his most significant achievements didn't come in that portfolio. Every time there was a big development on the international stage (international trade agreements, the end of apartheid in South Africa, or attaining membership in the Organization of American States or La Francophonie), it was the prime minister's fingerprints that were all over the file, as opposed to his foreign minister's.

No, if Canadians now hold a soft spot for Joe Clark, it's because of what happened in his next job. When the Meech Lake Accord failed in 1990, Mulroney was smart enough to realize he was the wrong man to lead the next effort at constitutional peace. So he tabbed Clark to be his constitutional affairs minister. If not loved, Clark was at least widely respected by Canadians for how he had handled the leadership transition. If, albeit after two majority government victories, Mulroney was now despised for such moves as over-presidentializing the prime ministership, Clark was seen as quite the opposite—a modest, trustworthy fellow who had demonstrated time and again the skill of keeping his ego in check.

So Clark spent two years crossing the country, and actually achieved the impossible: the first unanimous agreement among the federal, provincial, and territorial governments, and First Nations groups. It was called the Charlottetown Accord and it's not overstating matters to say that Clark may have been the only person in the country who could have pulled it together. And again, to Mulroney's credit, the prime minister must have known how damaged his standing in the public's mind was, because he let Clark run with that ball, even when he vehemently disagreed with him.

"He and I had had very sharp divisions in a couple of matters that fell within my jurisdiction, when I was a minister in his government," Clark now reveals. "And he could have stopped me. He's prime minister."

But Mulroney didn't.

"And I think that was not just an attempt on his part to avoid strain in the family," Clark figures. "I think he thought that I had sort of earned the right to do this. I think he allowed that I might know more about this than he did."

Canadians would also have their say on Charlottetown. A national referendum would take place on October 26, 1992, but the bar for success was set very high. Each province would hold its own vote and it would take just one province's turning thumbs-down to kill the accord. The first ministers gambled that the public was weary of constitutional wrangling and so, even if they didn't love the agreement, they would at least hold their noses and vote for it, if only to put the whole bloody issue behind the country.

No such luck. In one of the most confusing episodes in Canadian history, former prime minister Pierre Trudeau and Reform Party leader Preston Manning—who surely disagreed on virtually every other aspect of public policy—both campaigned hard against Charlottetown. In the end, it made no difference that the accord had the support of thirteen governments (the feds, the provinces, and the territories), two national opposition leaders (the Liberals' Jean Chrétien and the NDP's Audrey McLaughlin), and most of the business and cultural elites of the country. Mulroney was poison and voting no to Charlottetown became a way of sticking it to a thoroughly unpopular prime minister. In total, 54 percent of Canadians voted no. Only three Atlantic provinces (Newfoundland, Prince Edward Island, and New Brunswick), the Northwest Territories, and Ontario voted yes.

Forget Winnipeg in January 1983. Forget Ottawa in June 1983. The rejection of Charlottetown was the absolute lowest moment of Joe Clark's life in politics.

"It was the toughest loss I've ever experienced," Clark begins. "I really thought it was dangerous for the country. I *still* think it's dangerous for the country."

Clark has spent much time considering how the agreement fell off the rails.

"The strength of Charlottetown had been that real people, albeit people with titles, sat down and worked out a solution that made sense to them, piece by piece, item by item. And the public saw them do it. We should have run on that. Instead, we ran on an ad campaign. We turned it over to the advertisers. And I think that was significant. The public trusted the process. They saw it. They believed in it. And maybe, there may be some ego in this, but they saw me as the lead guy."

It's the one time in our lengthy conversation where Clark is close to tooting his own horn.

A year later, in 1993, Clark retired from politics. Perhaps he saw the writing on Kim Campbell's wall: the Tories were about to be slaughtered. More likely, he had just had enough. Many of the characters he had entered politics with more than two decades earlier were either going (Don Mazankowski, Elmer MacKay, Michael Wilson, Jake Epp, John Fraser, Harvie Andre, Stan Darling, Otto Jelinek) or already gone (Flora MacDonald, Sinc Stevens, Jim

Gillies, Sean O'Sullivan, Ron Atkey, Jack Murta, Walter Baker, Stanley Schellenberger).

So Clark left basically the only life he had known. He signed on as visiting scholar in the department of Canadian studies at the University of California at Berkeley. He and Maureen founded Joe Clark and Associates, an international business consulting firm in Calgary. And he chaired the boards of a couple of companies: SMG Canada, which operates trade and convention centres; and CANOP International Resource Ventures Inc., an Alberta-based oil and gas company.

But Clark found he just couldn't stay away. Approaching age sixty, and with another vacancy in the PC leadership thanks to Jean Charest's departure, Clark recaptured the party's top job in a one member–one vote system containing none of the drama of his previous two leadership experiences. For some, it was an inexplicable return to public life. After all, the Conservatives were still in fifth place in the House of Commons and, if not dead, then at least on life support. But Clark is one of those people who just don't burn for the art of the deal in the private sector. He's a public service and public policy guy through and through.

For some strange reason, despite a wealth of experience, there was one aspect of life where Clark continued to demonstrate little aptitude—interpersonal skills. Traditionally, after every leadership battle, the winner is supposed to call the runner-up to assure the second-place finisher he or she still has an important role to play in the party. But after Clark recaptured the leadership in 1998, he never once reached out to Hugh Segal, his most serious challenger. He never congratulated him on his campaign. He never urged him to find a riding and run for the PCs in the following election. In fact, he seemed to have more kind things to say about leadership candidate David Orchard, the Saskatchewan farmer who was (and still is) a thorn in the side to traditional Tories.

"Clark seems to have a lack of communication skill on a personal level," his old friend Sinclair Stevens says. "It was one of Mulroney's great strengths, but Clark seemed to have an aversion to phoning people." Numerous Tories have offered the same observation.

Nevertheless, Clark was back. And given how unpredictable Canadian politics has been over the past quarter-century, it wasn't completely ridiculous for him to hope for a return to the prime minister's job. Poll after poll showed how much Canadians respected and admired Clark's contributions to public life. But when the tallies were added up on election night, November 27, 2000, Clark's Tories were still in fifth place, barely hanging on to Official party status. They had won 12 out of 301 seats, garnering only half as many votes as the Canadian Alliance, and essentially were reduced to a rump in the Atlantic provinces. Miraculously, Clark won his own seat in Calgary Centre by more than 4,000 votes. It was the fourth different riding he had won during his career.

It would also be his last. In August 2002, Clark confirmed the third act of his political life would soon be coming to an end. The mix of events that propelled him to the country's top political job in 1979 would, he now knew, never happen again.

Why do Canadians admire Joe Clark, but were simply not prepared to return him to the Prime Minister's Office?

"Part of it is generational," Clark theorizes. "And I don't mean simply age. I think that the wellsprings of the respect are in terrain the country has . . . passed by. [Voters] are not sure that I am going to be as pertinent to new challenges that the country is facing.

"I think your frames of reference matter a great deal," he adds. "Political leaders who aren't sports fans and have to be coached as to who a quarterback is and what a spitter is . . . there is a lot about the modern world on which I have to be coached."

That's a pretty candid admission and it won't be his last during our conversation. In the next breath, Clark inadvertently confirms his unease at having to be in touch with popular culture. He speculates that Paul Martin may experience similar problems. "People will brief him on the latest development in the IMF, but they won't tell him who Nelly Furtado is," he says, mispronouncing the surname of one of Canada's hottest young singers (he calls her Fur-TAY-do). As Clark thinks of another example of what he's talking about—former U.S. president George Bush, the elder, reacting to a supermarket checkout scanner as though it were technology beyond anything he had ever imagined—he catches himself.

"Fur-TAH-do," he says, pronouncing it properly this time.

"The respect for me is in areas that people think are probably important but not fundamental to their lives," Clark continues, citing his strong performances in Parliament and keeping the government accountable. "They think I'm good at it, but they are not sure that I am going to be able to determine the most effective industrial strategy for the world that they are operating in."

"Does that gnaw at you?" I ask.

"Sure," he admits. "But against all of that, whatever the frustrations in all of this, it is worth it. Because you can't help but look at the people whose lives we've brushed, people of great talent and ambition and aspirations. They have at least as many frustrations as I do. They are not as widely celebrated. But they are often more corrosive. And they have very little sense of satisfaction, or if they have it now, it's the sort of thing that will not be as sustaining to them ten years from now, as they sit down to enjoy the view of their life's work."

It's true, Joe Clark never made it back to the top of the mountain. But he did get there, which is a considerable feat, considering only twenty Canadians have done it. And his tenure is by no means the shortest (Sir Charles Tupper gets that dubious distinction, at two months and seven days in 1896).

"Being prime minister requires something special," says Donald S. Macdonald, the former Liberal cabinet minister who might have fought the 1980 election as Liberal leader against Clark, if not for Pierre Trudeau's decision to come back for one more go.

"Particularly when you know what they go through. It goes beyond rational explanation. It's a sense of personal ambition, not ability, that I'm talking about. Joe Clark, Jean Chrétien, Brian Mulroney—they'd all think less of themselves had they not become prime minister."

Mountaineer Ed Viesturs said it right—getting down from the summit in one piece is actually more important in the long run than reaching the summit. And if anyone in Canadian public life can legitimately claim to have descended the mountain with his or her life and dignity reasonably intact, it's Charles Joseph Clark.

# THE MEDIA

Our liberty depends on freedom of the press,
and that cannot be limited without being lost.
—*Thomas Jefferson*

Four hostile newspapers are more to be feared
than a thousand bayonets.
—*Napoleon Bonaparte*

I believe in equality for everyone,
except reporters and photographers.
—*Mahatma Gandhi*

THERE IS NO EXPERIENCE in any other profession that can
compare to being a politician in the crosshairs of today's mass
media. I have never subscribed to the conspiracy theory that depicts
packs of reporters sitting in dark rooms, sharpening their fangs,
deciding which public figures they'll search out and destroy this
week. It simply doesn't happen. Having said that, something
perverse often does happen to a group of journalists and the prey
they zero in on, particularly during scrums—those occasionally
frightening and spontaneous encounters in which a single politician
is surrounded by dozens of cameras, microphones, notebooks, tape
recorders, and the machine-gun-like rat-a-tat-tat of question after
question after question. Reporters become emboldened. Their

interrogation can get downright vicious. The poor slob in the middle of this pas de deux (more like pas de trente-cinq) starts to perspire. Fear sets in. It can get ugly.

There isn't a politician anywhere in this country—from the prime minister to the proverbial dog catcher—who doesn't love a vigorous free press when it's offering praise by the truckful of newsprint. But when the press turns on you—and it's really something to behold—there truly aren't enough prisons to accommodate the journalists that our politicians think ought to be locked up.

Some politicians have had such extraordinarily bad experiences with the media feeding frenzy that I need merely list their names and their stories instantly come to mind. Richard Nixon. Gary Hart. Dan Quayle. Bill Clinton. The Canadian media may not be as salacious as our American cousins. But don't try telling that to Stockwell Day. Or Joe Clark. Or Kim Campbell. Or former British Columbia leaders Glen Clark and Bill Vander Zalm, both of whom had their premierships cut short by media-fed brouhahas, both of which ultimately turned out to be a lot less scandalous than they seemed at first blush.

In an earlier chapter, former Conservative cabinet minister Paul Dick spoke of coming to work on Parliament Hill every day in 1991, knowing reporters would be waiting to grill him about his marital meltdown. He and the press gallery joined a mutual detestation society.

"I am not very comfortable with the press, frankly, because the press, I don't think, has any understanding, compassion or feeling," Dick now says. "They love chewing you up and spitting out politicians, because they know they'll have a fresh one next year anyhow. The press loves confrontation and controversy."

Much of the time, the media set their sights on a politician because of some policy or issue that's going badly. Think of Bob Rae when the Ontario economy went south in the early 1990s.

Sometimes they descend on you because you've said something particularly stupid. Liberal MP Carolyn Parrish's comments in 2003 about the "damn Americans, I hate those bastards," would fall into this category. Then there are those occasions when your personal life becomes news. Witness Paul Dick's circumstances.

As onerous as these incidents with the media no doubt were, I believe they can't compare to the ordeal of one woman from Burlington, Ontario, who ran for elective office and experienced something unlike anything I'd ever seen before or since.

THE FIRST TIME I met Priscilla de Villiers, I now confess I was feeling something I almost never sense before an interview. I was nervous. She wasn't a president or prime minister. She wasn't heading up a Fortune 500 company. She wasn't some movie actress I'd secretly had a crush on for years. No, she was simply a woman who had endured something no mother should ever have to, and I was interviewing her for a television broadcast.

Her beautiful nineteen-year-old daughter had been brutally murdered by a man who was a dangerous offender out on bail.

De Villiers's daughter, Nina, had coincidentally attended the same school in Hamilton that I had, although many years later. I had arranged an appointment with De Villiers to discuss her work for CAVEAT, the acronym for Canadians Against Violence Everywhere Advocating its Termination. It was a group she helped establish to constructively channel her deeply felt determination that no other family should experience what hers had.

Born in South Africa, De Villiers and her family came to Canada, where, in her own words, she spent ten years ignoring the outside world and living a lovely life in Burlington, about forty-five minutes west of Toronto. "But, when an angry man came in and destroyed my family and took away my daughter, I couldn't ignore what was around me any more," she says, thus her efforts leading to CAVEAT.

The justice system in Canada had broken down with appalling consequences for this wonderfully talented family. (Nina's father, Rocco, is a prominent neurosurgeon, perhaps best known for successfully operating on Wayne Gretzky's father, Walter, after a stroke nearly killed him; her brother, Étienne, has attended three different universities, studying biomedical engineering and intellectual property law.)

I was concerned upon meeting De Villiers. I was sure the interview would go well—that wasn't the issue. She had a powerful message to deliver and I was pleased to be the vehicle through which hundreds of thousands of viewers would see and hear that message. However, with every taping, before the interview actually starts there are several minutes for the interviewer and the guest to engage in usually harmless (and occasionally mindless) chit-chat, while the technical crew set up the lights, cameras, microphones, and so on. Part of my job at that point is to make the interviewee more comfortable, because all of the technical requirements in a television interview ironically do exactly the opposite. My concern at that moment: how do you make small talk with someone whose every facial gesture or utterance is screaming "I'm in pain."

As we got to talking, De Villiers told me she hadn't experienced a single happy moment since Nina was murdered, and didn't expect to for the rest of her life. All of our hearts went out to this woman, who exhibited remarkable calm and dignity despite her horrible situation.

Eventually, the interview got under way, and at some point it occurred to me that Priscilla de Villiers would have a lot to contribute to public life. She had forced herself to become an expert on all of the intricacies of the justice system, particularly where she believed the balance between victims' rights and the rights of the accused had gone disturbingly out of whack. Her work with CAVEAT had taken her into schools, youth centres, mental health facilities, not to mention the corridors of power, giving her a broad range of experiences and knowledge.

Our interview complete, I left CAVEAT headquarters wondering how long it would take before De Villiers got frustrated with trying to influence decision makers from the outside looking in, rather than as a member of a government with more frequent access to cabinet ministers or first ministers.

I thought De Villiers would be a natural for politics, because there have been many people whose experience with a personal tragedy led them into public life. The theory is simple: I can do more about gun control, parole violations, or toughening sentences if I'm at the table where those issues are debated and the decisions are made.

Ida Ballasiotes found the best place to turn anger into action was in the Washington State Legislature, where she became a representative in 1988. Much like the De Villiers case, her daughter was stalked and murdered by a sex offender on a work-release program. And Carolyn McCarthy became a politician in 1996 after a crazed gunman killed her husband and nearly her son as well, on the Long Island Railroad. She found she could have a real influence on the gun control debate as a United States representative in Congress. In Canada, Chuck Cadman's sixteen-year-old son Jesse was killed in a random, unprovoked attack by a group of older teenagers in Surrey, British Columbia, not long after the murder of Nina de Villiers. Cadman ran for Parliament and won election for the Reform party in British Columbia. In 2003 he was still in Parliament, as the Canadian Alliance MP for Surrey North.

Surprisingly, however, De Villiers had never considered a run for office. She had worked in CAVEAT for almost ten years before anyone seriously approached her to consider it, and even then, she didn't exactly jump at the chance. She looked back at the real progress she had been a part of with CAVEAT—making victims' rights an essential part of the justice system—and thought about whether she could do more if she took her crusade to the next level. Ten years earlier, victims' rights were an afterthought. Now, every province in the country had a victims' bill of rights. Could she accomplish even more?

After six weeks of tossing around the idea, Priscilla de Villiers decided to go for it. When a by-election was called for September 2000 in the riding encompassing part of her own home community, she sought and won the Ontario Progressive Conservative nomination for Ancaster–Dundas–Flamborough–Aldershot (ADFA), a suburban/rural riding outside Hamilton.

What De Villiers experienced next is a classic cautionary tale of why sensible people avoid politics like the plague. She had never minded confrontation, intense debate, or rejection. She had experienced plenty of it with CAVEAT.

"But I didn't realize it would get so personal," De Villiers now admits. And the media reported every gory detail.

Despite her lengthy track record at CAVEAT of defending those victimized by the justice system, she was mercilessly attacked by some of her more ruthless opponents. The mayor of Dundas, a fixture on the local scene but clearly not the brightest bulb on the tree, accused her of exploiting her daughter's death for political gain. When De Villiers read those words in a headline in her local newspaper, *The Hamilton Spectator,* she broke down. Even as we discuss the incident two years later, she can't hold back the tears.

"He really hit a nerve there," she says. "I was devastated."

De Villiers doesn't need to, but she apologizes for crying during our conversation. "It's coming up to the anniversary of Nina's death," she points out, "and that's always a tough time of year."

Furthermore, De Villiers found herself caught up in a maelstrom of events not of her making. Even though Mike Harris's Conservatives had won their second consecutive majority government less than a year earlier, the Tories were constantly on the defensive during the campaign because of a white-hot local issue: municipal amalgamation. The previous member of the riding had quit the Harris government to protest what, in his view, was a broken promise to not force Hamilton's suburbs into a new super-city. Local residents were looking for a Tory to lash out at, and Priscilla de Villiers became the target.

On by-election night, De Villiers learned first-hand about the dark side of public life. She lost by almost ten thousand votes to the Liberal candidate, who ran the perfect "we'll-show-those-bastards-at-Queen's-Park-they-can't-jam-a-super-city-down-our-throats" kind of campaign. The winner, Ted McMeekin, was well positioned to run that campaign. He was the popular mayor of one of those smaller municipalities that was being swallowed up in the new Hamilton super-city.

WHAT LESSONS ARE there in Priscilla de Villiers's story? Sadly, the first lesson appears to be that politics is definitely a game for professionals. Rookies, beware.

"It's not a game for amateurs, yet every amateur thinks he can play," says Tim Murphy, a top adviser to Paul Martin.

"I admit I'm a contentious figure," De Villiers says, "and I left myself open to damaging criticisms. Where politics is okay is where you're a bland personality. My work was diminished in the political arena."

De Villiers doesn't intend to sound condescending when she says "bland" works. (Students of political history may well recall that former Ontario premier William Davis lived by those words.) She merely states a truism for the way the media cover election campaigns. She was well known. Her daughter's murder and the ensuing inquest ensured that. Deeply personal details of her private life were now public because of media interest in her daughter's tragic demise. When she refused to share the few remaining details of her private life, such as the fact that she and her husband were separated—questions to which no other candidates were subjected—she was accused of being cold and uncommunicative.

"I should never have allowed anyone to know that they had drawn blood," De Villiers now says. "But it took me by surprise when I was tired and being beaten up every day. I was a rookie indeed."

Timing is also key in politics. A decade of fighting for victims of crime will not win out over a less urgent but more timely issue. "I thought amalgamation was a done deal," says De Villiers, whose forecast has turned out to be right. "I'd lived in Aldershot for eighteen years and thought I could be a strong voice for my riding at the table."

In case we needed reminding, the ADFA by-election demonstrated how vicious and ugly politics can get when it's winner take all. And it all takes place in the eye of a media hurricane.

If it seems that the media take great delight in destroying public figures from time to time, rest assured they can take as much pleasure in doing the opposite. They had a field day with Joe Clark in the late 1970s and early 1980s. But Clark, through dogged persistence and longevity, won back much of the media's respect. He may not have returned to 24 Sussex Drive, his ultimate goal. But through his work to find constitutional peace during the early 1990s, and his return to the PC leadership in the late 1990s, he forced conventional media opinion to re-evaluate his time in public life.

The same fate may still await Priscilla de Villiers, if she ever gives elective politics another try. In the meantime, she has returned to a line of work where she is widely respected. She is special adviser to the Ontario government's Office for Victims of Crime, far from the prying eyes of today's mass media.

# THE UNHAPPY
# ENDINGS

The bigger they are, the harder they fall.
—*Celtic fighter Robert Fitzsimmons*

Lᴇsᴛ ʏᴏᴜ ᴛʜɪɴᴋ gut-wrenching, dramatic events are the sole
purview of premiers who've lost elections, think again. To be sure,
there are few things tougher to deal with in one's professional life
than knowing that millions of Canadians have, over the course of a
campaign, re-evaluated their love for you, and decided to reject you
in harsh fashion. But even premiers who have enjoyed great victories can experience deep emotional stings. Such was the case for two
Atlantic Canadians—Frank McKenna of New Brunswick and
Clyde Wells of Newfoundland—both of whom had successful runs
as premiers.

Frank McKenna virtually wrote the book on how to enjoy a
successful premiership. And yet, years after he left office on the
highest of highs, he still suffers pangs of guilt over the fate of his
party and former colleagues.

The history books will say McKenna did just about everything
right. In his first campaign as leader, he led the Liberals to fifty-
eight seats in the New Brunswick Legislature. There are only
fifty-eight seats in the New Brunswick Legislature.

"Not in my wildest dreams," McKenna tells me, when asked whether he saw the clean sweep coming.

"I thought that the seeds of our defeat were buried within that victory," McKenna now reveals, "that the public would immediately realize what they had done and bend over backwards to correct it in the coming years. So I thought it was a hugely satisfying win but a very dangerous win."

In fact, McKenna was quite wrong about the public's need to "correct" what it had done in 1987. They re-elected New Brunswick's twenty-seventh premier with forty-six seats in 1991, and forty-eight seats in 1995. Three elections. Three huge majorities.

But McKenna's greatest achievement was in getting Canadians, and New Brunswickers themselves, to rethink their stereotypes of that have-not province. McKenna brought in tough social policies such as workfare long before others did. He convinced hundreds of corporate executives to invest millions in a province they had never previously considered investing in at all.

"The ultimate thrill was in the governance," he says with Boy Scout–like sincerity. "It was in announcing hundreds of new jobs at a place. That used to just turn me on enormously." McKenna loved to open new highways. He got a charge out of securing money from Ottawa for new social programs or putting thousands of welfare recipients into training programs. It thrilled him to go into schools and see very poor, uneducated children learning how to read and write. "Those were the days that I just felt like I could walk on water," he says.

Contrast that, however, with the intense guilt McKenna felt, and still feels, over the demise of the Meech Lake Accord. McKenna was never a huge fan of the accord. So he started a process that would produce a companion accord, which dealt with many of the issues on which Meech was silent. Less than three months before the first ministers were to meet in June 1990 in Ottawa to ratify the Meech

Lake Accord, McKenna unveiled his parallel accord. Unlike Meech, it dealt with issues such as women's equality, Native and other minority rights, plus Senate reform, and a clarification of the controversial "distinct society" clause.

Prime Minister Brian Mulroney apparently thought enough of the effort that he sent McKenna's accord, dubbed "Meech Plus," to an all-party parliamentary committee chaired by Jean Charest, then a Tory MP.

McKenna was trying to be constructive. But his efforts to improve Meech set in motion a chain reaction of events that would prove to be disastrous to the accord, to the Mulroney government, to the PC party, and perhaps even responsible for the rise of nationalist sentiment in Quebec. When the Quebec government of Robert Bourassa saw the recommendations of the Charest committee, it dug in its heels. It passed a resolution rejecting any changes to the Meech accord. Lucien Bouchard, then a Mulroney cabinet minister, wanted to show his solidarity with the province, so he quit the cabinet, and refused to speak with either Charest or his old friend the prime minister, who had appointed him ambassador to France, then brought him home to enter the cabinet. Mulroney, in turn, pulled his support of the Charest recommendations, lest he be outflanked by the nationalists in Quebec.

When the eleven first ministers eventually gathered in Ottawa, the outlook was most pessimistic. McKenna knew it was pointless to try to put more pressure on Robert Bourassa to bend. Six months earlier in a private conversation, McKenna had confronted the Quebec premier, demanding to know why his support for Canada always seemed so ambiguous.

"Look," McKenna said, "wouldn't it help, Robert, if you just stood up and said, 'I am Canadian, I believe in a united Canada, and I am fighting for the rights of Quebec within that?'"

Bourassa's answer was so poignant, it cut McKenna to the quick.

"I was very close to Pierre Laporte," McKenna recalls Bourassa telling him, referring to the Quebec labour minister who was assassinated by the Front de Libération du Québec terrorist group. "I personally had to take a very hard stand in the hostage negotiations. The intransigence of the leadership in Quebec— really on the side of Canada—resulted in Laporte losing his life. When I went in to tell his widow that her husband—one of my best friends—had died, it was one of the hardest moments of my life. And so, Frank, unless you've walked in my shoes, you should not judge my commitment to Canada."

After conversations such as that one, McKenna gained a greater appreciation for Bourassa's position. When the accord ultimately failed to pass the Manitoba and Newfoundland legislatures, "I felt like this was the beginning of the end of Canada, and that I was a major part of the reason. I personally felt devastated, as low as low could be," McKenna recalls. "It was weeks before I felt better, where I didn't feel this huge sense that the country was going to be destroyed, a country that I had worked so hard to unify."

Ironically, the man who brought him out of his depression was Robert Bourassa. McKenna was at his cottage at Cap-Pelé, forty minutes east of Moncton, when the Quebec premier called.

"I just wanted to talk to you about what happened," Bourassa said.

"I feel absolutely terrible, Robert," McKenna replied.

"I know how you must feel," Bourassa said, "but it's not the end. We'll wait for the Latin blood to cool for a while and then we'll go to work again."

McKenna thought Bourassa was amazingly classy, despite having lost his cherished accord.

On October 8, 1997—ten years to the day after he became premier of New Brunswick—Frank McKenna announced he was quitting politics. He had promised his family and his province that he wouldn't overstay his welcome, and he didn't. McKenna would leave politics with one of the most successful political resumés ever crafted. Rex Murphy, the CBC commentator, paraphrased William Shakespeare when he cleverly said of McKenna, "Nothing became his term of office so much as his manner of leaving it."

If there was one aspect of his transition to private life that McKenna truly regrets, it's that the Liberal government couldn't survive his departure.

"I thought succession planning was a very important part of the process and I felt that I had the perfect situation," he says. And he did. His departure came in the middle of his third term, leaving his successor plenty of time to put his own stamp on the job before having to go back to the people. The Liberals already had 80 percent of the seats in the legislature, and a million dollars in the bank. They enjoyed huge leads over the other parties in the polls. The budget was balanced, the economy was good, and there was a decent team of contenders ready to duke it out to replace him.

But when McKenna's successor, Camille Thériault, counted the votes in the election of June 1999, the results were shocking. Conservative leader Bernard Lord took a party that had had no seats at all twelve years earlier to a landslide win over the Liberals, capturing forty-four of fifty-five seats. McKenna's former team was reduced to ten seats. Despite his careful succession planning, the days of Liberals governing his province were over.

"I've told the public of New Brunswick that I accept a share of the responsibility for the election loss," he says.

Frank McKenna has put together one of the most impressive post-political careers ever seen in Canada. He enjoys a mix of legal work (senior partner at McInnes Cooper in Moncton), corporate directorships (a dozen at last count), and public service (he did a stint on the Security Intelligence Review Committee, which oversees the Canadian Security Intelligence Service, CSIS). He was offered a seat in the Senate, but turned it down.

And still, six years after leaving public life, nothing else has come close to the highs and lows of being premier of New Brunswick.

"I miss it terribly," Frank McKenna sighs. "I miss it every day."

FROM AS FAR BACK as he can remember, a young Newfoundland boy born in Buchans Junction in 1937 wanted to be a lawyer. No one in his extended family, or his immediate family of nine, had ever been involved in the law or even gone to university for that matter. In fact, no one in the entire town had ever gone to university. He had never met a lawyer. Nor does he have any recollection of how the interest arose. He may have seen a lawyer in the movies or heard one on radio. Certainly he never saw one on television, since there were no TV sets in Newfoundland when he grew up. But somehow he just knew.

Sure enough, years later, he found himself enrolling at Dalhousie University in Halifax, where one of his law school classmates during first year was a charming and affable Quebecer named Brian Mulroney.

He would realize his childhood dream and become a lawyer, then return home to Corner Brook to practise. It took no time at all for him to make a name for himself, so Premier Joey Smallwood asked him to run for the Newfoundland House of Assembly.

"I was carried away by the excitement of it, and said yes when I probably ought to have said no," he says. His law practice was just getting off the ground and he had two young children. But he said yes to politics anyway. Smallwood brought him into cabinet right away as minister of labour. Then the voters of Humber East said yes to him in the 1966 election, held a month later. His friend and then fellow Liberal John Crosbie followed the same path, having been appointed to the cabinet at the same time, then winning a seat on election day.

That was about the last non-controversial thing this politician would do in his political career. He would go on to have a very public and nasty breakup with his premier. And nearly a quarter of a century after that, he would experience another public and nasty break with another first minister, this time the prime minister, his old law school acquaintance Brian Mulroney.

His name was Clyde Wells.

For better or for worse, Canadians remember Clyde Wells as the man who killed the Meech Lake Accord. He was against it from the moment he first heard about it on a radio broadcast in his motel room, in the middle of his quest for the Liberal party leadership in 1987. He left the first ministers' conference on June 9, 1990, having agreed only to put the accord to a free vote of the Newfoundland House of Assembly. He complained during that weekend in Ottawa that he was "constantly being pressured to agree to do something under fear and threat that failure to do it may do irreparable harm to the country."

The most dramatic moment in Wells's Meech Lake story didn't even happen in Ottawa. It took place upon his return to Newfoundland, where supporters greeted the premier at the airport and gave him a conquering hero's welcome home. Wells addressed the cheering throng, tried again to explain his reasons for not supporting the accord, and was in tears by the end of the impromptu speech. He may have been a pariah among pro-Meech advocates. He may have been representing a province with barely 2 percent of the Canadian population. But at that moment, he was the most important person in the country, giving voice to the anxieties many Canadians had about the accord.

Even though the accord was facing certain death in the Manitoba Legislature, thanks to Aboriginal MLA Elijah Harper's filibuster, Prime Minister Mulroney and his associates have perpetuated the version of history that blames the collapse of Meech on Wells and

Wells alone. Wells would love to dispel that myth, but feels somewhat hamstrung in doing so, because of his new job. In March 1999, he was sworn in as chief justice of Newfoundland and Labrador, also presiding over the province's Court of Appeal.

Some day, he will tell more about Meech and other events, but in the meantime, "I don't want to bring discredit upon the position that I now hold by doing that."

During the course of our conversation, Wells delves gently into talking about Meech more than he thinks he should, only to stop himself. He has pledged not to go mano-a-mano with Mulroney on the history of this time, until he's off the bench.

"I am the world's worst disciplinarian in sticking to this, because I am so involved in the overall issue, you know?" he says. It's killing him to bite his tongue. It's killing him to watch his old nemesis Mulroney giving interviews, possibly cementing in the minds of Canadians the notion that Clyde Wells is the villain. And so, for now, he waits for a day when the constraints of the bench are no longer there.

(Near the end of our conversation, I tell Wells a little piece of trivia he didn't know. There was actually another judge named Clyde Wells, who used to sit on the bench in Florida and once sentenced a man to death. "And you thought I went on vacation and got carried away," Newfoundland's Clyde Wells jokes.)

Wells does enjoy some things on the bench that he didn't experience in politics.

"Like what?" I ask.

"Civility and order and discipline," he says, naming three things that are in incredibly short supply in public life.

"There's nothing as exciting and challenging and exhilarating," he says of politics. "But it's wearying. And if you've got any real sense, you won't stay at it forever—unless you're a real glutton for punishment."

# THE CURVEBALL

Michael Jordan was a spectacular athlete with a great work ethic,
a competitive nature and a passion for baseball,
but he found that hitting a curve ball was no slam dunk.
—*Dave Murphy, Scripps Howard News Service*

ONE OF THE REASONS politics is such a fascinating spectator sport—and so frustrating for its practitioners—is that the best-laid plans are often knocked off the rails by that one issue no one sees coming. Politicians become accomplished at hitting the fastball. An issue might come at you at ninety miles per hour, but it's straight across the plate. You can handle that.

However, in politics you've got to be able to hit the curveball—the issue that sneaks up on you, handcuffs you, and can make the best home-run hitter look foolish if he's not prepared for it. You must learn to hit the curveball, or your success in politics will be as short-lived as Michael Jordan's career in baseball.

LYN MCLEOD ENTERED politics because she wanted to improve the education system in her province. Through the course of doing her job well, she eventually rose to become leader of the Ontario Liberals, the first female party leader in that province's history. Tim Murphy was one of McLeod's backbench MPPs. He loved being a politician because it provided him with an outlet for his deep interest in public policy, and at the same time scratched an itch—the love of the game. Bob Richardson was McLeod's 31-year-old chief of staff, who despite his tender age had quite a bit of backroom political experience and looked forward to helping make Lyn McLeod Ontario's first female premier. All three came to politics with big dreams and the best of intentions. All three saw their dreams crushed because at one time in their collective political lives, Lyn McLeod couldn't hit the curveball.

Tim Murphy is a forty-something, Irish Catholic from Barrie, Ontario, who has had his name in the papers a lot lately because of his close relationship with Paul Martin. He was the one-time finance minister's chief of staff, until Prime Minister Jean Chrétien fired Martin on that bizarre spring weekend in 2002.

Murphy grew up immersed in current events. He subscribed to *Time* magazine as a kid; watched the rise of Trudeaumania and the fall of Richard Nixon with fascination; and, growing up when he did, only ever remembered William Davis being the premier of his home province ("the colossus astride Ontario politics," as Murphy jokingly refers to Davis).

Murphy was all over the place when it came to politics. He joined the Young Progressive Conservatives in high school. In the first two national elections for which he was of age—1979 and 1980—he voted for the NDP. But he really got turned on to partisan politics in 1984, while he was a legislative intern at Queen's Park. A Liberal MPP named Sean Conway, from Renfrew, near Ottawa, became his mentor. Everybody expected Bill Davis to run in the upcoming election and make short work of David Peterson and Bob Rae, after which another leadership contest might be required. Murphy at this time witnessed first-hand the behind-the-scenes machinations of politics. He and Conway were having breakfast in the basement of the Ontario Legislature, discussing what the MPP planned to do if Peterson failed.

"If we win, great, but if we lose, I'm thinking about running for leader," Conway said.

Then Murphy learned how to put on his best poker face. Who should walk around the corner at that very second but David Peterson, who pulled up a chair and joined the pair for a bite. Mum was the word.

Meanwhile, Murphy decided once and for all that he was a Liberal. He went to the 1984 leadership convention in Ottawa and voted for John Turner.

He then established a pattern that would become familiar in his professional life. He was to bounce back and forth between the law and politics, knowing the former would pay the bills but the latter would fill his heart.

In 1985, Murphy got himself a job working for Conway. That little scheme in the basement of the legislature became moot when Davis retired, Bob Rae made Peterson the premier after the ensuing election, and Conway became minister of education. In this case, it may have been the government's most important portfolio. Conway's job was to give legislative voice to the policy that Bill Davis introduced but never actually implemented—full public funding for Catholic schools. Murphy was the minister's legislative assistant, directly negotiating with his NDP counterpart on what the bill should look like. Since the Liberals had a minority government at the time—and this was clearly the most potentially explosive issue on the agenda—the stakes were high and the consequences huge if negotiations with the NDP broke down.

It may have been the Davis Tories who introduced full funding, but after Davis retired it was the Frank Miller–led Tories who were its staunchest critics. As long as the Liberals and NDP continued to sing out of the same hymn book, all was well. But if a significant difference in that alliance arose, it could kill not only the bill but perhaps even the government. Murphy had all this in his head when he saw his NDP and PC counterparts leave a meeting for a private chat. In fact, all sides were headed for a showdown over the issue of whether the separate school system would be allowed to favour Catholics when hiring new teachers. The separate schools wanted that right, but was it discriminatory considering all taxpayers would now be funding the Catholic system?

Murphy's warning bells went off. He contacted Peterson's chief of staff, Hershell Ezrin.

"Something fucking horribly wrong is happening here, Hershell," he recalls saying.

Peterson got on the line, made some suggestions, then sent Murphy, Ezrin, and Conway off to negotiate a compromise, which they did. (The separate school system could favour Catholics for ten years—long enough to figure out whether that was constitutionally acceptable.) The other parties bought the compromise. The bill was saved. So was the government, from a potentially toxic combination of religion and politics. The more Murphy thinks about that moment in time, the more he thinks it's representative of everything that is desirable in public life.

"Those are the moments for which you do the job," he says. "You're having an effect. It's fun for your ego, challenging intellectually. You're trying to figure out the right thing to do politically, and the right thing to do from a public policy perspective. You're riding two horses at the same time. It's an ethical and moral challenge. You face up to your own moral and ethical boundaries in making those decisions, too.

"If you believe that the value of life is experiencing the things that life has to offer, then those are the kind of moments that give meaning to life," he says. "Where do I stand? Why do I have these views? And how far will I go or not go in compromising? Where do I draw the line? To have the opportunity to make those decisions to face up to them, that's big issue stuff. French existentialists write about them. And we actually get to live it."

As challenging as the Catholic school funding issue was, in baseball parlance it represented fastballs all the way. The issue was front and centre of everyone's agenda. It wasn't going to sneak up on anyone.

Murphy later switched jobs to work for Attorney General Ian Scott, and got involved in Scott's riding. He worked on Bill Graham's second run for Parliament in 1988, which ultimately came up sixty votes short in Rosedale riding. (Graham would eventually win a seat, and become foreign minister during Jean Chrétien's third mandate.) Murphy then took a leave of absence from his legal career at Blake, Cassels & Graydon to become Ontario campaign director for Paul Martin's leadership run in 1990.

But his days in the backrooms would soon come to an end. In 1990, the Liberals were sent packing by Bob Rae's New Democrats. Ian Scott, much to his chagrin, managed to hang onto his seat by seventy-two votes. But life on the Opposition benches did not suit the brilliant lawyer, who was getting crustier by the day, watching his former law student Bob Rae in the premier's chair. So, almost two years to the day after that 1990 election debacle, Scott quit, forcing a by-election in St. George–St. David, his diverse downtown Toronto riding. Tim Murphy saw an opening to realize a childhood dream—to win an election and become a politician.

St. George–St. David had one of the largest and most influential gay communities in the country. In order to secure that vote, Murphy campaigned on a promise of dramatically enhancing the civil rights of gays and lesbians. When the Liberals under David Peterson formed the government in 1985, they passed a law prohibiting discrimination against homosexuals. It would be illegal to deny jobs or housing to anyone on the basis of their sexual orientation. Murphy was proposing to take the next step that the community was seeking—same-sex benefits, the right of gays and lesbians to adopt an even greater legitimacy for same-sex unions. Although these tenets were in conflict with his Catholic upbringing, Murphy saw Canadians as an essentially tolerant people who wouldn't oppose extending to homosexuals many of the rights everyone else already enjoyed.

Lyn McLeod is also a tolerant person. But she probably wasn't prepared to go as far as Murphy was in taking the next legislative steps for gay rights. Mind you, who would know? McLeod represented a riding in Thunder Bay, a long way geographically and spiritually from Church and Wellesley Streets in downtown Toronto—the heart of the gay community. The issue of same-sex benefits tends not to come up in the all-candidates' meetings on the north side of Lake Superior.

But the pending by-election was hugely important to McLeod. The riding had been safely held by Ian Scott since 1985. It would look terrible, just one year after McLeod's taking over the leadership of the party, if the Grits were to lose it. McLeod knew it. So did Murphy. And so did the gay community.

What happened next is open to a myriad of interpretations. Only one thing is clear. Whatever did happen ruined Lyn McLeod's chances of ever becoming premier of Ontario. It ended Tim Murphy's career in elective politics. It forced Bob Richardson to return to the private sector much earlier than planned. It also helped make Mike Harris the winner of the next election. And nobody saw it coming. It was the most dangerous of political curveballs.

April 1, 1993 was a joyous night for Toronto Liberals. With significant support from the gay community, Tim Murphy kept St. George–St. David Liberal red. The margin of victory was significantly higher than in the previous campaign, which McLeod appreciated. Somewhere in the victory speeches that night, both

Murphy and McLeod gave the distinct impression that significantly extending gay rights would be high on the Liberals' agenda.
The duo believed it was not only good policy but good politics.
They believed it was the right thing to do, and they knew to whom
they owed a considerable part of their by-election-night triumph.
Murphy promised that the first bill he introduced as the new
member of provincial parliament would extend rights for gays and
lesbians. His leader was up on the podium, beaming beside him,
and giving everyone the impression that there wasn't a sliver's worth
of difference between their positions on gay rights.

"We did put that out," admits Bob Richardson. "If you read the
fine print it wasn't quite that clear, but the impression was certainly
left by the candidate and, given the leader's participation in the by-
election, the inference was there."

In the days ahead, a very different truth would emerge. It quickly
became abundantly clear that, while Murphy and McLeod may
have supported championing gay rights, the rest of the Liberal
caucus didn't care for the issue very much at all. Neither did a
sizable part of Premier Bob Rae's NDP caucus. And Mike Harris's
entire PC caucus, though small and in third place in the legislature,
was united in its opposition to any extension of same-sex rights. If
Murphy intended to advance the case for more rights for homosexuals, it was going to be a hell of a struggle.

Nevertheless, two months after winning the by-election, and true
to his word, Tim Murphy introduced Bill 45, the "Human Rights
Code Amendment Act." As the title suggested, the bill offered
greater protection to gays and lesbians through Ontario's human
rights code. It allowed gay couples to list their "significant others"
as beneficiaries, for example, on life insurance policies. Only a
handful of Liberal MPPs voted for the bill, and Lyn McLeod was
one of them. But it was a far cry from the full equality that Murphy
had promised during the campaign he would try to implement. He

knew he had promised that. But he also knew it was impossible to get the Liberal caucus to support that. In fact, caucus members started to get increasingly irritated with the fact that the issue was dominating their political lives.

"Almost every member hated the issue, wanted it to go away, were mad at me for raising it, were mad at Lyn for letting it be raised, but since they couldn't be mad at her, they were mad at me," Murphy recalls. "It came up at every caucus. They whined and bitched and moaned about the issue." Even though he had been an MPP for only a few months, Murphy stopped going to weekly caucus meetings, so intense was the anger at him. He got constant pressure to withdraw his bill. His response was always, "No way in hell."

Having said that, the pressure he was getting from within caucus was matched by that he was encountering from without. The gay community was equally angry because Murphy's bill was a lot less ambitious than what he'd promised. He tried to reason with community leaders. *Let's take a two-step approach. We'll get half the agenda passed now, and half later. If we shoot for the whole thing now, we'll get nothing.* It all fell on deaf ears.

"The whole same-sex debate was without any question the most difficult point for me in politics," admits McLeod, who personally favoured extending same-sex benefits. "I was really compromising my personal beliefs in order to carry out my leadership role." McLeod, like Murphy, wanted to be ahead of the curve on the issue. But she simply couldn't get her caucus to move rapidly toward full equality either.

"You can't be a leader and be out there on your own," she says. "And I wasn't ready to leave the leadership over it."

The Liberals were all over the place on the issue—just like an oil slick. And then Bob Rae's government tossed a match on that oil. Almost a year after Murphy introduced his bill, the NDP government unveiled one of its own—Bill 167, the so-called Equality

Rights Statute Law Amendment Act. However, this bill was much more ambitious. It offered to redefine marriage to include spouses of the same sex. It allowed gay couples to adopt. It matched Murphy's same-sex benefits provisions. And to show how open-minded the government was on the issue, it was offering its MPPs a free vote.

At first blush, the Rae government's plans seemed bold and decisive. The NDP was proposing to get ahead of public opinion on a very contentious issue, but allow individual members to follow their consciences if they disagreed with the government's direction. However, the politics of the move was also brilliantly ruthless. The effect was to drop another grenade on the Liberal caucus.

The bill went much further than most Liberals were prepared to go. Only three Grits voted in favour, one of whom was Tim Murphy, who even worked behind the scenes to help the NDP bring more Liberals on side.

But many New Democrats opposed the bill. They struggled with the notion of what was the right versus the pragmatic thing to do. Many of them, particularly those representing so-called ethnic communities, feared that supporting the measure would cost them their seats. (Most of them lost their seats a year later anyway.)

Even though the NDP had a large majority government, its Bill 167 failed to pass the legislature by nine votes. Ten New Democrats voted against the measure. So did Lyn McLeod. It would prove to be the beginning of the end of her time as Liberal leader.

Fairly or not, the biggest loser in the entire drama was not the attorney general, whose name appeared on the bill that failed to pass. It was not Premier Rae, who ultimately looked weak offering a free vote because he knew he couldn't depend on his caucus to support the bill. It wasn't even Tim Murphy, who was clearly wounded by the fiasco, but whose "aye" vote still kept the faith with his election promise.

It was Lyn McLeod.

By voting against the bill, McLeod allowed herself to be tarred with the allegation that she had "flip-flopped" on the issue—that she had supported full equality when it came to securing votes for a by-election win, but not when the rubber actually hit the road.

"We supported moderate legislation on the issue," says Bob Richardson in reference to Murphy's bill. "The NDP brought in a bill that included provisions that weren't explicitly stated during the by-election. The impression left by their bill was that if you weren't in favour of it, you weren't in favour of same-sex spousal benefits. Ergo, you flip-flopped."

Tim Murphy still gets irritated when he remembers the politics involved. "For all their climbing on their high horse about the issue, the government was entirely cynical about the way in which it dealt with this bill," he says. "It knew exactly what was going to happen, and it dumped it on Lyn."

Richardson shares that analysis.

"The Rae government was far more interested in damaging Lyn McLeod than in passing human rights legislation," he insists. "That was their number one motivation. Let's remember who had the majority government. Had they taken a more moderate approach, which is how you make progress on these issues, the legislation would have passed.

"I've had discussions with people who've been significant aides in the NDP government and there's no question, they saw us as on the ropes on the issue and they weren't going to let us off," Richardson says.

"I actually think that most of my political life I've been able to stay pretty true to who I believe I am," McLeod says. "But I wasn't comfortable with myself on that issue. The reason it distressed me so much was because I knew that wasn't being true to myself."

"I think it makes her mad because she's a progressive liberal," Richardson adds. "To be demonized and become the poster child for opposition to human rights legislation does not sit well with her. I think she found that difficult on a personal basis because it's not who she is."

Personally, McLeod felt quite comfortable supporting the tenets of the legislation. Politically, she simply felt her position, as leader, would be undermined by being so offside with the rest of her caucus.

"We were all intimidated by the calls, the letters, the faxes, the reaction of caucus," Richardson says. "All those things combined. We were also a little spooked by the Conservatives. It made us far too weak-kneed on the issue."

Having said all that, McLeod agrees with both Murphy's and Richardson's assessment. "How it became my fault is because it was a very deliberate strategy to make it my fault," she says.

That's something the premier of the day adamantly denies.

"Nothing could be further from the truth," insists Bob Rae, a decade after the fact. "I can't tell you how wrong that is. I would reject that absolutely, completely, and totally. We were desperate to do a deal with Lyn McLeod and find a solution that would be satisfactory."

NDP cabinet minister Frances Lankin's job on the day of the vote was to find as many Liberal supporters as possible. Even today, she regrets the fact she was able to find so few. When told of McLeod's comments, Lankin's response is astonishment.

"Are you serious?" she says. "Oh God." Lankin is either genuinely surprised at McLeod's comments or she's one hell of an actor. She denies that hobbling McLeod politically was part of the game plan. However, she does allow that she can see why McLeod feels that way. (For the record, Richardson believes Lankin acted genuinely on the issue. "I think Frances was straight up in the whole process," he says. "The problem is, she wasn't necessarily driving the political train on this.")

When all is said and done, the NDP seems to have simply preferred a glorious death for its own bill to the alternative of working out some kind of compromise, which surely could have passed the House. After all, the only party unalterably opposed to any extension of gay rights was the Conservative party. But it represented only twenty votes in a legislature of one hundred and thirty members.

"The reality is that Bob [Rae] couldn't have whipped the caucus on this one, so he chose to make a virtue of it by doing the free vote thing," says Frances Lankin. "It was a mistake as far as I'm concerned. I thought that then, I think that now."

"The fact is, we didn't have a majority in the legislature," says Richardson, who is sipping coffee at his neighbourhood Starbucks near Bathurst and Bloor Streets in downtown Toronto, and gets really animated as he remembers the futility of the time. "The fact is, we didn't bring in the bill. The fact is, we supported moderate legislation. But no one gives a rat's ass. If you brought up the term 'Bill 167' [among members of the public], you'd get 'Lyn McLeod flip-flopped' eight times out of ten."

"I was always convinced—wrongly at a certain point—that a compromise would emerge," remembers former premier Rae. "But the issue became too partisan and we lost some of our own people. We were always trying to see if there was a way to fashion something everyone could live with." At the end of the day, Rae says, "We couldn't even get people in the same room to negotiate a possible compromise. I had an enormous sense of frustration."

Lankin speculates that if Rae had whipped the caucus to support the bill, the legislation would have passed. The NDP dissidents would have either voted in favour of it, or been absent from the vote. Either way, the outcome likely would have been different.

But Rae felt he couldn't whip his caucus on the vote. The NDP's poll numbers were terrible. The issue, in Lankin's words, "was tearing caucus apart." The majority supported the measure, but those who were opposed were violently opposed. No one could tell them that supporting more rights for gays and lesbians was a way to win votes.

As much as the Liberals didn't approve of the NDP's bill, they hated what it did to McLeod personally and the party politically.

"The issue was so poorly handled by Bob Rae," says Greg Sorbara, one of the Liberal MPPs to vote against it. "And our leader had shamelessly changed positions." But there was plenty of shame to go around. Many gays and lesbians took the overwhelmingly negative vote by the Liberals as a rejection of their entire community.

"In my heart I knew we were doing the wrong thing by voting against that bill," says Richard Mahoney, the Ottawa lawyer and president of the Ontario Liberals at the time. "I kept my mouth shut. I actually regretted that. I regret it now. I'm not asking for forgiveness or anything. But I remember being very troubled by this."

"I just felt so awful, and that still bothers me," says Sorbara, who remembers walking down Bay Street in Toronto shortly after the vote. He stopped at a phone booth to make a call, and someone rapped on the glass.

"How could you?" the person said with utter disgust.

"And then I got home to have dinner with my kids, and my kids said, 'How could you?'" Sorbara recalls. "How do you explain it to teenagers? I tried explaining it to them and they said, 'Okay Dad, you're just wrong. You're stupid.'"

As the bill was being shot down, Rae says it didn't occur to him that McLeod would eventually suffer the most over the controversy.

"We'd put people through turmoil on this for weeks," he says. "I felt the only tarring going to be done was to me. I didn't come out of this with any feeling that this was a clever strategy [to ruin McLeod]."

"I accept my share of the responsibility," says Bob Richardson. "I was the leader's chief of staff. It was a disaster from start to finish. We have no one to blame but ourselves."

What was the prime lesson Richardson learned?

"When it comes to human rights legislation, you should damn the torpedoes, do what's right, and accept the political consequences later," he says. "What we tried to do is be all things to all people, and ended up alienating everyone in all sides of the issue—caucus, party, you name it, we alienated them."

While the NDP bill was dying a very public death, Murphy's bill was actually still alive, although in limbo. After passing second reading, it had been referred to the justice committee of the legislature, where it was awaiting further deliberation. However, rather than try to bring Murphy's bill back and restore some trust with the gay community, the Liberals and NDP had decided enough was enough.

"The ground had been scorched; we can't wade back into this turf with a compromise bill," Murphy says, recalling the arguments advanced by most elected members at the time. For her part, McLeod was certain Murphy's bill would have had Liberal support if only the NDP had called it back for a vote. She told that to Frances Lankin. But the NDP had turned the page. The issue was dead.

Murphy himself now had a difficult dilemma on his hands. Should he be the team player, claim that he had given it his all, and fall quietly back into the Liberal fold? Or should he articulate the rage of the gay community and become a maverick burr in the side of his leader and colleagues?

"It's the Burkian dilemma," Murphy says. "Am I their representative or am I independent? Part of me felt the responsibility to articulate that rage. Part of me felt that would do no good."

Murphy is honest enough to acknowledge that if he did raise hell and challenge his party, any hopes for future political advancement would be over.

"Guess where I'm sitting if we win the next election?" he asks rhetorically. "I'll be sitting so far back I'll have to heckle the spectators." Murphy's analysis wasn't completely self-interested. If he crossed his leader and his party, he knew he would never make cabinet in a future Liberal government. If he held his fire, he could argue the case again, potentially more effectively, inside cabinet.

"Every politician comes to the point where they know when they're making the decision to compromise their own principles for ambition," Murphy says. "The danger in politics is not that you get to make that decision all at once. You have to make it a thousand times, step by step by step. And the challenge in politics is when you finally get to the one thousandth decision, is there anything left in you? That's the truth of politics. You don't make one big compromise in politics. You make a thousand little ones."

Regardless of the NDP's motives behind putting forward their same-sex rights bill for a vote, one thing was clear. Tim Murphy saw his political career, which was fourteen months and eight days old, flash before his eyes.

"There was no way around the train that was coming at me," he says. What he hated most about his predicament was that almost none of it was of his making. The NDP determined to bring in a bill they knew would fail. The Liberals almost happily stepped into the trap that was set for them, and Murphy and McLeod got caught in the crossfire.

"Helplessness is what I hate and the reality is, there's a fair amount of that in politics," Murphy says.

The NDP's same-sex rights bill died on June 9, 1994, but the issue would live on for another year. The gay community (and the Tories) labelled Lyn McLeod the queen of flip-flops. Someone even dressed up as a huge pair of beach flip-flops and dogged McLeod at a couple of her campaign events on the election hustings a year later.

Meanwhile, Tim Murphy could still feel the gay community's rage. Doors were slamming in his face as he campaigned in the 1995 general election. The Liberals started the campaign twenty-five points up on the second-place Tories, but Murphy could feel the tide turn. Two weeks before election day, he came home after a day of pummelling and told his wife he thought he was going to lose. He was right.

"One of the fun and challenging parts of politics," Murphy says, is that you don't get to pick when decisions will be made about where your boundaries are. "I'm sure there's no point in her long life that Lyn McLeod ever thought her ethical boundary, her moral boundary, her political core would be called into question on same-sex legislation. And yet from a public perspective it clearly did."

McLeod herself admits to being a victim of a tornado she couldn't control.

"The worst decisions in politics, I'm sure, are the ones that you got caught in, accidentally, and you don't have any time to re-frame the thing," she says.

Her opponents happily re-framed the issue for her. It was the worst time of McLeod's political life.

Every great political story has some degree of irony to it, and this one is no exception. Guess who finally passed the legislation that would significantly expand gay rights in Ontario? You guessed it. Mike Harris's Conservative government. The courts told the Tories that dozens of provincial laws discriminated against gays and lesbians. So the Tories amended those laws to comply with the courts without a peep. They could have used the notwithstanding clause of the Charter of Rights and Freedoms to fight the court decision, but they didn't because, fundamentally, the Harris Tories, while a fiscally conservative party, weren't as socially conservative a party as their critics painted them. And, in a further ironic twist to the story, the Conservative attorney general whose name was on the

bill extending gay rights was none other than Jim Flaherty. Flaherty secured his place in the neo-conservative pantheon by running one of the most unabashedly right wing, socially conservative campaigns in history, in his bid to succeed Harris at the 2002 PC leadership convention. Go figure.

THE SAME-SEX BENEFITS BROUHAHA ended three promising political careers with extreme prejudice. The issue "confirmed in people's minds that a woman wasn't ready to be premier," according to Richardson, whose public opinion research indicated 20 percent of voters admitted those sentiments to pollsters. No doubt even more felt that way but were too politically correct to admit it. Tim Murphy's life as an elected politician ended after just two years and two months. And Bob Richardson's career in the public service ended as well.

As miserable as that time was for all three of them, it's also worth pointing out that all three did rebound from the situation. McLeod may not have won the province, but she did hold her Thunder Bay–area riding by increasingly huge margins in the 1995 and 1999 elections. She went on to become one of the most respected and effective critics of the Harris government, before announcing in 2002 that she wouldn't run again.

Tim Murphy replaced the drama of Ontario politics with that of the national stage. In mid-2003 he was Paul Martin's chief of staff and excellently placed to be a top adviser to everyone's odds-on favourite as Canada's next prime minister.

Bob Richardson re-crafted his resumé outside public life, but still maintained links to significant public issues. After the Liberals' defeat in 1995, Richardson hooked up with the Ipsos-Reid marketing research corporation, then became deeply involved with Toronto's bid for the 2008 Olympic Games, which ultimately went to Beijing. These days, he's one of the founding partners—along with fellow Liberal backroom boy Gordon Ashworth—of a new communications consulting company called Afrm$^2$.

And, at the end of the day, what lessons does one learn from Lyn McLeod that other politicians should heed? McLeod certainly wasn't a bad leader. In fact, quite the contrary.

She simply couldn't hit the curveball.

# THE FAMILY

To put the world right in order, we must first put the nation in order.
To put the nation in order, we must first put the family in order.
To put the family in order, we must first cultivate our personal life.
We must first set our hearts right.
—*Confucius*

WITH THE NOTABLE EXCEPTION of show business, is there another field of endeavour that puts as much stress and strain on marriages and families as politics? Certainly there are other occupations that require as much, if not more, time away from home. But public life adds another element that almost no other job features. As Brian O'Kurley, the former Alberta MP, quite correctly pointed out in a previous chapter, nobody criticizes the truck driver if he runs a red light. "He doesn't have the same pressure to be accountable to such a diverse group of interests."

Furthermore, it's one thing for Willy Loman rarely to be home because he's off selling ladies' garments across the United States. It's another thing to miss an anniversary or birthday party because you've convinced yourself you're contributing to the exercise of nation building. And that doesn't begin to address the temptations that some politicians experience being a long way from home. Believe it or not, sex, drugs, and rock 'n' roll are still a feature of public life and a test for any political marriage. As the twice-divorced former Liberal cabinet minister John Munro says of marriage, "Public life made it immeasurably more difficult."

Political consultant David Goyette has seen the appeal to ego and vanity, which is a constant feature of politics, threaten many political marriages.

"We don't have a traditional Hollywood star system in Canada," he says. "Our stars, to me, are hockey players and politicians. So some guy from a small town who is not a hockey player can get to be a star by being a cabinet minister. All of a sudden, they get into this lifestyle that is far more onerous and far more difficult than they thought it was going to be. It leads to stress, the loss of privacy, the loss of family life, and the loss of intimacy. And it leads to alcoholism. I have seen substantial amounts of alcoholism."

Goyette adds that when one partner in a marriage gets a political promotion, he (and it's almost always he) brings that home with him.

"A substantial majority of marital problems involves one partner losing power, exercising control over the other partner at home, as if this was a political office," he says.

"The resentment grows, the disparity grows, the lack of mutual respect grows. This is already going to happen because of the demands of the office. He's going to be in the paper. The wife's not. Playing second fiddle is part of being a political wife. But that attitude that you can do no wrong is transferred to the home and does a lot of damage to relationships."

Jane Stewart is a third-generation politician from Brant County, Ontario. Her father, Robert Nixon, was an Ontario Liberal party leader and her grandfather Harry Nixon was a former Ontario premier. In 1993, after being determined *not* to enter the family business, Stewart changed her mind and successfully ran for the Liberals in Brant. Like all rookie members of Parliament on their first day on the Hill, Stewart attended an orientation session, where the basics of being an MP were outlined. One of the more important points that emerged from the session focused on marriage.

"Look around this room," the guide told Stewart and the other rookies assembled, "because by the end of your political careers, 70 percent of you will either be divorced or have done serious damage to your marriages."

Stewart felt sure she would be the exception. But she wasn't. She's been a parliamentarian for ten years, a cabinet minister for seven of those years, and during the course of that political career, her seventeen-year-long marriage came to an end. She insists politics didn't kill her marriage, that there were other problems independent of public life.

"I think it's not a factor of politics," she says. "I think it's a factor of life cycle. It's tough."

But spending as much time away from your spouse as politics almost requires cannot be conducive to keeping marriages together.

In fact, in his autobiography *Think Big,* former Reform Party leader Preston Manning said public life placed unconscionable pressures on his three-decades-long marriage to his wife, Sandra. For five years, he lived in Ottawa and travelled the country, trying to build a new political movement. She spent most of her time in Calgary, dealing with family matters and trying to maintain her career in real estate. The Mannings are deeply Christian people, quite apparently still in love, and seem to have one of the great marriages and partnerships in Canadian political history. But if politics could do damage to their marriage, imagine what it must do to the relationships of couples who don't have the Mannings' deep foundation of love, respect, and faith.

Lest you think that no successful marriages such as the Mannings' are left inside the arena, let me start by shining a light on some that are. While no one can truly know what happens inside someone else's marriage, some politicians seem to have that aspect of their lives amazingly under control.

WILLIAM VANDER ZALM spent much of his time as premier of British Columbia away from his wife, Lillian. She ran the family business in Richmond while he ran the government in Victoria.

"I would tell her each day how much I loved her," Vander Zalm recalls. "I'd give her a hug or a kiss at every opportunity."

In addition, every night at eleven, Lillian would get a phone call from Bill, just to check in and see how she was doing. "Never failed once for all of the years."

On June 27, 2003, the Vander Zalms celebrated their forty-seventh wedding anniversary. "And Lillian and I intend to go another forty to fifty years," Vander Zalm laughs. "We're still in love."

Heather and David Smith are another two-career couple. She has been a judge for almost twenty years, he a lawyer and Liberal back-room boy who in 2002 was appointed to the Senate by Prime Minister Chrétien.

"She's always had her own career," Smith says of his wife, the chief justice of Ontario's Superior Court of Justice. "It was never as if she was sitting around waiting for me. And I think that's a big advantage."

Smith's other secret? "It irritates my wife when I say this, but she can't dispute it. She's never cooked me a meal in thirty years," he says. "Not one. Not bacon and eggs. And probably wouldn't know how." Smith became a short-order cook in a restaurant when he was fifteen. He's always had the knack of cooking well and quickly. What woman wouldn't love that?

Canada's great political couples include Jim and Heather Peterson. He has been the Liberal MP for Willowdale, Ontario, since 1980—with the exception of the 1984 Tory landslide. She worked for Pierre Trudeau and headed up the appointments office for Jim's kid brother, David, when he was premier of Ontario. The Petersons live in a gorgeous and tasteful home in the Forest Hill neighbourhood of Toronto. They have known each other since Grade 9 in London, and married at age twenty-one. As we talk in their living room, adorned with beautiful art and a crackling fire, they still appear to be quite a cute couple. They finish each other's sentences and laugh at each other's jokes.

When they were both working full-time, Heather at Queen's Park, Jim on Parliament Hill, "that wasn't the easiest time for us," admits Heather, who scaled back her career so the couple could spend more time together.

In another part of Ontario, Neil McLeod is a successful doctor in Thunder Bay. Yet when his wife, Lyn, became a Liberal MPP in 1987 (and later the Ontario party leader), he rearranged his lifestyle to meet the needs of her political career.

"He met me at the airport every week when I came home," Lyn says. "I thought the novelty would wear off after a while." Sixteen years later, he was still doing it. Neil also went to all the community festivals and wedding anniversaries to which Lyn, as the local MPP, was invited. It's one important way they've stayed in each other's lives, despite the fact that much of the year, he lives in Thunder Bay and she lives in Toronto.

Some couples take that collaboration even further. John Carstairs canvassed in every neighbourhood in River Heights, Manitoba, even though his wife was the candidate.

"He used to knock on doors and say to people, 'I want you to vote for Beauty Wonder,'" former Manitoba Liberal leader Sharon Carstairs recalls. "He just charmed every woman in my constituency. They knew this guy to be a lawyer and senior corporate person who thought his wife was the best thing since sliced bread. I've had a uniquely special relationship."

Sharon Carstairs estimates she and her husband have attended sixty-five political conventions over the course of their marriage.

"This was a real hobby for the two of us," she says. "Others play tennis. John and I play politics."

Perhaps the most scrutinized marriage in Canadian history—next to Maggie and Pierre's—is that of Joe Clark and Maureen McTeer. Can you think of a political couple who have sustained more vicious comments about their union? Not likely. It started with McTeer's decision, back in the 1970s, to keep her birth name (as if that were some kind of indictment of Clark's manhood) and continued because she had the temerity to be as interested in politics and public policy as he was. McTeer even ran for Parliament in the 1988 election, although she lost the Ottawa-area riding of Carleton–Gloucester by seven thousand votes.

In June 2003, this uniquely political duo celebrated their thirtieth wedding anniversary.

"I've got to be very careful, how I say this," Clark says. "It could sound impersonal, and I want it to be the opposite of that." Clark explains that the couple's daughter, Catherine—who was born in 1976, the same year Clark became PC party leader—helped sustain his relationship.

"She gave us a common place to go that was ours," he says. "She was our daughter, she wasn't the party's. When she was with us, it was our time. It wasn't anybody else's. Would we have worked to find time to be together had Catherine not been there? I doubt it. Because the trouble with the wear and tear of public life on private life is that there are so many priorities that are forced on you from the outside. You can have all the plans in the world that you're going to be together, but they always get pushed aside."

If Clark and McTeer are the best example of a very *public* political marriage, some are quite the opposite. You'd be hard pressed to see any pictures in the newspaper of Roy and Eleanore Romanow together, despite their having been married for more than thirty-five years. Of course, for much of that time she lived in Saskatoon and he in Regina.

"My wife made a conscious decision to be her own person," says Romanow, the former Saskatchewan premier. "She doesn't want the limelight and to be on stage waving. She always said, 'They elected you Roy. You do the job.'"

Romanow admits one of the many sacrifices his wife has had to make is the simple pleasure of going out to dinner together.

"We don't like to socialize because you do so much in your job," he says. "Sometimes my wife would like to go to dinner and I just don't want to, 'cause some guy's going to hassle me about the tax rates. But it's not impossible to have a reasonably happy marriage and be in politics."

Romanow's predecessor, Allan Blakeney, always thought one of the great advantages he enjoyed in his marriage to Ann was the fact that he lived and worked in the same city, something the vast majority of provincial and federal politicians don't do.

"I'm a fairly careful liver," Blakeney says. "But who knows what would have happened [if we were in different cities]?" Blakeney says that in his day, alcohol was the worst temptation. Members would meet after the day's proceedings and share a bottle. Before long, someone would have a drinking problem. Blakeney also expresses a truism about his generation: "The expectation was that husbands and wives would stay together," he says. "We knew it wouldn't always be beer and Skittles."

Clyde Wells recently celebrated his fortieth wedding anniversary. He acknowledges his wife, Eleanor, frequently told him during his time as premier of Newfoundland that his career was placing intolerable strains on his family. At one point, early in his political life, Wells even walked away from politics and resumed his career in the law, figuring it would put less stress on his home life. But it didn't.

"I kept telling my wife that this was going to change, and it did," Wells says. "It got worse."

On one occasion, Wells arrived home at four o'clock in the morning, unable to fly back to Corner Brook from St. John's because of bad weather. A letter from his youngest son, then ten years old, was waiting for him.

"Dear Dad," the letter said. "You shouldn't be away from home so much. You've been away twenty-three days so far this month. You should try and reduce it to no more than fifteen. You have to think of the rest of us, you know." The letter was signed by Wells's son, who added the names of his mother, his brother, his sister, and the dog, Piper.

"That kind of tears at you," says Wells, who has kept the letter to this day.

Somehow, the Wellses' marriage got through it all. What's their secret?

"The special tolerance of my wife, and understanding on her part. A reasonable level of sensitivity on my part. And the love that was shared for a very long time," he says.

"It's hard to write some of these things because they sound so pompous," said John Savage, the former Nova Scotia premier, who was thinking ahead to this interview appearing in print, "but sure it's been difficult at times. Fancy having seven kids in nine years. And we founded the Family Planning Association of Nova Scotia in 1969," he laughed.

"You obviously didn't believe in birth control pills, did you?" I asked him.

"Only for other people," he smiled.

Margaret and John Savage were married for forty-five years, until they both succumbed to cancer in 2003.

"It makes sense to me, as Mulroney said, to dance with the one that brung ya. Plus," Savage said, echoing Allan Blakeney, "we're from a generation that worked its way through things."

Frank and Julie McKenna are in the thirtieth year of their marriage.

"You really need a rock when you're in public life," the former premier of New Brunswick says. "I know you can ignore 'the rock' and find comfort somewhere else. But in my case, my family really were a rock for me and a very important haven."

Part of what allows Julie McKenna to be that rock is that she's not at all impressed with politics or politicians. The former premier has heard the following lecture a number of times:

"That's enough. That is absolutely enough. You've worked every night this week. You've worked every day and you now want to go into the office. It's seven o'clock on Sunday morning. You are not going to the office."

Did McKenna go?

"No! When she would put it like that I didn't go," he jokes. "She's not impressed by kings and prime ministers. She's impressed by just being with people that she happens to like, because they're good people. And so she has no pretension and no illusions of grandeur. So she would keep me very rooted."

Back in Ontario, for almost three decades Floyd Laughren lived in Toronto while his wife, Jeanette, raised their three children in Walden, near Sudbury. When he was elected to the Ontario Legislature in 1971, the couple had three children under the age of four.

"We had an agreement way back," the former Ontario finance minister says. "We tried to make sure that when I headed to Toronto we weren't still mad about something. It may be a little thing, but I didn't leave angry."

Laughren also made a point of not bringing home some of the stories from due south.

"Boy, I used to see lots of things," he says. "To go home and talk about so-and-so having this affair—you know, that doesn't really help the sense of security and well-being here."

David Smith says one of the keys to his thirty-year marriage was coming home on weekends while he was an MP. He saw too many MPs who didn't.

"The guys are up there getting . . ." he pauses. "I was gonna use the word 'laid,' but that can be misinterpreted," he smiles. "But getting *involved*. And I always went home every weekend."

David Goyette shares a quite bizarre story about just how far some politicians take their extracurricular activities. He was once chief of staff for a cabinet minister in the Ontario government in the 1980s who was having an affair with a woman from his hometown. "The lure was that this woman, whom he had known on and off, all of a sudden saw him as a powerful figure and became attracted to him."

Before long, the minister shared his secret, and said he wanted his paramour to receive the same treatment as his wife: Goyette would be expected to arrange free meals, taxicabs, tickets for shows, even send her clothes out for dry cleaning.

"I said I wouldn't do it," Goyette recalls. "I said, 'It's not a moral question. It's just that we have enough to do without that, and really you're doubling our workload because you're still married!'

"The point of this story," Goyette continues, "is that the lure of politics can be sexual, but the management of the lure can be a real pain in the ass."

Former Ontario premier Bob Rae had a tin ear when it came to criticisms about his wife, Arlene Perly. The Raes very much disliked Bob's time in Parliament in Ottawa.

"We didn't like living apart. It's never worked," he says. "So when I was premier, I always insisted we travel together. And people said, 'Oh there'll be criticism.' And I said, 'Look I don't care, I'll take that criticism. That little headline in any newspaper that says, "Premier's Trip Cost $86.52." I don't care about any of that.'"

Rae saw too many examples in the labour movement of marriages that fell apart. One of the spouses moves up the union chain of command, starts going to conventions, and the next thing you know, husband and wife no longer know each other.

"It creates huge pressures and strains because people just grow apart," he says. "But we never had that. We just always slept together. Always. And still do."

Norman Atkins, who managed Brian Mulroney's landslide victory in 1984, chalked up the failure of his marriage to that "growing apart" Rae mentioned. "It contributed," he admits. Mulroney appointed Atkins to the Senate in 1986. Atkins says his wife didn't want him to take the job. But, after twenty-seven years in advertising, he'd had enough of the business and was looking to try his hand at something else.

Pam Barrett had already experienced one divorce in her life. Then politics claimed her next relationship.

"He hated me being in politics," says the former leader of the Alberta New Democrats of the industrial electrician who was the man in her life in the 1980s. It did not sit well with him that public life competed almost unceasingly with real life. He'd cook her a birthday dinner. She'd get up in the middle to take a call from a constituent.

"Stop answering the phone," he'd say to her.

"I can't," she'd reply. "I have to answer the phone. It's my job."

Interestingly, now that Barrett is out of politics, that man is back in her life, "and it's extremely comfortable," she says of the relationship.

"Honey, I'm home," Barrett chortles.

Sometimes, it isn't politics in general, but one issue in particular that ruins relationships. Frances Lankin was a member of Bob Rae's cabinet from 1990 to 1995. She hated the Social Contract, which unilaterally abrogated collectively bargained agreements with public servants to save $2 billion. But she voted for it nevertheless.

"My guy left me as a result of that," she says. "The relationship could not survive that."

Lankin's beau even had a poster up on the wall, printed by one of the unions affected by the Social Contract. The poster featured pictures of "Traitors" (those who favoured the policy) and "Heroes" (those who voted against it). Lankin's picture was on the traitors' side. The couple split up for three years, then tried getting back together again, but it wouldn't take. Whenever they had a fight, Lankin's vote in favour of the Social Contract would come up again. (Interestingly, when Lankin quit politics to take a job heading up the United Way of Greater Toronto, the two got back together and this time, things seem to be clicking. The couple married two years ago.)

Nevertheless, Lankin definitely has a love–hate relationship with politics as it relates to her personal life. Politics has provided her with some of the most interesting, stimulating moments of her life. But its relentlessness, particularly during her years in the cabinet, caused her to postpone having a family. As long as friends of hers were having children in their early forties, she held out hope. Then, sadly, her health took a turn for the worse and she was forced to have a hysterectomy.

"It's all gone," she says with evident bitterness of her inability to have children. "It's just all gone."

Pierre Marc Johnson, the former premier of Quebec, knows the non-stop nature of politics all too well. "You're consumed by your job. You're consumed by your constituents. You're consumed by everything except your personal life," he says.

Most politicians are also focused on a myriad of policy issues, and their long- and short-term prospects within their party. Add it up, and Johnson says he found himself tackling at least half a dozen heavy-duty issues every day of his political life. There was little room for anything else.

"Even in my professional life as a lawyer, I don't find one-tenth of what I had in politics on an everyday basis which is challenging to my mind, to my emotions. So sharing that with someone else is so difficult, so difficult," he says.

Johnson remembers being asked by a recently married friend whether he should run for a seat in the Quebec National Assembly. Johnson advised him not to.

"I know you and I know your wife," he told his friend, "and it will kill this marriage before it takes off the ground."

The man took Johnson's advice on that occasion. But in the following election, which Johnson and the Parti Québécois lost, Johnson's friend *did* run, and he won, winding up on the Opposition benches.

Three years later, he was divorced.

"The problem is you don't have the time; the tensions you go through and the incapacity to convey what you go through every day, it's just impossible," Johnson says. "So, rapidly, you grow in two different lives because you can't share on fundamental issues enough."

Pierre Marc Johnson's marriage did not survive. Neither did the two marriages of his brother Daniel, also a former premier of Quebec.

"I think that strong marriages survive politics, weak marriages don't," says Joe Clark. "Some marriages are not meant to last, and those that were, will [survive] the politics and those that won't, won't.

"Most people who are involved in politics are combative and spouses can't fight back," adds Clark, pointing out one of the worst injustices of being a political spouse. "That adds to the frustration."

Politics isn't just tough on couples. It's tough on singles, or perhaps more particularly, on single women. Former NDP leader Audrey McLaughlin demonstrated her wonderfully dry sense of humour in describing the relationship game in the capital.

"If you're a male MP, married or not, or in a relationship or not, of course you will be assailed with offers," she says. "This is not a trap into which women MPs fall, nor are they challenged ethically by this in particular."

One time, McLaughlin and fellow New Democrat MP Lynn Hunter were on a flight together, having just heard that author Salman Rushdie had become engaged.

"Well, there's our social life," McLaughlin said to Hunter. "Here's a guy in hiding, under threat of death, and he gets engaged. We don't even get asked out for coffee."

Did McLaughlin want more of a social life when she was in politics? Yes and no. "Being a party leader and representing the Yukon was an enormous responsibility. Mind you, it's always nice to think you might be the object of some interesting fellow's desire. Having said that, frankly, there's just not a huge call for menopausal grand-mothers," she jokes.

I'm constantly surprised how many politicians are in relation-ships with people who don't like politics. Greg Sorbara, the former leadership hopeful for the Ontario Liberals, is such a person. His wife, Kate Barlow, "hates politics and she hates politicians," says Sorbara. Perhaps she's seen too much close-up of how politics infringes on family life. The Sorbaras have six children, who are now producing ever more grandchildren.

"The best way to maintain a relationship is to devote time and energy to it," Sorbara says. "Even if you do have the time, you don't have the energy, because the lure of public life has taken so much out of you."

Sorbara remembers life as a cabinet minister in David Peterson's government of 1985 to 1990. Breakfast every morning with ministry officials or people doing business with your ministry. Then, perhaps, a cabinet meeting. Then a lunch meeting. Then the parry and thrust of question period. Then more meetings with other officials.

"Then you go to a dinner party where everyone says, 'Geez, you're doing a real great job.' And so you get home at nine o'clock at night and maybe you have two hours, but you don't have one bit of emotional capacity left," Sorbara remembers of his experience. "It's been drained."

Part of the glue that held the Sorbara family together was an annual drive to Florida in February. They did it every year, even in 1992 when Sorbara was running for the leadership of his party and really couldn't afford the time away.

"But there were times when I thought this marriage is just not going to survive, it's just really at the edge," he says. "I attribute it to the difficulty of maintaining a relationship, and politics can add to that difficulty."

In fact, Sorbara says if he had been an MP instead of an MPP—in other words, unable to live and work in the same city—"my marriage wouldn't have survived. I'm convinced it wouldn't have survived."

WHEN YOU CONSIDER some of the pressures on political marriages, a basic question emerges: Is there anything we can do, as citizens who have an interest in helping make our representatives as effective as possible, so they can do a better job for us? The answer is yes, and the simplest place to start is with travel budgets.

I suspect there will be howls of outrage from some short-sighted constituents or special interest groups to the following suggestion, but I put it forward in the interests of kick-starting a discussion on how to keep political marriages together. Let me have the temerity to suggest that taxpayers ought to foot the bill to allow a politician's spouse to travel with him or her, if not all the time then at least some of the time. The costs would be minimal, the benefits significant.

For those who believe this so-called perk is too generous, consider the following. In many cases, taxpayers are already footing the bill to send politicians and their mistresses or paramours around the world, because of course, some politicians are having affairs with members of their staff or other political associates. We puff out our chests and feign massive outrage when someone suggests that taxpayers ought to pay for a minister's wife to accompany him on foreign business. But no one offers a peep of criticism when taxpayers pick up the tab to bring along several ministerial staffers, one of whom may very well be that politician's mistress. (I don't mean to be sexist here: the reality is, far more male politicians are having affairs with female staffers than vice versa.) Ironically, we subsidize philandering, but won't spend a dime to help these folks keep their marriages together. I think that's stupid.

Unless you're representing a riding in your capital city, being a politician almost automatically means you will experience lengthy and potentially debilitating absences from your spouse. I'd like us not to be a petty people who begrudge these frequent flyers this simple perk. Let 'em travel with their spouses and let's pick up the tab. Who knows? If their personal lives aren't falling apart, they may actually do their jobs better.

THE FAMILY EXPERIENCE of politics is, of course, a multi-faceted affair. In fact, perhaps surprisingly, the stresses of public life can produce some very amusing anecdotes. Dalton McGuinty tells a story that is probably more widely experienced than most politicians would admit. In 1998, McGuinty made history of sorts when he came from an improbable fourth place on the second ballot to win the Ontario Liberal leadership on the *fifth* ballot at 4:30 the next morning. But before he became leader, he was an ordinary MPP, occasionally touring the province on legislative committees. Once, McGuinty found himself immersed in a long week of constant and lengthy travel through the vastness of northern Ontario and, by the end of it, he was completely bushed. He picked up the phone to call his wife Terrie in Ottawa, but was so tired, he inadvertently forgot to dial the area code. After a few rings, a woman picked up the phone.

"Hello?" the voice on the other end of the phone said.

"Hi," McGuinty answered.

"How ya doin'?" the woman asked.

"Tired," McGuinty said. "Kids in bed yet?"

"Yeah," came the response.

"You okay?" McGuinty asked.

"Yeah," the woman answered again.

Suddenly, a long pause and a revelation.

"You're not my wife, are you?" a confused McGuinty asked.

"And you're not my husband either, are you?" the woman inquired back.

True story.

Since McGuinty's leadership victory in 1998, he's lived much of the time in Toronto and travelled across Ontario, while his wife and their four children lived in Ottawa. Never mind not recognizing one another's voice. It's a wonder they still know each other's names, given that kind of time apart.

McGuinty wasn't the only family member to experience a moment out of *The Twilight Zone*. His father, Dalton McGuinty Sr., held the same Ottawa seat as Dalton Jr. for three years, until the older man's death in 1990. Back in 1966 when the elder McGuintys had eight children (two others had yet to be born), they decided to drive to Florida for a vacation—all of them in one vehicle. It was cramped but manageable. The family also had a buddy system to ensure everyone was present at all times, but like many foolproof systems, it broke down. One time, the family stopped for gas somewhere in Georgia and everyone took a bathroom break. When the break was done, everyone piled back into the car and drove off. About half an hour down the road, McGuinty's mother, Elizabeth, asked, "Where's Michael?" Sure enough, they had forgotten the four-year-old back at the gas station.

"Back then," McGuinty laughs, "we thought it was all pretty funny and thank God it worked out. Today, we'd have been busted for child endangerment."

Jokes aside, public life, of course, can be brutal on the children of politicians as well. Neil Davis, the oldest of the five offspring of Ontario's eighteenth premier, says the Davis kids simply got used to the fact that their father was never around.

"He was a terrific father. But he didn't have the time to devote to us that other fathers had," says Davis, whose father, William, was a cabinet minister from the time Neil was three years old.

Bill Davis made it a point to be at the breakfast table every morning and in his own bed almost every night. But there wasn't much in between, something he now acknowledges.

"I'm seeing more of my grandchildren now, in some respects, than I saw of my children," says the former premier, who turned seventy-four in mid-2003 and still keeps a full corporate schedule.

Peter Lougheed always thought his four children had a tougher time in the schoolyard than they'd ever let on to him. They didn't complain much, but "my instinct tells me it wasn't easy," the former Alberta premier says.

In politics, the sins of (overwhelmingly) the fathers (but increasingly the mothers) are often visited upon their children. During the worst of the education wars between the Mike Harris government and the teacher unions, it was not uncommon for students to bring home inflammatory literature from their teachers, pointing out what terrible stewards of the education system the Tories were. Chris Stockwell, who became a cabinet minister in Mike Harris's government, has a daughter named Victoria who was known among her school friends as "Tory." One day at school, she saw one of her teachers wearing a button that featured the word "Tory" in a circle, with a red slash through it.

"She came home from school and was convinced the teacher didn't like her," Stockwell says. "That kind of impression on an eight-year-old girl was overpowering to her. And I remember saying to her, 'Look, your teacher doesn't hate you, she hates *me*!'"

ONE OF THE NUTTIEST examples of politics descending on the normalcy of family life is the story of Tim Murphy, whom we met in the last chapter, and his wife, Jane Thompson.

When they met, the attraction must have been fairly immediate, since three months later they were engaged to be married, and three months after that, they were on a flight to the south of France to elope. Thompson knew she was involved with a man who enjoyed politics. After all, Murphy was trying to get Paul Martin elected as Liberal leader in his first showdown with Jean Chrétien in 1990. She didn't necessarily know she was getting involved with a future politician. But she learned quickly.

"The day after we got married in Corsica, he said, 'We may have to host coffee parties.' That was my shock about what politics was really about," Thompson says. "Meeting voters. Pressing the flesh. And that's when I started to hyperventilate. I wasn't buying into that part of the life. I was buying into him being *in office*."

Why didn't she just take off?

"'Cause I was in the south of France," she smiles. "And I thought maybe it won't happen."

No such luck. In the summer of 1992, it was looking increasingly likely that former Ontario attorney general Ian Scott would retire from politics, opening up a nomination fight for his St. George–St. David riding. Rather than take off for a summer vacation, Thompson and Murphy hung around Toronto in anticipation of the news.

Except it didn't happen. Lesson number one: "Never book your summer holidays on what you think might happen in politics," Thompson says.

The summer, however, was not a total write-off. The couple discovered Thompson was pregnant and due to deliver their first child the following February. Soon after, Ian Scott did retire. Murphy ran for, and won, the nomination to carry the Liberal colours into the by-election, whenever it would be called.

If Jane Thompson thought politics was already unfairly dominating her life, she hadn't seen nuthin' yet. In February 1993, right on schedule, she went into labour.

"I was pushing in the delivery room and they put a call through, while I was pushing, to say the by-election had been called for April 1st," she recalls. "I couldn't believe that."

Emma Farewell Thompson-Murphy was born on February 23, 1993. She was named after Emma Peel, the female star on the television series *The Avengers* ("the first sexy feminist," according to Thompson). The middle name came from Jane's maternal grandfather, Farewell Fletcher. And speaking of farewell, that's exactly what Tim Murphy said to his family immediately after his daughter's birth. He called his mother-in-law to say he would be busy for the next six weeks running for office and could she please help? She arrived the next day and off went Murphy to engage in his first campaign as the candidate.

At that moment, did Thompson absolutely hate her husband's guts? She doesn't hesitate for a second.

"Oh yeah," she says. "He'd come in at ten or eleven at night, lie on the couch and look at Emma. And that sweet thing about having the baby in your bedroom? That lasted one night. Then he said, 'She's gotta get out of here.' He needed the sleep."

Murphy, a lawyer, was in the middle of a six-month-long trial when the by-election was called. Then his daughter was born.

His wife was telling him to be home. His office needed him to work the case. And the Liberals were telling him to start knocking on doors.

"It was as insane a time in my life as has ever been," says Murphy. "There was no way I could do all three things. I was the April fool."

The only thing worse than having your entire life turned upside down by politics is having it turned upside down by politics and losing. None of the participants to this drama wanted that to happen.

"He checked in at night and he never saw Emma naked again until after he won," Thompson says. "He missed the first six weeks of her life. He just wasn't there for all those things. Thank God for my mother."

By-election night was a classic. As Murphy, Thompson, and their new baby waited to mount a podium to give the victory speech, Emma just wouldn't stop crying.

"We brought her up to the stage," Murphy recalls with a smile. "All the cameras turned on. She stopped crying. The cameras turned off. She started crying again. She's her father's daughter."

Even when he was a behind-the-scenes staffer, Tim Murphy always knew he wanted to be the candidate. "You have to like being in the public eye a bit. You have to like the exchange. You also have to like people," he says. Murphy discovered he liked all three, particularly dealing with the problems of some of Toronto's poorest citizens, who were his constituents.

"They were the people who actually needed your help, for whom you could actually make a difference," he says. "That was a really enjoyable part of that job."

Murphy was now the newest member of the Liberal team and a caucus mate of his former mentor and boss Sean Conway. He soon found himself piling up the interview requests from members of the media. He was young, intelligent, well-spoken, and a quick study on the ways of the fourth estate.

"I was being interviewed by Heather Bird of *The Toronto Sun*," he remembers. "I was giving some answer that was too long, and she took her cassette recorder, put it in front of her mouth, and said, 'Would you say it was too little too late,' then stuck it in front of my mouth."

Murphy was no idiot. "I said, 'It's an outrage, this government attempting to do this. It's just too little too late.' She turned off her microphone and walked away. I said, 'I get this game.'" After twenty years of immersing himself in politics and policy, he finally understood the art of giving a good ten-second clip.

"Deep down it's shallow," he howls.

Murphy loved being a politician, but it was definitely taking its toll on his family life. He missed one of his wife's birthdays to attend a dinner for Paul Martin. Then he left her thirtieth birthday celebration to attend a riding event in the Philippine community. But the worst was yet to come. On the day of his daughter's first birthday, Murphy almost missed the entire party, again because of a Philippine community event.

"At that moment I realize, what the hell am I doing?" Murphy recalls. "My daughter has one first-year birthday party. The Filipino community will have many events. So at that point I decide, for major [family] events, I'm going to be there."

It's also becoming increasingly clear to the couple that Emma is going to be an only child. "Tim's just too busy," says his wife, who took a couple of years off from her career in journalism to be a full-time mother to Emma.

Meanwhile, Jane Thompson wasn't becoming any more enamoured with politics. She appreciated the constituency work her husband did for many downtrodden people. ("He really helped people. That's the good part about it.") But she couldn't abide the internal politics of the Liberal party.

"The backstabbing, the manoeuvring, all that shit, I hate that," she says. "And I'll never forget that. Some people are just not decent. It's really awful."

Murphy chooses his words carefully in echoing his wife's sentiments. "There are some hard lessons in politics and one of them is, no one does you any favours no matter how many you do for them." His statement begs several follow-up questions, but Murphy makes it clear that's all he'll say about that.

And how does a woman such as Thompson, who hates politicians so much, end up married to one? As one of the couple's friends, John MacMillan, says: "Jane hates politics, but loves contradictions."

As much as Murphy loved public life, his tenure in it would be short-lived. Just two years after winning his by-election, he was back at the polls fighting a general election, which Mike Harris would win for the Common Sense Revolutionaries. Murphy lost his seat by just 337 votes to Al Leach, the former chief general manager of the Toronto Transit Commission who would become a cabinet minister in the Harris government.

Murphy was depressed for a good four months after the loss. He had no money in the bank, and no job. The law firm he had previously worked for didn't want him back when he was an Opposition backbencher looking for part-time work, so he didn't think he could return there now.

Eventually, he got a job at McCarthy Tétrault, one of the bluest of the blue-chip law firms in Canada. After being turned down by several law firms that weren't sure politics was totally out of his blood, Murphy was given a chance because he assured McCarthy Tétrault he wouldn't be running again soon.

"We don't want to hire a politician, we want to hire a lawyer," they kept telling him.

But they never said he couldn't be a backroom boy. So Murphy returned to his roots, working behind the scenes. He became president of the Ontario Liberals in time for the 1999 election campaign, which saw the Liberal vote rise significantly, but not enough to knock off Mike Harris.

"Last year, I devoted six hundred hours to the presidency of the Liberal party. But I nonetheless billed two thousand hours of legal work," Murphy smiles. "So they're happy. The sad reality is, the loser in that equation is my family."

Ah yes, the family. Murphy returned to working one six-day week each month, to the delight of his wife, Jane, whose own career was taking flight. She became the style editor at the *National Post*. Why did she green-light his taking the party president's job?

"Just to keep him happy," she says, not entirely joking.

The great irony of Murphy's short stay in politics was that, after he lost the 1995 election, his life got immeasurably better in many respects. He and his family were able to buy a house for the first time. They also bought their first car. And Murphy's income was at least three times higher than what it was in politics.

Just when it looked as if some kind of normalcy might set in, Murphy got another one of those this-could-change-my-life phone calls. I saw him at a party shortly thereafter.

"Don't tell anyone, but Paul Martin's people are asking if I'm interested in being his chief of staff," said Murphy, looking as if he were about to burst from the excitement of it all, but tempering that enthusiasm with a new reality. If he accepted Martin's offer, he'd have to quit yet another law job. Would any law firm take him after quitting twice? Plus, he would not only be putting his family on the political treadmill again, but asking them to move to Ottawa, where Jane and Emma knew virtually no one.

"Jane is absolutely going to kill you, you know," I told him.

"I know," Murphy whispered back.

He took the job as executive assistant to one of the best finance ministers in Canadian history, but the job didn't last long. Martin and Chrétien went through a well-documented divorce in June 2002, and before you knew it, Murphy had lost his title, his office, his email account, and all the other trappings of power in Ottawa. The best indication of his change of status was his new email address: formerEA@hotmail.com. From that moment on, Murphy began devoting 100 percent of his professional time to making Paul Martin prime minister.

And what about the future? Is Thompson worried her husband will want to run again?

"I know that he will," says Jane, who with the move to Ottawa lost her perch at the *National Post* and then became vice-president of communications at the Canadian Film and Television Production Association. "I'm hoping it won't be for ten years."

Does she worry about the strains that might put on her family again?

"It doesn't look good for the long term," she says candidly. "Marriages don't last very often. But I don't worry about it. He's Catholic, too. Lot of guilt there."

I'd bet on the Murphys. If nothing else, her sense of humour will pull them through.

# THE
# CONCLUSIONS

Speak the truth, but leave immediately after.
—*Slovenian proverb*

I INTEND TO DO the above right now.

Some of the most gratifying by-products of writing my first book, *The Life: The Seductive Call of Politics,* were the heartfelt letters, emails, and phone calls I received from people who had read it. I wanted to tell stories about politics and politicians that one doesn't typically read in the newspapers, in hopes of showing people another side of public life. What surprised me was the large number of people who considered *The Life* influential in helping them decide whether to run for public office.

"About a year ago, a friend of mine who had run for the Liberals told me to read your book before I made my decision," wrote Dan Yake in an email to me. "After reading your book it made me realize a few things: that average people, from average backgrounds could take a leadership role in this province or country; that it would not be easy on me or my family, but that it could be very rewarding; and that when you get involved in politics, it gets in your blood and it's hard to get out.

"Between my wife Kim, my kids Greg and Jenna, and your book, you all had some influence in my final decision."

Yake sought and won the Liberal nomination in the Ontario riding of Dufferin–Peel–Wellington–Grey. He clearly doesn't mind a stiff challenge, because his choice of riding pits him against the premier of Ontario, Ernie Eves.

A precedent having been set, I now have similar hopes for this book. By telling tales from the dark side of politics, I hope to give the reader in general, and prospective candidates in particular, a greater insight into how this game works. If the result of this book is to discourage good people from seeking office, frightened off by the experiences contained in these pages, then I'll consider this effort somewhat of a failure. From the outset, my motive has been to describe the good, the bad, and the ugly of politics, so that interested parties might seek this life with open eyes, greater understanding, and more realistic expectations.

Having said all that, I'd like to suggest that we, as citizens, and the politicians we elect to do our business need to have a more candid and serious relationship. I am frequently appalled at how vociferous the electorate can be on the items I feel are irrelevant, but in the next breath they're prepared to ignore what I think should be of more serious concern.

Now, if I haven't offended you yet, let me push you a little further. Every independent study has shown that politicians are underpaid—in some cases, rather dramatically. Yet virtually every time a government tries to rectify the situation, even by just discussing the issue, proponents of pay hikes are drowned out by columnists or opposition politicians exploiting the easiest and cheapest headline one can get.

The results are predictable. Politicians in many legislatures haven't had a raise in a long time. They, therefore, do whatever they can—cartwheels and other forms of financial gymnastics—to exploit the current system and get as much compensation out of it as they possibly can. In 2002 in Ontario, Premier Ernie Eves's tourism minister, Cam Jackson, had to resign after his lavish expense accounts became public. Jackson, who lives in Burlington (just forty-five minutes from the Ontario Legislature) was spending many nights after work in pricey downtown Toronto hotels and charging expensive meals and in-room movies to taxpayers. I don't bring this to your attention to pick on Jackson, who has paid a steep price for his misdemeanours. He was ridiculed by opposition members and newspaper columnists. The premier criticized him on a live radio phone-in show. His career as a cabinet minister is certainly over, with no indication it will ever be resuscitated. I raise this because I suspect Jackson developed a sense that he was entitled to these perks, since cabinet ministers work long hours for relatively little pay. Once you get it into your head that no one appreciates what you do, ethical corners tend to get cut.

I believe our penny-pinching ways with politicians encourage them, if not to cheat, at least to work the system every way they can. It's not unusual for some backbenchers to show up for committee meetings only long enough to be marked "present," thereby becoming eligible for an extra per diem. Then they head out the door. They don't all do this, but too many do because they're trying to squeeze nickels out of a system that doesn't adequately reward or acknowledge what they do.

And I know you've heard this a million times, but the more I watch politics, the more I know it's true: it's nearly impossible to attract a higher-calibre group of candidates, with a wider range of backgrounds and experiences, if we constantly talk down the value of what the job entails or how much it pays. We decry the professional politicians, the "lifers" who can't or won't do anything else. Or the rich egomaniacs who can afford to walk away from their jobs and take a flyer on politics. And then we're shocked that these groups are overrepresented in our system. As former Ontario

Liberal leader Lyn McLeod puts it, "If you're looking at people who have distinguished themselves in their field and are setting aside a career in which they were distinguishing themselves by going into politics, it's a short list." I don't wonder why.

But what about those gold-plated pension plans, you ask? Good point. These pensions are becoming increasingly indefensible. The pension was meant to compensate people for putting their careers (and earning potential) on hold while they offered themselves up for public service. The reality is, the vast majority of politicians are not forgoing any income at all by entering politics. If anything, they may be making more in politics than they would have had they stayed in the private sector. A tiny percentage of politicians parlay their experience in public life into big-paying jobs: those such as Brian Mulroney, Peter Lougheed, and William Davis, who retire from politics and are coveted by numerous boards, are unquestionably the exceptions. So the pension need not be as rich to compensate politicians for their so-called lost income. (I note with interest the Ontario and Alberta governments under Mike Harris and Ralph Klein respectively eliminated their pension plans a few years ago, replacing them with ordinary registered retirement savings plans. Theoretically in Ontario, under the old system, someone as young as forty, with fifteen years of service, could receive a full pension for life provided he or she had served as few as five years on the job. That seems absurdly generous.)

Having said all that, can you imagine politicians giving up their right to a gold-plated pension as long as the salary is as low as it is? On the contrary. Several Canadian Alliance politicians have hypocritically opted into the pension plan they spent months trashing while trying to get elected. Why? Because they belatedly recognized that members of Parliament are undercompensated in the short run, and if you're not in the pension plan, you've given up long-term security as well. However, if we're going to pay politicians a salary that better represents their contributions to society, they have to stop making the job of their critics so easy. Politicians should not be able to draw on their pensions until they're closer to a pension-able age, and at the very least, out of public life. After he resigned from the House of Commons, former Liberal cabinet minister Brian Tobin justifiably came under harsh criticism for accepting his MP's pension, even though he was remaining in politics as premier of Newfoundland. The taxpayer was doubly compensating Tobin, and he wasn't even fifty years old yet. With that greedy misstep, Tobin set back any rational efforts to discuss compensating politicians.

One of my chief goals in writing these two books has been to remind people that the work politicians do is important, even if most of what the public hears about politics from the media and the politicians themselves ridicules the profession. I fervently believe we need to put the lure back into public life. When airlines buy adver-tising, they don't spend millions of dollars bad-mouthing their competition. They wouldn't think of boosting their own images by pointing out how many fatal crashes other airlines had experienced. If they did, no one would fly any more because of the loss of confi-dence in the entire industry. But politicians are different. They think nothing of venturing out on search-and-destroy missions against their opponents, and then are surprised when the public concludes that they're all a bunch of bad apples. If all sides toss the mud—and the media lovingly report every luscious detail—how can we be surprised when the public stops voting, or loses faith in the entire political process?

Heckling is a lost art. In days past, politicians of all stripes tossed barbs across the floors of various legislatures. But the purpose was to be clever and display some intellectual wit. Nowadays, panache has disappeared, replaced with profanities and goonish behaviour that would be more appropriate at a British soccer match. Things have deteriorated so much that Gary Carr, as Speaker of the Ontario Legislature, has set a Commonwealth record by ejecting more than three dozen legislators from the chamber.

Carr, a Conservative MPP from Oakville who has decided against seeking re-election, begins every session at Queen's Park with a prayer that includes the following admonition: "Give to each member of this legislature a strong and abiding sense of the great responsibilities laid upon us."

Rarely has this advice been followed. David Young, the then Ontario attorney general, was upbraided in 2002 for calling an Opposition member a "moron," a word that has gained considerable currency since Prime Minister Jean Chrétien's former director of communications, Françoise Ducros, used it to describe the president of the United States. Liberal MPP Sandra Pupatello got the toss for calling a Conservative member an "asshole." Similarly, Ontario cabinet minister Brad Clark was chastised by the Speaker for shouting "You're a puke, you're a puke" across the floor at a New Democrat. Extended middle fingers have been appearing at regular intervals. Tory MPP John O'Toole was the most unfortunate of the middle-digit flippers, having been caught by every television station in the province doing so in the middle of question period. (Then he made matters worse by trying to deny he'd done it.) And all the while, schoolchildren are watching these august proceedings from the public galleries above.

"You're an embarrassment, all of you," Speaker Carr shouted at MPPs in November 2002, in a rebuke unprecedented for its harshness and directness. "It's an absolutely disgraceful performance by all of you. You should be ashamed of yourselves."

Carr threatened to eject every single member if the level of decorum didn't improve immediately. He later mused about implementing a new system where politicians would be fined every time they got the boot. (Carr's disciplinarian ways have paid off with an interesting new job. In June 2003, the former Memorial Cup–winning goaltender signed on to coach the London Racers, a professional hockey team in Britain. He was to remain as Ontario Speaker until the next election.)

The point is, politicians have to be more careful about what they say and do because, more than anyone, they're the ones who are tarnishing the job. Why should the public respect what they do when they so clearly have such disrespect for the job and one another?

It's an issue that Carr's predecessor, Chris Stockwell, has thought about.

"I'm not an old man," Stockwell says, "but when I got into this business in '82, there was so much more respect for politicians then. Today I don't know a profession that has a worse reputation than politicians. And we deserve it. That's the one thing that makes me so mad. We've done it to ourselves."

It's fashionable to think that politicians and diapers have one thing in common: they should both be changed regularly, and for the same reason. I'd like to change the way Canadians view their public servants.

But, in all honesty, I can't do it alone.

# THE BACK OF THE BOOK

FIRST AND FOREMOST, I owe a debt of thanks to all of the politicians who agreed to be interviewed for this book. Understandably in life, everyone prefers to talk about his or her successes. These folks also agreed to discuss their failures, candidly I think, so that we might better understand our shared history and perhaps offer some cautionary advice to the next generation of leaders.

I feel very fortunate to be able to work with some of the finest people in the book business. From the outset, Cynthia Good, the recently retired president and publisher of Penguin Group (Canada), has shared my desire to tell stories about how we do politics in this country. She has a wonderful way of saying *This really sucks— rewrite it* in a way that doesn't crush my spirit ("Steve, this needs some work"). Cynthia, for your always-constructive criticism and enthusiastic support, I thank you.

Cheryl Cohen was the copy editor on this book. Lucky for me. She spent countless hours improving my manuscript's grammatical failings, and even tried to teach me the difference between "that" and "which" (I still don't completely get it). Amazingly, she did it all through cyberspace. Cheryl, some day we actually have to meet.

It has also been a delight to work with the team at Penguin. From Lesley Horlick, publicist extraordinaire (whose only fault is an affection for a certain hockey team in Ottawa), to senior production editor, Joe Zingrone (whose delightful and easygoing manner got this project over the finish line so smoothly), I thank you too.

Thanks to my literary agent, Denise Bukowski, whose approach four years ago allowed me to fulfill a lifetime dream of writing books.

My friend David Lockhart has written the words that some of the most influential politicians in this country say. He helped me find some of the words I needed for this project. Thanks, Daver.

To my parents, Marnie and Larry Paikin, to whom this book is dedicated: despite having been asked by PCs, Liberals, and New Democrats to run for office under their banners, my mother has always refused, preferring to make her contribution to her community in other ways. Now that I've written this book, I truly understand why she took the route she took. That she wears the Order of Canada, and deservedly so, suggests she made the right choice for her. However, as a proponent of good people getting into politics, I'd remind my mother that Louis Saint-Laurent became prime minister of Canada at the same age she is now. So it's still not too late for her to change her mind. As for my father, I couldn't have asked for a better role model as a parent. This year, 2003, was a big one for him. He turned 70. Talk about a gift from above. My Dad's father only made it to 51. I feel so blessed still to have him in my life. His musicianship, as fourth clarinetist in the Dundas Concert Band, is admirable, although Phil Nimmons may be able to cling to top spot on the Canadian clarinetists' totem pole for just a wee bit longer.

To my brother, Jeff, who never ceases to amaze me with his contributions to our hometown, Hamilton. I think he'd make a fabulous mayor, but I suspect we'll never get to find that out. Like most Canadians, he can't stand politics or politicians.

There cannot be a more perfect place on earth to write a book than Maple Point on Manitoulin Island in Lake Huron. Fortunately my in-laws, Caroline and Roberto Grosso, have a cottage there. I thank them for allowing me, in the summer of 2002, to infringe on their vacation time while I constantly had my nose in my computer. (My father-in-law passed away during the summer of 2003, but his spirit lives on, on Manitoulin, and I'd like to think in these pages as well.)

To my friends at TVOntario: I could not possibly work for a more supportive organization. The head of current affairs, Doug Grant, gives me the freedom to be myself on the air, and to indulge in these other projects when I'm not. He understands that at the end of the day, writing books makes me a better broadcaster, while doing *Studio 2* and *Diplomatic Immunity* makes me a better writer. To our chair, Isabel Bassett, from whom frequently is heard an encouraging word; and to TVO's membership department, which kindly agreed to put this book and my previous effort, *The Life*, into the hands of TVOntario members. Thank you Roberta Garcia, Bob Baker, and their very gracious former on-camera host Joanne Souaid.

As if that weren't enough, just a few weeks before the deadline for this book was up, I inexplicably herniated a disc in my back. The pain was like nothing I'd ever experienced. I ended up flat on my back for more than six weeks, almost three of them in hospital, pretty much incapacitated. Fortunately my wonderful *Studio 2* co-host Paula Todd held the fort, doing double duty until the cavalry arrived. Thanks to Paula and my many friends at TVO, who did so much to keep my spirits up.

To Hamilton Hall, "The Back Doctor," whose care and advice got me on the road to recovery, enabling me to finish this book sooner than otherwise would have happened. I also owe a debt of thanks to Cheryl Richardson, physiotherapist at Dr. Hall's Canadian Back Institute; and to my wonderful cousins, the Kesslers: Syd and Ellen, Jacob and Isaac, who gave me unfettered access to their pool (and their love), enabling me to do my hydrotherapy exercises, thereby allowing me to finish this book sooner than otherwise would have happened—my deepest thanks.

Let me also express appreciation to Diane Turbide of Penguin, for being so kind to relax deadlines that, because of my back, couldn't be met. Somehow, those amazing Penguins, led by Joe Zingrone, got the book out on time anyway, a testament to their professionalism.

I need to thank five other people, who frankly had little to do with the writing of this book but who simply make every day I'm with them better: my wife, Francesca, and my children, Zachary, Henry, Teddy, and Giulia. There is no dark side when it comes to life with them.

And one last thing. While writing this book on Manitoulin Island, Ted Williams died. He was my favourite baseball player, after whom my third son is named, and whose death provided a sad moment in an otherwise thoroughly enjoyable endeavour. I had the pleasure of meeting him once. He was curt and crusty—just the way I hoped he'd be. Rest in peace, Teddy Ballgame, the greatest hitter who ever lived.

# THE NAME INDEX